GOLF'S
BEST-KEPT SECRETS

DEDICATION

To Ashley Rae, the light of my life; and to Kelle, my best friend.
A nod and perhaps even a hug to Anthony and Brady, who have given me
laughs when I needed them most.

Published by Sellers Publishing, Inc.

Text © 2009 Jeff Barr
A list of photo credits appears on p. 220
Cover design and interior by Cooley Design Lab
All rights reserved.

Sellers Publishing, Inc.
161 John Roberts Road, South Portland, Maine 04106
For ordering information:
(800) 625-3386 toll free
Visit our Web site: www.sellerspublishing.com • E-mail: rsp@rsvp.com

ISBN: 13: 978-1-4162-0772-6
Library of Congress Control Number: 2009923844

10 9 8 7 6 5 4 3 2 1

Sellers Publishing and the author represent that all course information
and statistics are accurate, to the best of the author's knowledge, as of
the original date of publication. All scorecard information containing
yardages and pars included in *Golf's Best-Kept Secrets* was provided
by the staff of each course prior to the 2009 golf season.

Printed and bound in China.

GOLF'S
BEST-KEPT SECRETS

Awesome and Affordable
Public Courses Anyone Can Play

JEFF BARR

SELLERS
PUBLISHING

CONTENTS

Pacific waves crash as the sun sets on the Waikoloa Beach Resort in Hawaii.

Ratings: In each "Chip Shots" section throughout the book, you'll find a course rating and slope rating. The course rating is the United States Golf Association's evaluation of the playing difficulty of a course for scratch golfers under normal course and weather conditions. Slope (or slope rating) is the USGA's measurement of the relative playing difficulty of a course for players who are not scratch golfers, compared to scratch golfers. It is expressed as a whole number from 55 to 155.

"On the green" price-point key

◖ = $75 and under
◖ ◖ = $76–$135
◖ ◖ ◖ = $136–$199
◖ ◖ ◖ ◖ = $200 and over

Fees shown are to be considered general ranges, and are affected by time of day, time of season, and special packages and discounts. Contact the pro shop in advance to obtain exact prices.

Brian Hewitt serves as a Golf Channel insider for Golf Central and golfchannel.com. His weekly segment, "From The Tips," in which he delivers behind-the-scenes reports from the PGA Tour and other areas in the world of golf, appears on Golf Central. He often reports live from on-site tournament locations. Before joining the Golf Channel team in 2003, he spent six years writing and reporting for Golfweek magazine. During that time, he was a frequent guest on the Golf Channel's "Viewer's Forum." Before that, he served as the golf writer for the Chicago Sun-Times.

PREFACE

Affordable public golf is a commodity even more precious in times of tumbling world economies and shrinking disposable incomes. It's everywhere you want to look in Australia. And, if you get far enough off the beaten paths of Scotland and Ireland, you will find plenty of it in those places too. I have been lucky enough as a golf writer and golf television reporter to play a lot of nicely priced hidden gems in those three countries.

Public golfing opportunities are harder to find in North America and the Caribbean. I'm not sure why that is so. But I can tell you that Jeff Barr's discriminating compilation in these pages is a complete one.

I have worked, talked, and argued with Barr about the craft of golf writing and reporting since our days as staff members at *Golfweek* magazine.

I have also played golf with Barr. And I have had beers with him. The latter, arguably, is the time you really discover the heat of a person's passion for the game and the depth of the well of his golf knowledge.

In short, he knows how to bring the deep heat.

There is nothing wrong, by the way, with expensive, good golf other than the fact that most of us aren't on expense accounts or in the same financial league with the T. Boone Pickenses of the world. Jeff Barr does offer a couple of the pricey public wonders of the world, simply because it wouldn't be a complete collection without them. But he writes about them in a way we commoners can understand. Most of the courses in this book, however, are very affordable and are the cream of today's crop.

My early interest in golf came about because my father played. He wasn't very good — he only broke 90 a few times — but he never failed to amaze me when we watched golf on TV. He could pick out the players faster than the announcers could.

"Miller Barber," he would say with unfailing accuracy. "Ted Kroll . . . Julius Boros. Look at how little time he needs to hit the ball."

As a kid I played junior tennis. One day, as I was on the way home from winning a fourteen-and-under tournament in Janesville, Wisconsin, my father surprised me with an unplanned stop at a roadside muni near the Illinois border. The eighteen holes that followed were more fun than the tennis. That's when I should have known which sport I really loved.

I have since played Augusta National, Pebble Beach, Cypress Point, Pinehurst No. 2, Riviera, San Francisco Golf, Pacific Dunes, Medinah...the list goes on.

But enough with the name-dropping. I have also played my share of goat tracks. I have played golf where the tee boxes were AstroTurf mats and the greens were slower than the second cut of rough at Baltusrol. In near-darkness, I have snuck onto courses of private clubs with membership rolls that would make Judge Smails blush.

I am happy playing golf just about anywhere, even happier to play golf well; and I'm always curious about this new course, or that redesigned one, or the one I just read about in *Golf Digest*.

Now my friend and professional colleague, Jeff Barr, has produced book that I will return to when planning vacations or just sipping a glass of white wine in my study. (No, I don't do sherry, port, cognac, or cigars.)

Many of my favorite golf memories involve simply showing up by myself at a local public course and meeting three new people. For me, public golf has a way of encouraging you to seek out the best characteristics of a perfect stranger during the course of a round. Public golf, of course, is also crucial to the development of the game, especially on the junior level.

And, oh the stories. My home course for years was a neat little park district eighteen-holer in the north suburbs of Chicago. I once saw a man make a hole-in-one on a long par 3 and argue with his wife all the way up to the green. He insisted it *hadn't* gone in the hole.

"There," she snapped when they peered in the cup and the ace was confirmed. "I told ya."

We used to call that place, affectionately, "Winnetka National," even though its official name was different.

Jeff Barr has given us a book full of "Winnetka Nationals." And for that I thank him. I know I will use this book as a reference when considering my schedule, my wallet, and my vacation time.

— Brian Hewitt

Bradley S. Klein is a preeminent expert on golf course architecture and design. He is the longtime architecture editor of Golfweek magazine and has written five books on golf course design. Klein was inducted into the International Caddie Hall of Fame in 2007.

FOREWORD

About a dozen years ago my hometown of Bloomfield, Connecticut, came to me with the hare-brained scheme of creating a public golf course. Our town was lagging in economic development and the local real estate market needed a boost.

Long story short, we now have a Pete Dye-designed golf course in the middle of town, on what used to be a farm field. It's called Wintonbury Hills Golf Course, and I'm proud to say that the course, opened in 2003, is among the fine facilities featured in this book. More importantly, it's an asset that meets its own operating costs and makes high-quality golf available to town residents for less than $50. The cart fee is built in, but because we wanted the layout to embody the true nature of public access, we made the course easily walkable. Also, it's not terribly difficult in terms of forced carries. That's no easy feat when you're dealing with a site that has 90 acres of wetlands. But Dye and his associate, Tim Liddy, complied with our insistence that the golf course be fun, not beat you up. There's not a single hole where you actually have to fly the ball in over a pond or wetland to get to a green.

It's easy to forget that golf is a public game and that it started that way – in Scotland, on links tracts, on courses that anyone could play. In the U.S. today, 70 percent of the country's 15,500 golf courses are public access (whether resort, daily-fee, municipal, or privately owned and open to the public), and 75 percent of the half a billion rounds played annually take place on public layouts.

That means real people are playing on these courses, not PGA Tour pros. Golfers whose handicaps are 11 and 18 and 29 are playing them. And it means the vast majority of golfers who have no handicap, who would be hard-pressed to be able to play by the lawyerly rule book, are also playing them. They simply want to go out and have fun and enjoy the outdoors for a few hours and hope they can make some good swings and get a few pars or bogies. Some of them would be happy just to finish all eighteen holes.

Not that public golf has low standards. It simply must be able to meet the diverse abilities and interests of a wide range of players. And when you head out on the first tee at a place like Wild Horse Golf Club in Gothenburg, Nebraska, in the middle of the state, in the middle of the country, and in a place that looks and feels very much like a windswept prairie, you get a sense of what public golf is all about. It's about a first tee where guys in jeans and carrying a six-pack can get paired up with a twosome who just stepped off their charter plane.

Even the staid old U.S. Golf Association is catching on to the lure of public golf. Remember, this is the country's governing body for golf, founded in 1894, and it didn't hold a U.S. Open on a public-access golf course until 1972 (Pebble Beach Golf Links). Since then, the U.S. Open has been back to that resort layout three times (1982, 1992, and 2000). In 1999, the USGA added Pinehurst No. 2 in North Carolina to its championship roster (1999, 2005), and in 2002 took the bold step of holding its championship on a municipal layout (Bethpage State Park-Black Course in New York). Now we're in the middle of an extraordinary, three-year run of public tracts for the U.S. Open (Torrey Pines-South, California, 2008; Bethpage-Black, 2009; Pebble Beach, 2010), with two newly opened public courses slated for future U.S. Opens (Chambers Bay in Washington in 2015; and Erin Hills in Wisconsin in 2017).

If the bluebloods comprising the USGA can get the spirit of public golf, then there's no excuse for any golfer anywhere to miss out on this considerable sector of the golf universe. For too long, public-access golf has suffered under the misperception that it's somehow second-tier. But as you're about to see, the courses profiled throughout this book reveal just how first-rate many public courses truly are.

— Bradley S. Klein

INTRODUCTION

Golf is a game of secrets, of hidden niches and blind tee shots. There are unusual undulations and unnoticed slopes. Those who uncover and solve the mysteries of these unique nuances are on their way to returning to the clubhouse with satisfying scorecards in their pockets. But even more important secrets are the ones that offer knowledge on places to play, sights to see, money to save, and rounds to enjoy.

These are the nuggets shared in *Golf's Best-Kept Secrets*. They are stories, I believe, that are surely worth telling.

I have loved public golf since my first swing thirty-five years ago at Warren Valley Golf Club, a county-owned muni in Dearborn Heights, Michigan. My mom and dad made a comfortable living, but we weren't rich. The closest I ever came to a round on a private course as a teen-ager was when I picked up my little brother after his shift as a caddie at Dearborn Country Club.

As a kid, I played courses that were pretty scruffy, but it didn't matter because I felt lucky to have discovered such a fascinating game. Besides, I could get on the rough-edged tracks for less than ten bucks, which was easily in reach if the customers on my *Detroit News* route came through with some decent tips.

Some of my best public-golf course memories involved no greens fees at all. I loved to go out by myself, before Warren Valley was open for the season, with my bag on my back and nine holes in my sights. I'd wait for the first hint of a respite from Midwest winter weather — usually mid-March or so — and enjoy what became an annual cathartic ritual. It was cold, the course was mushy; there were no pins in the holes, no carts to ride. But I loved the solitude, the unadulterated immersion in a game I loved, on the No.1 course in my limited golf universe.

I remember sitting on a bench beside the No. 5 green, where nothing but pure public golf course was visible. Peace and quiet was my world. I'd get up from the bench, happy that I had four more holes to play. But I was saddened to realize that the weather would sour in a day or so and I wouldn't be able to play again until spring became the genuine article. Golf — I thought then and perhaps even now — doesn't get any better than this.

The country-club set may scoff at the notion, wondering how anyone could have that much fun playing golf without a shoeshine and a massage. Admittedly, there are hundreds of magnificent private golf courses in the world, where dues are high and intrusions low. During my years of travel for *Golfweek* magazine and as an author, I have been fortunate enough to play some of these fantastic private clubs. I've admired their fairways, tees, and greens, but a country-club atmosphere just ain't my cup of tea. I do not judge those who enjoy it, but it isn't for me.

I'd rather pay my money and go public — whether it be thirty bucks for a regular-guy's muni, a little more for mid-range public courses, or a good chunk for some of the famed public tracks of the world. It seems more a privilege to play when you don't have to be privileged to play.

In thirty-plus years of enjoying this great game, I have been lucky enough to play public golf in Hawaii and the Bahamas, Mexico and Jamaica. I've smiled and trod public-access fairways in Alabama and Arizona, Kansas and Kentucky, Nevada and New York. I know firsthand the joy of finding charming, little-known public golf courses and the delight of playing at some of the finest public courses in the world.

Golf's Best-Kept Secrets reveals great bargains and excellent public courses that you may have never heard of before. There also are tips on sights to see and places to check out after your round. But these aren't the only secrets revealed.

This book presents courses you'll be surprised to discover are available to us public-Joes and Janes — U.S. Open venues, ocean beauties, and mountain gems that rival the courses at any of the nation's private clubs. Included is at least one public course in every U.S. state, plus Canada, Mexico, Jamaica, and the Bahamas. I've set the bar high, but I've found more than 100 courses that make the grade. Many will leave you with plenty of walking-around money when you're done, and only a few might require you to break into your piggy bank. But when you consider how much it costs to join the top-rated clubs, even the most expensive public gems remain bargains.

In addition to the courses presented in detail, I've also included other courses in each state that are well worth a visit. By providing you with these listings, I hope you'll find this book a user-friendly resource that covers the wide range of public courses that are available to you.

Travel with me through these pages as we tour the wonderful world of public golf — its joys and quirks. The bang-for-your-buck courses we will traverse together offer soft fairways under your feet and scenic vistas in your sights. They'll also help you keep a few extra dollars in your wallet. These are rich rewards you won't want to miss.

— Jeff Barr

ALABAMA

FARMLINKS GOLF CLUB AT PURSELL FARMS
SYLACAUGA, ALABAMA

Alabama is filled with public golf, mostly on the ever-popular Robert Trent Trail, which includes many golf courses open to anyone. But those courses tend to lack strategic options.

This isn't the case at FarmLinks at Pursell Farms, which opened in 2003 and continues to stand the test of time. Its excellent conditioning and feel of being a "secret hide-away" contribute to it being one of golf's glimmering – but still somewhat "undiscovered" – gems. At FarmLinks, strategy and beauty are constant companions.

One of the joys of FarmLinks is that it affords golfers the opportunity to customize the course to their abilities. There are five sets of tees that allow the course to be played anywhere from a friendly 5,176 yards to an ultra-challenging 7,444 yards. A scratch player and a double-digit handicapper can enjoy a quality round on the same course, another facet that sets FarmLinks apart from many of the more well-known courses in Alabama.

The course is the brainchild of David Pursell, CEO of a local fertilizer company called Pursell Technologies, Inc. He had the vision to build the layout on 3,500 acres of rich Alabama land. At first his father, who controlled the land, had other ideas. He didn't see the reason to plow up the land to make a golf course.

It is fortunate for Alabama golfers that the younger Pursell is a convincing speaker. Neither father nor son will let on to the extent of the debate, but the heat is irrelevant today – unless you're playing FarmLinks on a particularly broiling day in August.

The front nine is generally at a higher elevation than the back, and it has more rolling terrain that requires players to understand that where their ball hits the ground isn't necessarily where it will lie. The greens on the front also are smaller than the back (6,560 square feet average to 7,130 average on the back).

If you have a good score after playing the front nine, you have a good chance to put a solid round together because the inward nine isn't quite the same test as the outward nine. The aforementioned large putting surfaces, comfortably wide fairways, and fairway bunkers actually enhance a player's chance to reach a green in regulation.

Many players view fairway bunkers as nothing but a penalty for an errant shot, but they actually can be used to a player's advantage if he or she understands the way to use them – and stay out of them, of course. Fairway bunkers are almost always placed in a spot where players should fall short of them to have an open shot to the tee. If a player manages to do this, a perfect angle to the green awaits.

Distinctive looks on every hole are also a FarmLinks plus. Course architects Dana Fry and Michael J. Hurdzan pride themselves on avoiding the "cookie cutter" look, and they have absolutely succeeded with this Alabama beauty. There are several structural facets to the golf course, but they have managed to blend them into quite an appealing finished product. There are grassy bunkers, where the scruffy elements are more dangerous than the sand. It is an example of the architects taking advantage of the original elements of the land and not eliminating them.

CHIP SHOTS

Course contact info:
(256) 208-7600,
www.FarmLinksgolfclub.com

Par: 72
Yardage: 7,444 yards

Rating: 75.5
Slope: 140
Notable: The ambience of the round is established before reaching the golf course. The entrance into the property begins a mile-long country road that is surrounded by soothing open countryside, a great preface to the enjoyment that lies ahead. Another bonus: the log-cabin style clubhouse is a rustic pleasure.

On the green
◐ ◐ $125

All eighteen holes at FarmLinks are beauties but the most-discussed is the memorable, par-3, 210-yard 5th. The back tees rest 158 yards above the green, and the view is gorgeous, and just a bit distracting. Generally, players should have two clubs from their regular striking distance, and then take in the scenic cart ride down to the green. Like most of the rounds at FarmLinks, it will be an easy thing to enjoy.

AFTER YOUR ROUND

The Big Cave: If it's adventure and a look at a natural wonder you crave, then take a tour of DeSoto Caverns, "Alabama's Big Cave." The guided tour takes you into the

No. 5 at FarmLinks offers a large green at which to shoot, but there is little room for error on this rugged par 3.

main room, which is twelve stories high and larger than a football field. The caverns are decorated with thousands of formations, making them among the most concentrated collections in America. Calcium carbonate and other minerals have formed thousands of ancient stalactites, which hang like rock icicles from the cavern's ceiling.

SCORECARD

Hole	1	2	3	4	5	6	7	8	9	out	
Yardage	576	422	365	478	210	532	428	254	458	3,723	
Par	5	4	4	4	3	5	4	3	4	36	
Hole	10	11	12	13	14	15	16	17	18	in	total
Yardage	547	433	488	381	444	228	388	196	616	3,721	7,444
Par	5	4	4	4	4	3	4	3	5	36	72

OTHER PUBLIC COURSES IN ALABAMA WORTH A VISIT

- Capstone Club of Alabama
- Grand National GC, Opelika
- Limestone Springs GC, Oneota

Huge greens and immense bunkers are staples at Kiva Dunes, as exhibited by No. 18.

ALABAMA

KIVA DUNES GOLF COURSE
GULF SHORES, ALABAMA

In order to give proper perspective to Kiva Dunes Golf Course in today's Gulf Shores, Alabama, it is imperative to take a look at the Gulf Shores of yesterday. Highlights then included NASCAR and crawfish, Oakland Raiders quarterback Kenny Stabler, sugar-white sand beaches and the Mullet Toss Festival. Those not familiar with the Mullet Toss are told by Alabamans that it ranks right up there with Mardi Gras and the Kentucky Derby. The idea is to take a live mullet and see how far you can throw it.

OK ...

These were the hot items in Gulf Shores. Kenny Stabler, long retired from the NFL, is still a celebrity on the Alabama coast. The other staples still are prevalent, but outstanding golf – virtually nonexistent twenty-five years ago -- must now be added to the equation.

Kiva Dunes Golf Course is top dog of several new public golf courses that have changed the face of Gulf Shores.

Kiva Dunes and the others are not just obligatory additions to the area's tradition. Yes, they were built to diversify the coast, but the business planners and golf designers went beyond token course design – particularly at Kiva Dunes.

The Jerry Pate design not only changed the face of Gulf Shores when it opened in 1993, but it paved the way for a transformation of opinion.

Kiva Dunes sits on a thin strip of land cradled between Bon Secour Bay and the Gulf of Mexico. Even before Pate began his work, he realized he had a piece of raw material land that would afford him great opportunity to create.

There is a feeling of seclusion upon entering the course, which altered but didn't intrude upon the land's natural feel. There still are dunes, natural grasses, and stately elms and oaks, along with a golf course that remains intriguing for all eighteen holes.

Kiva Dunes faces competition in Gulf Shores, including quality public tracks like Craft Farms and Peninsula Golf & Racquet. The neighbors aren't quite in the same class as Kiva Dunes, but they provide a decent second tier and also keep Kiva Dunes management on its toes.

Kiva Dunes was one of Pate's first designs, but the inexperience is undetectable. By virtually all accounts, this is the best course in Alabama, and anyone can walk up and get a tee time. Reservations might be necessary, but it's not often that a state's top course is purely public.

Golf Digest, *Golfweek*, and *GolfLink* have included Kiva Dunes in various forms of recognition. The course has been rewarded with much acclaim, and playing it is a reward in itself.

In addition to the thoughtful layout, Pate took into account the windy conditions that are predominant in the region.

No. 1, which generally heads into the wind, adds extra burden by forcing a player to make a choice when approaching the green. Left is the easier shot, but the pin is often placed on the right of the green. A shot at the pin, and a sloping putting surface awaits.

Other holes, such as the par-4 10th and the par-5 14th, feature greens that will result in balls rolling off if they don't land softly. Slopes are not protection at Kiva Dunes. Often, they'll earn you penalties. These penalties, however, are a small price to pay. Winds from the sea, along with dunes and grasses, add to a golf test that is unequaled in Alabama.

AFTER YOUR ROUND

Skipping along: Wahoo Watersports and several other companies offer hydroplaning, airboat trips over the swampy waters. The rides bring sights and sounds unique to the bayou that you've probably never experienced before. I still don't know the species of some of the creatures I saw.

Don't forget, it's wet: Waterville USA is a water park that is quite a departure from a quiet round of golf. It's fun and full of frenetic energy. I didn't have my kids with me when I visited Gulf Shores, so I skipped Waterville. But I did take a peek, and if the teenagers are with me on my next visit, I'm taking my trunks.

CHIP SHOTS

Course contact info:
(866) 540-7000,
www.kivadunes.com

Par: 72
Yardage: 7,092 yards

Rating: 73.9
Slope: 132
Notable: Kiva Dunes designer Jerry Pate has been a big winner on the PGA Tour, capturing the 1974 and 1976 U.S. Open.

On the green
◯ $75

SCORECARD											
Hole	1	2	3	4	5	6	7	8	9	out	
Yardage	415	541	228	313	576	428	465	161	428	3,555	
Par	4	5	3	4	5	4	4	3	4	36	
Hole	10	11	12	13	14	15	16	17	18	in	total
Yardage	357	353	452	175	570	540	417	215	458	3,527	7,092
Par	4	4	4	3	5	5	4	3	4	36	72

ALASKA

MOOSE RUN GOLF COURSE
(CREEK COURSE)
FORT RICHARDSON, ALASKA

Often, golf courses use misleading names when marketing themselves to attract as many players as possible. The practice is palatable if the golf is good, but sometimes it becomes obvious rather quickly that there are no pleasant ridges, hills of elms, or fields of oak.

The moniker given to Moose Run Golf Course in the northern hinterlands in the coldest region in the United States is no illusion. There is a very good chance that a moose will be spotted running through, or at least around, the course.

The marketing folks could have named the club Elk Run, Fox Run, or Wolf Run. Bear Run also might have been in the running — pardon the expression — because course architect Robin Nelson needed to carry bear repellent while surveying the land to build the course.

But it's not just the name that makes Moose Run true to its reputation. It is the longest track in Alaska and has been rated as one of the fifty toughest golf courses in America by *Golfweek* and *Golf Digest*. The frontier-like feel one gets while working through a round is no accident. Designer Nelson is always conscious of atmosphere as well as playability.

Nelson's layouts have required a diverse knowledge of how to make golf blend with various natural settings. Among his designs around the world are Mauna Lani Resort Golf Course on the Big Island of Hawaii, Mimosa Golf and Country Club in the Philippines, and the Bali Golf and Country Club in Bali, Indonesia.

Nelson has been around the world, and it is this experience that helps him create a northern masterpiece at Moose Run. The two-course complex, which also includes the Hill Course, opened in 2000. The next year, Nelson was named "Golf Course Architect of the Year" by *The BoardRoom* magazine.

The Creek Course is scenic, but it is its challenges that will leave players gasping for air. The monstrous par-5 11th checks in at 640 yards, and Nos. 6 and 11 play through astonishing gravel pits formerly used by the U.S. Army. Standing on the 4th tee, there is a clear view of Anchorage and miles beyond.

A quick and helpful tip on the differences between the two layouts at Moose Run: players with high handicaps might want to stick to the Hill Course, which is more forgiving but still breathtaking. The Creek Course is where skilled players will relish the test.

Besides the wildlife and the stiff golf challenge at Moose Run, there are a few special features that will grab a player's eye. Two suspension bridges are used to get players where they need to be, there are views of mountains on virtually every hole, all holes are surrounded by forest, and Ship Creek runs right through the middle of the

CHIP SHOTS

Course contact info:
(907) 428-0056,
www.mooserungolfcourse.com

Par: 72
Yardage: 7,324 yards

Rating: 78
Slope: 142
Notable: Moose Run's Creek Course was rated in 2008 as "The Best Public-Access Course in Alaska" by *Golfweek*. It might surprise some in the contiguous U.S. that the course was also named the forty-ninth toughest course in America by *Golf Digest*. The golf season is only four months long, so it's a small window to enjoy a great public course.

On the green
$45

On the last hole, a cluster of saguaro cacti, foreground, are just a few of thousands that surround their namesake course at We-Ko-Pa Golf Club.

Saddle up: There are several horseback-riding stables in the Fountain Hills area, almost all of them offering rides through cactus-filled desert. Peaceful beginner rides are available, and experienced riders can find a stable that will send them a' galloping.

SCORECARD											
Hole	1	2	3	4	5	6	7	8	9	out	
Yardage	469	316	416	631	161	442	314	415	137	3,301	
Par	4	4	4	5	3	4	4	5	3	36	
Hole	10	11	12	13	14	15	16	17	18	in	total
Yardage	337	197	476	470	538	255	328	402	508	3,511	6,812
Par	4	3	5	4	3	4	4	5	4	36	72

ARIZONA

WHIRLWIND GOLF CLUB AT WILD HORSE PASS

(DEVIL'S CLAW/CATTAIL COURSES)
CHANDLER, ARIZONA

Many public courses highlighted in this book are rich in golf tradition and history, and while Whirlwind Golf Club features an exquisite golf experience, the sport is not the only focus here. The course's design is influenced by the heritage of the Native American community and the club's surroundings.

The Gila River Native American community was intent on keeping its traditional home as true to its original look as possible, while splashing championship-quality golf into the desert ambience. Architect Gary Panks was hired to strike the mixture, and he has absolutely succeeded.

The Gila River, which once flowed through a reservation, now follows a path through Whirlwind. The thirty-six-hole complex also features countless native vegetation—including mesquite, cottonwood, saguaro, and palo verde — that emerge alongside and among native grasses. Much of the growth is natural, and more has been added to give the Gila River a similar appearance to the days when it ran through the old reservation.

The Devil's Claw Course was Whirlwind's original design, and it incorporates many of the property's natural elevation changes — including mounds, both gradual and pronounced, which add undulation and challenge to fairways throughout.

The undulations don't stop with the fairways. Devil's Claw greens are multi-tiered, making it vital to stick approach shots on the same level as the pin. Reaching the green in regulation is no guarantee of par; being on the wrong tier can leave you with one devil of a putt, or perhaps two or three. The Devil's Claw has hosted the Gila River Buy.com Classic, bringing top players to face a challenge that is becoming increasingly familiar to locals.

Panks came back to add a second eighteen holes in 2002, and when the Cattail Course opened in the fall of that year, it was an instant and perfect complement to its big sister. The Cattail doesn't depend so much on mounds to provide its test, although there are some natural slopes throughout the layout. In a direct contrast to Devil's Claw, Cattail features cavernous canyons and shimmering lakes strategically placed to keep even the most skilled players on their toes.

It is the diverse design offered by Panks's second

Whirlwind layout that gives the complex a rare combination. Often, when a property adds a second eighteen, it is very similar to the original and doesn't give players much of a reason to give it a try. Not so at Whirlwind. Because Cattail heads in a different direction on the property, where the land is so different, so too is the player's experience.

Cattail attracted the attention of the PGA Tour, which brought the Nationwide Gila River Classic to be played on Whirlwind's second eighteen the year after it opened.

The influence of the Gila River Native Americans can be felt even after players are finished with their round. The original 8,500-square-foot clubhouse has a truly Southwest American feel, and Native American mementos and artifacts are displayed throughout.

Also on tap in the clubhouse is a first-rate golf shop, a pair of spacious locker rooms, and the Sivlik Grill featuring Arizona favorites. When 3,000 square feet were added in 2004, so was much more individual as well as group seating, adding elbow room and ambience to the restaurant.

The Native American touches, an attention to detail, and a dedication to the natural look of the Gila River make Whirlwind one of the most unspoiled settings for high-quality golf you'll find, not only in the Phoenix area but also throughout Arizona and beyond.

CHIP SHOTS

Course contact info:
(480) 940-1500,
www.whirlwindgolf.com

Par: 72 (both courses)
Yardage: Cattail - 7,218 yards
Yardage: Devil's Claw - 7,029 yards

Rating: Cattail - 72.8;
 Devil's Claw - 72.6
Slope: Cattail - 131;
 Devil's Claw - 129
Notable: True to the culture of its surroundings, Whirlwind hole names have a Native American connection — including names that are translated from the Gila River community's native language. Among the hole names (which appear both in Native American dialect as well as English): "Ilpa Kyaam" – Arrow Shot; "QaaQ" – Mud Hen; and "Avehan" – Rattlesnake.

On the green
⛳ ⛳ ⛳ $165

AFTER YOUR ROUND

Take a chance: The Gila River Casino, just a touch over one mile away from Whirlwind, is a target for many players after completing a round at either the Devil's Claw or

Sand and mountains in Arizona should not surprise, but the water and lush grass on the 14th fairway at Whirlwind's Cattail Course aren't your usual desert staples.

Cattail. All the standard games are featured, including blackjack, roulette, and Texas hold 'em. If you want to give yourself a better chance, and you are a believer in the spiritual, perhaps a thirteen-mile drive to Mystical Cove is in order. There, you can make an appointment with a medium who might just tell you what lies ahead on your trip to the casino. If gambling or the spiritual world aren't your activities of choice, a twelve-mile mile trek to the Arizona Railway Museum is another fun option.

SCORECARD - CATTAIL

Hole	1	2	3	4	5	6	7	8	9	out	
Yardage	413	517	162	462	337	180	599	402	431	3,503	
Par	4	5	3	4	4	3	5	4	4	36	
Hole	10	11	12	13	14	15	16	17	18	in	total
Yardage	245	481	578	441	389	143	428	560	450	3,715	7,218
Par	4	4	5	4	4	3	4	5	4	37	72

SCORECARD - DEVIL'S CLAW

Hole	1	2	3	4	5	6	7	8	9	out	
Yardage	424	399	593	190	410	564	160	317	441	3,498	
Par	4	4	5	3	4	5	3	4	4	36	
Hole	10	11	12	13	14	15	16	17	18	in	total
Yardage	407	444	222	361	172	507	425	551	442	3,531	7,029
Par	4	4	3	4	3	5	4	5	4	36	72

The par-4 4th is a scenic tester during the day, and becomes even more cosmetically pleasing during twilight at Mountain Ranch.

ARKANSAS

MOUNTAIN RANCH GOLF CLUB AT FAIRFIELD BAY
FAIRFIELD BAY, ARKANSAS

They say golf is a gentleman's game, and designer Edmund Ault adhered to that principle in 1983 when he built Mountain Ranch Golf Club at Fairfield Bay. The front nine gives players a chance to settle in, providing a welcoming, gently sloping introduction to the course.

But Ault proves that even gentlemen can hide a few tricks up their sleeves. The back nine wakes up a player who may have laid back in the opening nine's ambience. Danger, drop-offs, and bogeys await for those who aren't prepared. And unless you're playing with a local or are privy to some inside information on Mountain Ranch, it is difficult to be ready for what lies ahead.

The front nine is no piece of cake, but other than the rugged 2nd hole, it isn't as tough as the back. No. 2 requires a tee shot of at least 200 yards over a rock quarry,

which covers most of the fairway. The final 200 yards into the two-tiered green is a dogleg left. The putting surface is protected by a pond and two large bunkers. The 2nd hole should be used as a precursor to the unveiling of the back nine, eight holes later.

Perhaps the most striking example of wake-up golf on the incoming nine is the par-5 14th, which presents an eighty-foot drop from the tee. Then comes the par-4 15th, which is a 395-yard uphill climb. This back-nine pairing is considered to be among the toughest consecutive holes in Arkansas, but they aren't alone in positioning Mountain Ranch at the peak of the state's golf horizon.

Nestled in the hills of North Central Arkansas, the terrain sets the tone for the round. Ault didn't shy away from the rugged land; instead he embraced a chance to let Arkansas show off a little. Ault gives you a chance to golf Fairfield Bay's Mountain Ranch in all its natural splendor, with its natural challenges too.

Golfweek rated Mountain Ranch "The Top Resort Course in Arkansas," as well as one of the best public courses (ranked No. 2) in the state, and among the best bargains in America. It's there for the public to play; no membership required.

The Ozark Mountain layout is among Arkansas' best courses for good reason. It forces strategy amid the mountains, even though it isn't overly long by today's standards. It compensates for its lack of length by creating angles amid slopes and valleys.

Not one single fairway at Mountain Ranch is flat from tee to green, and nearly all of the holes feature a dogleg of some degree. Twists and turns and cants and curves make for a delightfully dizzying challenge at Mountain Ranch.

When Mountain Ranch was built more than twenty-five years ago, Arkansas public golf was dominated by municipal courses running on tight budgets. Without much money to spend, conditioning of the courses deteriorated. The enjoyment level of those who played public golf in Arkansas suffered right along with the scruffy fairways and greens.

That's when LinksCorp, a Chicago-based company that owns dozens of resort courses nationwide, came in to

CHIP SHOTS

Course contact info:
(501) 884-3400,
www.tboxgolf.net

Par: 72
Yardage: 6,780 yards

Rating: 72.7
Slope: 1139
Notable: Mountain Ranch has been the site of five Arkansas state championships, and is in line for events that might give it even more exposure on a larger golf stage.

On the green
◯ $50

offer the Razorback State public golfer a saving grace. Not only did LinksCorp hire Ault to create an outstanding track, but it kept the greens fees at a level that was affordable for those playing public golf in Arkansas.

Mountain Ranch offers the best of both worlds — excellence at a fair price.

AFTER YOUR ROUND

Fairfield fare: You don't even have to leave the Fairfield Bay property to continue with a day of recreation and activity. Golf is the main draw but it is far from the sole attraction. Tennis, swimming, fishing, and boating at nearby Greers Ferry Lake can also be part of a day of leisure. Activities close to Mountain Ranch include horseback riding, horseshoes, mountain biking, and miniature golf.

OTHER PUBLIC COURSES IN ARKANSAS WORTH A VISIT
• Hot Springs CC (Arlington Course), Hot Springs
• Hot Springs CC (Park Course), Hot Springs
• Prairie Creek CC, Rogers
• Thunder Bayou Golf Links, Blytheville

SCORECARD

Hole	1	2	3	4	5	6	7	8	9	out	
Yardage	375	540	155	370	405	165	415	565	380	3,370	
Par	4	5	3	4	4	3	4	5	4	36	
Hole	10	11	12	13	14	15	16	17	18	in	total
Yardage	385	415	315	160	560	395	200	440	540	3,410	6,780
Par	4	4	4	3	5	4	3	4	5	36	72

CALIFORNIA

NAKOMA GOLF RESORT
CLIO, CALIFORNIA

After a change in ownership, a new name, and the temporary closing of the facility during extensive renovation in 2006, the folks at Nakoma Golf Resort were looking to put a new face on an old beauty.

Since reopening in May, 2007, this facility, about forty miles from Reno, Nevada, has offered golfers along the majestic Sierra Nevada yet another venue in which to enjoy their game. Ownership of the course has been juggled in recent years, but it seems that no matter who operates the place, this is a great golf course to play.

Now, after more ownership turmoil at the end of 2008, there is uncertainty about the course's status. But there is hope among the golf community that Nakoma can remain viable. It is one of the most challenging layouts in the western part of the country, despite past efforts to amp it back a little.

Sightseers who don't even play the game have been known to visit the facility. Frank Lloyd Wright designed the Nakoma clubhouse in 1924, and the 23,000-square-foot structure includes a cozy restaurant and bar, private meeting rooms, a full-service spa, and an immaculate setting that allows you to soak in the magnificence of the mountainous scenery.

Breath-taking sights are as plentiful as poker chips in nearby Reno. Nakoma Golf Resort is nestled between pines and peaks, just north of Truckee, California and Lake Tahoe, Nevada. There are a few features worth viewing on the course as well. The tree-lined fairways are sleek and true, and the tee boxes are well maintained. Manicuring doesn't only apply to the tee boxes; there are five sets of tees to allow players to feel comfortable no matter what their skill level may be.

The course was softened somewhat during the 2006 renovation, backing off from the original layout that sometimes proved torturous. Many players in the area maintained that it was the difficulty of the course that kept golfers from coming and they ultimately forced the old owners to sell. The course is a beautiful track, and the renovation made it more playable.

Nakoma's reputation for being "too tough to play" has proved hard to shake, even after the renovation. Word hasn't traveled as quickly as staffers would like, and the information about the reduced greens fees also hasn't quite made the rounds. So, this public course definitely deserves to be rediscovered.

Nakoma staffers have gone out of their way to make the atmosphere as friendly as possible. Though this resort was formerly known in town as a place for the rich to congregate, its crew now wants people to know that all are welcome. All you have to do is show up and walk from the Frank Lloyd Wright clubhouse to the first tee and swing away.

CHIP SHOTS

Course contact info:
(877) 462-5662,
www.nakomagolfresort.sports.officelive.com

Par: 72
Yardage: 7,077 yards

Rating: 74.2
Slope: 147
Notable: Nakoma Golf Resort is the new name for a course that was formerly called The Dragon at Golf Mountain. The name may have changed but the golf course remains superlative. So, if you're looking for the old Dragon, here it is.

On the green
◔ $50

Wildlife and weeping willows provide the scenery, and the course provides the tough golf at Nakoma, which is undergoing ownership change.

The half-dozen water hazards are indeed hazardous, and they don't do anything to harm the scenic ambience. Nothing like a pond or a fountain to remind you to take a deep breath of the fresh mountain air.

Whether you elect to play the course from the front tees or take the ultimate, 7,077-yard challenge from the tips, Nakoma is full of tricky risk-reward situations. The bunkers, contours, and ponds have been placed in areas that will force you to use your best strategic thinking.

Speaking of strategy, it begins long before reaching Nakoma. The intelligent route is to forget the ownership difficulties, and past reputation of maniacal difficulty. Be smart: tackle Nakoma.

AFTER YOUR ROUND

Here, there, everywhere: Recreation takes several paths near the California-Nevada line, depending on your preference. Nature lovers can enjoy hiking, biking, or even a picnic in the Sierra Nevada.

Smart bet: Those with a little adventure in their blood can venture over to Reno for all the gambling they can handle. There's Atlantis Casino Resort Spa, Silver Legacy Resort Casino, Circus Circus Hotel and Casino-Reno, Sands Regency Casino & Hotel, and many more.

Gone are the blind tee shots, the greens have been slowed, the massive slopes on the fairways have been eased, and the rough has been cut. Nakoma is now as playable as any of the other golf courses in the area.

With such beautiful raw material with which to work, the region is rife with quality golf courses. There's Lake Ridge and Edgewood-Tahoe in Nevada; and Coyote Moon, Squaw Creek, and Whitehawk just a few miles away in California. There's quite a selection, and Nakoma fits in nicely.

OTHER PUBLIC COURSES IN CALIFORNIA WORTH A VISIT

- Barona Creek GC, Lakeside
- The Club at PGA West (Stadium Course), La Quinta
- DarkHorse GC, Auburn
- Pasatiempo GC, Santa Cruz
- Saddle Creek GC, Copperopolis
- Spyglass Hill GC, Pebble Beach

SCORECARD

Hole	1	2	3	4	5	6	7	8	9	out	
Yardage	533	458	400	320	164	456	499	192	398	3,420	
Par	5	4	4	4	3	4	5	3	4	36	
Hole	10	11	12	13	14	15	16	17	18	in	total
Yardage	433	553	390	216	443	393	495	175	559	3,657	7,077
Par	4	5	4	3	4	4	4	3	5	36	72

CALIFORNIA

PEBBLE BEACH GOLF LINKS
PEBBLE BEACH, CALIFORNIA

A book focused on public-access golf wouldn't be complete without including what might just be the most beautiful public course in America. Pebble Beach Golf Links, an oceanside wonder filled with stately trees and breaking waves, takes golf landscape to a level that few courses can even pretend to match.

Oh, and there's a little history, too. For more than eighty-five years, Pebble Beach has been displaying its muscle along with its beauty. It has been the site of many major championships, and the annual PGA Tour's AT&T Pebble Beach National Pro-Am is one of the most-watched golf events, rarely missed by any of the top names in the field, not to mention several celebrities who test their game alongside the pros.

So, you'd think Pebble Beach ownership would be crazy to mess with a course of this magnitude. But that's where you would be wrong. In January 2009, owners Arnold Palmer, Clint Eastwood, Peter Ueberroth, and friends announced that significant renovations would be made to the course to give it a facelift for the 2010 U.S. Open.

One of the most storied courses in the United States is getting an overhaul for what seems to be diverse reasons. The alterations are intended to restore the layout more to the philosophy Jack Neville had in mind when he designed Pebble Beach in 1919. But at the same time, it will stiffen Pebble's challenging course to help it keep up with today's PGA Tour players' skill and their interest in greater length.

Neville's original design was hazardous and treacherous. Over the years, the alterations incorporated at Pebble Beach softened the challenge. New bunkers, tees, trees, and shorter rough will add significant difficulty. A shorter rough to make things tougher? At a 1.5-inch-cut, the rough will no longer prevent errant shots from running into the ocean. Stay in the fairway or find watery perdition.

Changes include five bunkers down the left side of No. 6 rather than one large mass of sand. The par-4 3rd is much more difficult off the tee, and the 13th is thirty-five yards longer, which makes for an excruciating test when played into the whipping wind coming in from the sea.

These are not minor changes, and they get even more drastic. The fairways at Nos. 4, 6, 8, 9, 10, and 18 will be moved to create abutments to the ocean that will increase roll-offs into the water.

The purists have been howling since the announcement was made of the changes, but Palmer and Co. have stuck to their guns. Pebble remains a wonderful piece of American golf history, and it is also positioning itself to remain relevant for years to come.

"As we approached our fifth U.S. Open, we felt strongly that Pebble Beach should be strengthened to heighten the challenge of today's players and today's equipment," said R.J. Harper, the senior vice-president for golf at Pebble Beach Resorts, when announcing Pebble's transformation. "To do this we've scoured the archives to get a clear understanding of the overall original design principles. The location of new bunkers, tees, and trees all fall within the original concepts of the design. They are, for the most part, simply placed to accommodate today's standard of championship play, from the championship tees."

Whether or not you agree with the changes, there will be opportunities in store. A wonderful piece of golf history remains available for all of us public-access golfers to enjoy, and now there is a chance to play a new Pebble Beach.

CHIP SHOTS

Course contact info:
(866) 654-9300,
www.pebblebeach.com

Par: 72
Yardage: 6,737 yards

Rating: 73.8
Slope: 142
Notable: The $400-plus price tag at Pebble Beach may be a shocker, especially since no other course in this book comes close to that range. However, I thought Pebble Beach absolutely needed to be included in these pages because golfers may not be aware that it's accessible to the public. So save up for this once-in-a-lifetime golf experience.

On the green
◔◔◔◔ $400-plus

AFTER YOUR ROUND

If Pebble isn't enough: Amazing golf abounds on the Monterey Peninsula, and not all of it is expensive. Poppy Hills, Monterey Peninsula Country Club, and Spanish Bay are gorgeous and pricey. But Cypress Point is one of the best deals in golf; an oceanside course in double figures.

Mild West: There is plenty of ocean and beach and horseback riding, and the Pebble Beach concierge will make arrangements. Guided rides are available through wooded trails and along the Pacific — definitely not the Wild West.

Waves crash into the coast adjacent to the 7th hole at Pebble Beach, just a few feet from the green.

SCORECARD											
Hole	1	2	3	4	5	6	7	8	9	out	
Yardage	376	502	374	327	187	500	106	416	462	3,250	
Par	4	5	4	4	3	5	3	4	4	36	
Hole	10	11	12	13	14	15	16	17	18	in	total
Yardage	430	373	201	393	572	396	401	178	543	3,487	6,737
Par	4	4	3	4	5	4	4	3	5	36	72

Sunset at Pelican Hill North's 18th hole, 430-yard, par-4 seaside beauty.

CALIFORNIA

THE RESORT AT PELICAN HILL
(NORTH/SOUTH COURSES)
NEWPORT COAST, CALIFORNIA

California's got it all: sunshine, ocean, movie stars, glitz, glamor, and golf. There's so much going on in California that golf might get left behind. But the game in this state is earthquaking good.

Newport Coast, home to Pelican Hill Golf Club, is an almost unimaginably striking locale for golf. Pelican Hill, where holes meander and sometimes jut into the Pacific Ocean, is one of those beautiful places in California. And that's saying something.

There are thirty-six holes at Pelican Hill, and none of them are an imposition on what nature has spawned. The fairways weave in harmony with surrounding peace, and the pristine greens seem to be part of the coastline. The beauty of the area is not reserved just for the courses. Pelican Hill is set on over 400 acres of awesome coastal land and is next-door neighbor to the Irvine Ranch Land Reserve, which comprises thousands of acres of permanently preserved land.

Many times, one course on a thirty-six-hole property is the obvious choice of the two layouts. Not so at Pelican Hill. The North Course is a little tougher, and the South might have better scenery. The folks at Pelican Hill like to say, "The courses complement each other, they don't compete." Both courses are set high above the Pacific Ocean. They feature towering eucalyptus and pine trees, and carpet-like Bermuda fairways. White sand bunkers, while not natural, blend in with coastal sand while protecting gorgeous greens.

Pelican Hill is set on softly sloping terrain, encompassing fearsome tee shots over canyons, and many holes that make their way along the rocky cliffs of the coast. Natural vegetation and wandering canyons are constant companions.

Tom Fazio and Andy Banfield designed both courses on Pelican Hill — the South in 1991 and the North in 1993 — and Fazio reworked portions of each layout in autumn 2008. It's hard to imagine why Fazio wanted to touch his original design, but it wasn't a facelift. It was just a tweak here or there.

One of the most enjoyable pieces of the South Course

puzzle is the back-to-back par-3s at Nos. 12 and 13. Both short holes run along the Pacific Ocean and offer decent chances at par if the wind isn't kicking up too hard off the Pacific.

The highlight of the North Course is the par-5 17th. The fairway is lined with water on one side and a canyon on the other for all of its 558 yards. It takes three perfect shots to get to the green in regulation. Staffers and locals call No. 17 the "Gut Check."

Those who pass the Gut Check surely have accomplished something. Achievements don't come easy when playing Pelican Hill because of the courses' sometimes severe landscapes, but the club itself has earned plenty of accolades and awards.

The North Course has been ranked 40th by *Golf Magazine* in its "Top 100 Courses You Can Play" list, and *Golfweek* ranked it 72nd on its list of "100 Top Modern Courses" (of courses built after 1950).

The South Course also earned its share of awards. It has been as high as No. 30 in *Golf Magazine*'s "Top 100 Courses You Can Play" list, and No. 59 in *Golf Digest*'s list of "75 Upscale Public Courses."

The courses wear their medallions proudly, but the staff members place rankings in perspective. There is a realization that the golf courses, as perfect as they are, take a back seat to what nature has provided.

CHIP SHOTS

Course contact info:
(877) 735-4226,
www.pelicanhill.com

Par: South 70; **North** 71
Yardage: South 6,580 yards;
North 6,945 yards

Rating: South 72.1; **North** 73.3
Slope: South 133; **North** 133
Notable: Twilight golf is sometimes considered a rushed time to play, and often courses have trouble filling the evening slots. But playing at that time of day at Pelican Hill is a little different. Not only is the golf great, but twilight players are in store for the sunset of a lifetime.

On the green
◯◯◯ $165

AFTER YOUR ROUND

Island (s)hopping: A quick ferry takes you to Balboa Island, where there are more than seventy gift shops and galleries. Ferry hours go from 6:00 a.m. to midnight daily, extending to 2:00 a.m. on weekends. The fee starts at fifty cents. Another island of shopping adventure is Fashion Island, and it's actually right on Newport Center Drive. More than 200 stores and two movie theaters allow shopping outdoors amid fountains, palm trees, and ocean breezes.

See the sea: The Newport Aquatic Center offers an opportunity to go rowing, canoeing, kayaking, and outrigger canoeing. If visitors choose, they can enter one of the competitions sponsored by the aquatic center. Kayaks and canoes are rented by the hour. Another sea-worthy sight is the Newport Harbor Nautical Museum, the largest in Orange County. The museum features ship models, ship paintings, and hosts special events, so be sure to check their schedule.

SCORECARD - NORTH COURSE

Hole	1	2	3	4	5	6	7	8	9	out	
Yardage	542	197	409	433	441	170	450	540	424	3,606	
Par	5	3	4	4	4	3	4	5	4	36	
Hole	10	11	12	13	14	15	16	17	18	in	total
Yardage	421	369	202	345	411	445	158	558	430	3,339	6,945
Par	4	4	3	4	4	4	3	5	4	35	71

SCORECARD - SOUTH COURSE

Hole	1	2	3	4	5	6	7	8	9	out	
Yardage	443	353	346	142	359	402	193	562	455	3,255	
Par	4	4	4	3	4	4	3	5	4	35	
Hole	10	11	12	13	14	15	16	17	18	in	total
Yardage	475	367	159	131	544	407	219	570	453	3,325	6,580
Par	4	4	3	3	5	4	3	5	4	35	70

CALIFORNIA

RUSTIC CANYON GOLF COURSE
MOORPARK, CALIFORNIA

There aren't as many golf courses being today as in past years, but if golf architects took one look at Rustic Canyon Golf Course and followed its pattern, that trend might change. High-end, more widely known golf courses in the Los Angeles area charge triple greens fees and often don't fill up their daily schedule.

Rustic Canyon, believe it or not, charges in the $50 range and can stand up to any public course not only in L.A., but throughout the entire state of California. Word is getting out, but it's still what we would call a "little secret" of golf. Players unfamiliar with the area might not think they could play this top-notch golf course at such a reasonable price.

Golfers who live near L.A. know about the course, but those outside the metropolitan area should take a look at this affordable beauty. It's definitely worth the ride and almost certainly will spur a return trip.

Perhaps Rustic Canyon's low profile can be attributed to the fact that is has chosen to go with a classic design, filled with wonderful options and strategy, steering clear of outlandish, unnecessary illusion.

There are plenty of places on the course where decisions are required: go over the vegetation for the green or play it safe for a chip on the next shot. You have to think it through at Rustic Canyon. And there are no transplanted palms. The few native coastal oaks and all the vegetation at Rustic Canyon were in place long before the golf course arrived in 2002.

Rustic Canyon plays to a par-72 and can play to around 7,000 yards (it says 6,988 on the scorecard, but that changes according to maintenance requirements of the day). Double-digit handicappers shouldn't let the yardage keep them from playing the back tees.

The course is 800 feet above sea level, which doesn't require adjustment on most shots, but it's something to be aware of when deciding to hit a long 6-iron or a short 5. Then just stand back and enjoy the ball's flight through the majestic backdrop.

Gas prices could be a factor for Los Angeles residents taking the fifty-mile northward drive to the peaks above Simi Valley. But if you live in L.A. and you play golf, chances are you're willing to spend a few pennies on gas to take on Rustic Canyon.

There is no attempt to mimic classic holes, but designer Gil Hanse most certainly achieved the classic elements of golf: the course can be walked easily; there are vast chipping areas around the greens; the par-3s are long; and the par-4s offer variety. These features are but a few examples of retro-design at Rustic Canyon. Perhaps the greens are more contoured than courses in the old days, but that is one of the rare departures from golf the way it used to be.

After hearing the details of the course's construction, it seems Hanse's team enjoyed the design process. Jim Wagner is a regular associate of Hanse's, but there was one rather unique member of the team. Famed golf writer and golf historian Geoff Shackelford contributed to the project. Based in L.A., Shackelford offered input on what might be thought of as his home course.

Shackelford has been to virtually every classically designed golf course in the world, and it was wise of Hanse to bring him into the project. Who better than a historian to recreate history?

The golfers of L.A. should be thankful to the architects behind Rustic Canyon. The developers came in under their budget of $3.1 million, so they didn't have to make up any deficit by hiking up greens fees. Rustic Canyon is an affordable gem — and it's the genuine article.

CHIP SHOTS

Course contact info:
(877) 735-4226,
www.rusticcanyongolfcourse.com

Par: 72
Yardage: 6,988 yards

Rating: 75.5
Slope: 140
Notable: The awards and ratings speak to the high quality of Rustic Canyon. *Golfweek* has rated it the "No. 3 Best Public Course in California," and *Golf Digest* has ranked it the "No. 1 Affordable Golf Course in North America."

On the green
○ $50

AFTER YOUR ROUND

Glitz and glam: Rustic Canyon is just down the road from Hollywood, so there is no shortage of movie-star related things to see. Tours of movie studios, and bus rides past celebrity homes, are the standard activities for stargazers. Grauman's Chinese Theatre offers a little more history than most other sights in Hollywood. Famous handprints in the

The par-5 10th plays nasty if your shot happens to stray right.

sidewalk date all the way back to Mary Pickford's in 1927.

From tee to sea: The Aquarium of the Pacific in Long Beach offers as much quiet as a round of golf on Rustic Canyon. While you're enjoying the peace, you'll learn a little something about aquatic mammals, ecology, and the history of the sea.

SCORECARD

Hole	1	2	3	4	5	6	7	8	9	out	
Yardage	540	457	315	166	570	216	362	127	565	3,318	
Par	5	4	4	3	5	3	4	3	5	36	
Hole	10	11	12	13	14	15	16	17	18	in	total
Yardage	571	452	336	555	485	147	479	189	456	3,670	6,988
Par	5	4	4	5	4	3	4	3	4	36	72

Parasailers over the South's 12th green show there is more than one way to enjoy the beauty of Torrey Pines.

CALIFORNIA

TORREY PINES GOLF COURSE
(SOUTH COURSE)
LA JOLLA, CALIFORNIA

The beautiful sights in and around the San Diego area are plentiful and the climate is said to be the most pleasant in America. A golf course must be outstanding to be counted as a highlight in such a place. Torrey Pines Golf Course, in nearby La Jolla, more than holds its own.

There are two courses on the property — the South is longer and more difficult, and the North is considered more scenic. Both, however, are good enough to be used by the PGA Tour when it comes to visit each year. The South is indeed a stiffer challenge, but the North is plenty difficult. And the North may have more mountain and ocean views, but the South is privy to plenty of scenery. In early 2009, Torrey Pines was selected to host LPGA's 2009 Samsung World Championship on the South Course. It marks the first LPGA event held at Torrey Pines since the 1983 Inamori Classic.

Regardless of the debate about the "dueling courses," we will concentrate on the South Course because of the great challenges it offers. Its rating and slope are both higher than its sister to the north, lending credence to the difficulty factor. High-handicap players are well advised to play the North Course, which will offer plenty of tests as well and even more panorama. More skilled players will enjoy either course.

The courses stand proud on cliffs that tower above the Pacific Ocean. Wildlife abounds, and trees and brush fill both layouts. Truly, it is a sight that goes beyond golf. Playing the game is why players visit, but the views and memories they will take home might just render the game secondary.

The fact that Torrey Pines is a public facility is shocking enough when you consider that there are so many private clubs throughout the country that can't come close to matching what the La Jolla twosome have to offer. When you consider that the club is a municipal facility owned and operated by the City of San Diego, it is almost impossible to believe.

City officials are to be commended. Not only do they run one of the most beautiful cities in America, they find a little time to run one of the best golf courses in the nation. Nice work, San Diego.

The wild card at Torrey Pines is the weather. If winds

are sweeping in off the ocean, it is best to play with someone who is familiar with the course. Direction and strength of the wind are major factors when devising strategy, and those who've played the course a time or two are able to suggest which club might be best.

If you can't get a regular to play in your foursome, it would at least be wise to talk to someone with experience on the course before approaching the first tee, even if it's asking how many clubs to go down if you're into the wind, or vice-versa if the wind is at your back. It could make for a difference of several strokes on the scorecard, and that's why you came to Torrey Pines. Your challenge is to see if you can tame the monster that challenges PGA Tour players every January. The South Course is the more ferocious of the two.

The par-5 9th is among the most beastly. At 613 yards, its length can intimidate regardless of wind direction. If the winds are swirling or happen to be in your face, the hole is one of the stiffest challenges a public player will ever face.

Other memorable tests are the 198-yard, par-3 3rd and the 504-yard, par-4 12th. Like the 9th, the combination of length and wind make the holes extremely tough to master. A par on any of the three should be tucked away in the memory banks as one of the finest moments a public player will ever achieve. There is no room for imperfection on these, and as all players know, a series of perfect golf shots is a rarity to be remembered.

AFTER YOUR ROUND

Wild times: The world-famous San Diego Zoo is a must-see for animal lovers. Even those who don't find themselves particularly interested in wild beasts will leave amazed at the wide variety of mammals, fish, and reptiles that inhabit the zoo. Within the zoo is a 2,100-acre preserve, where animals wander freely in surroundings that are made to resemble their native environment as closely as possible.

Close to the course: La Jolla is just outside San Diego proper, and it is a destination in itself. Pelicans roam along Coast Boulevard, and world-class art galleries, exceptional shopping, and spectacular coastline views fill the landscape.

CHIP SHOTS

Course contact info:
(800) 985-4653,
www.torreypinesgolfcourse.com

Par: 72
Yardage: 7,608 yards

Rating: 78.1
Slope: 143
Notable: Both the South and North courses are used for the PGA Tour's annual stop — the Buick Invitational, which historically has been the Tour's fourth tournament of the season.

On the green
◯◯ $125

SCORECARD											
Hole	1	2	3	4	5	6	7	8	9	out	
Yardage	452	387	198	483	453	560	462	176	613	3,784	
Par	4	4	3	4	4	5	4	3	5	36	
Hole	10	11	12	13	14	15	16	17	18	in	total
Yardage	405	221	504	541	435	477	227	442	572	3,824	7,608
Par	4	3	4	5	4	4	3	4	5	36	72

COLORADO

THE GOLF CLUB AT REDLANDS MESA
(MONUMENT COURSE)
GRAND JUNCTION, COLORADO

This might be a chance to know what it feels like to sit on top of the world.

The Monument Course at the Golf Club at Redlands Mesa sits at 5,000 feet above sea level, offers views that are breathtaking — and it's one of those times that the cliché truly fits. There are several areas throughout the course that literally produce gasps.

The face of the Colorado Monument practically shadows the western side of the grounds of the golf course, which has rugged, rocky areas comprised of exposed sandstone. The sun bouncing off of the omnipresent stone produces a red-brown gleam that surrounds a player during certain times of the day.

It may be unusual to acknowledge this in a book dedicated to golf, but the scenery alone — even without a round of golf — is almost worth the modest price of admission.

Almost.

To arrive at the Monument Course is a beautiful trip into Boulderville, and the golf stands up proudly to its scenic surroundings. Course designer Jim Engh has never retreated from the challenge of creating a course in the rugged American West, which requires precise advance planning because of the obviously unlovable features.

The par-72 layout plays to 7,007 yards from the back tees, which is fairly short for a talented player. The air is ultra-thin at this elevation, and the driver can stay in the bag on most tee boxes. This might seem to work well for the average daily-fee golfer, but a longer-than-usual drive actually can hinder a player who doesn't hit it straight. An errant drive might not reach a hazard at lower elevation, but at this nearly mile-high course, it has a better chance to reach the rocky walls.

The Monument Course offers an unusual perspective for those who are in tune with their surroundings. The rocks are virtually everywhere, and the golf course seems laid out gently within the jagged natural terrain. After a recent round at Redlands Mesa, one player said the course made him feel like he was playing in dinosaur tracks and should have been partnered with Fred Flintstone and Barney Rubble. The comments may have drawn a laugh, but the golf is seriously solid. The front nine presents challenges, angles, and hazards that are difficult to read from the tees. And even if you can see them, knowing what club to draw takes a few holes to figure out if you're not used to mile-high golf.

The par 5s are particularly interesting, offering varying imagery and diverse challenges in shot-making. For instance, No. 5 is a treacherous, uphill bear, and No. 10 plays downhill all the way and is reachable in two.

Golf purists often disdain golf paths, and for this reason many designers attempt to hide them behind trees, or in the case of Redlands Mesa, stones. But Engh makes the cart paths work for him, and they form an attractive part of the golf course, the result of obvious craftsmanship and attention. The Monument may be the most enjoyable riding course in golf.

Redlands Mesa's Monument Course is a recommended ride, and it should be thought of as a vehicle to adventurous golf amid the mountains.

AFTER YOUR ROUND

Unwind with wine: Just west of Grand Junction, the Grand Valley stretches from Fruita to Palisade and averages 4,700 feet above sea level. The valley is the heart of Colorado wine country, and includes eight wineries composing the Grand Valley Winery Association. Grapes in the valley receive sun three hundred days a year, which, combined with the region's warm, dry days and cool nights, produces a perfect microclimate for grapes. The valley is a great place to buy wine, and also to view the vineyards.

Rev it up: After your round at Redlands Mesa, you have a chance to go from the tee to the Model-T by taking a trip to the Gateway Colorado Auto Museum. The museum is a slick,

---

CHIP SHOTS

Course contact info:
(970) 263-9270,
www.redlandsmesa.com

Par: 72
Yardage: 7,007 yards

Rating: 72.1
Slope: 137
Notable: The Monument Course at the Golf Club at Redlands Mesa has been named the best public-access course in Colorado – four times – by *Golfweek* magazine. Course designer Jim Engh is no stranger to Western golf. He also created The Sanctuary in Sedalia, Colorado, and Hawktree Golf Club in Bismarck, North Dakota.

On the green
◐◐ $84

Redlands Mesa is a meshing of nature's rugged ground and golf's manicured sands and grasses.

modern facility, but it gives you the history of automobiles dating back to 1907. After your day at the museum, you will have put a century's worth of cars in your rear-view mirror.

Not what to eat, but where: Canyons and red-rock formations make Colorado National Monument the area's biggest draw, not to mention a great place to eat. Breakfast on the Monument offers delicious entrees with a delectable view of the canyon. If you're more of a hands-on type, you can picnic near the Saddlehorn Campground or in the Devil's Kitchen picnic area.

OTHER PUBLIC COURSES IN COLORADO WORTH A VISIT
- Broadmoor GC (East Course), Colorado Springs
- Fossil Trace GC, Golden
- The GC at Bear Dance, Larkspur
- Haymaker GC, Steamboat Springs
- Lakota Canyon Ranch & GC, New Castle
- Raven GC at Three Peaks, Silverthorne
- Red Sky GC (Fazio Course), Wolcott
- Red Sky GC (Norman Course), Wolcott

SCORECARD

Hole	1	2	3	4	5	6	7	8	9	out	
Yardage	419	429	197	373	575	401	466	164	389	3,413	
Par	4	4	3	4	5	4	4	3	4	35	
Hole	10	11	12	13	14	15	16	17	18	in	total
Yardage	527	397	151	541	370	568	412	218	410	3,594	7,007
Par	5	4	3	5	4	5	4	3	4	37	72

COLORADO

KEYSTONE RANCH GOLF COURSE
KEYSTONE, COLORADO

Golfers looking to unlock a chance to play with the snowy peaks of the Rocky Mountains as a backdrop, not to mention take advantage of the thin mountain air, should take a look at Keystone Ranch Golf Course.

The course is set at 9,300 feet above sea level, which gives it an edge-of-the-world atmosphere that is nearly surreal. After you snap out of the temptation to simply stare at the surroundings and grab a club out of your bag, you're in for a picturesque round and a stiff challenge.

Besides the scenic views, there's another advantage to being so high in the sky. You'll enjoy at least a club-and-a-half distance advantage, and it doesn't take a Ph.D. in geology to tell you it's easier to hit a soft 7-iron into the green than a hard 6.

Even though this course is surrounded by mountains, it somehow manages to belie its surroundings — at least for the first half of the round. On the outward nine, this Robert Trent Jones, Jr. design more closely resembles Scottish links than pure mountain golf.

The front nine includes all the features of links-style golf. Brush, mounds, deep bunkers, and large, undulating greens are the player's challenge from the 1st to the 9th. The linksy feel might surprise first time visitors expecting a rocky surrounding, and you can almost see Jones smiling every time a player thinks, "Hey, I thought I was in the Rocky Mountains."

The front nine has a consistent feel to it, and that consistency includes some tough golf holes. None is more difficult, and memorable, than the signature 5th. It's rare that a par-3 is remembered for its challenge, but it's a different story when it's every bit of 190 yards and forces a long carry to reach the green.

Natural meadowland stands between the tee and the green, although there is a slight break for players. The ball doesn't have to reach the putting surface to avoid penalty. There are about thirty yards of landing area in front of the green, showing that Jones had a soft spot for those who couldn't quite pinpoint their tee shots to 190 yards.

The historic Keystone Ranch barn is part of the 5th's landscape, which offers players a brief history lesson on the way to the green. The property that is now Keystone Ranch was once an expansive lettuce farm and cattle ranch. The former ranch's rolling terrain has not been altered, which is a staple of the course's challenge.

The barn isn't the only historic structure on site. At the center of the course is a log homestead that is now the clubhouse. It has been restored to perfection and houses the four-diamond Keystone Ranch Restaurant. When Luke Smith built the homestead as a fishing and hunting retreat at the turn of the century, he would have been stunned to think that someday it would be the site of one of the finest restaurants in the Colorado/Utah region. The *Zagat Survey* rated it No.1 in the region from 2001-2003, and it remains one of the top dining experiences in the Rockies.

Players shouldn't start looking ahead to dinner until after they've finished the round, however. It takes full concentration to get through the Keystone Ranch challenge.

Just as you get used to links golf, the inward nine slaps you in the face with traditional mountain valley layout. Players face a whole set of conditions that contrast with the front nine: the fairways are more lush, the rolling slopes are now rocky formations, the landing areas are a little tighter, and the greens a bit smaller.

History, two courses in one, and outstanding dining are premium reasons why Keystone Ranch is consistently recognized as one of the can't-miss courses in Colorado.

AFTER YOUR ROUND

Summer face: Imagine a quaint ski resort without snow and you have a perfect picture of Keystone, Colorado, during golf season. The golf season is approximately four-and-a-half months long, but don't think this is a town that shutters up in the summer, waiting for the slope-seekers. There's plenty for golfers to do, and they're not considered second-class citizens. There are shops and activities to suit every budget, including rafting, fishing, and horseback riding.

CHIP SHOTS

Course contact info:
(970) 496-4250,
www.keystone.snow.com,
click golf.

Par: 72
Yardage: 7,090 yards
Rating: 71.4
Slope: 130
Notable: The Keystone property was a farm and ranch before it was a golf course, but its history goes back further than that. The land was an area where Ute and Arapaho Indians once hunted buffalo.

On the green
◐◐ $125

The 9th hole displays the highlight of twilight at Keystone Ranch Golf Course.

SCORECARD

Hole	1	2	3	4	5	6	7	8	9	out	
Yardage	528	433	429	412	190	564	207	422	368	3,553	
Par	5	4	4	4	3	5	3	4	4	36	
Hole	10	11	12	13	14	15	16	17	18	in	total
Yardage	463	351	171	552	172	403	422	414	589	3,537	7,090
Par	4	4	3	5	3	4	4	4	5	36	72

Lake of Isles offers a stunning, nature-hike ambience combined with a mixture of public and private golf.

CONNECTICUT

LAKE OF ISLES

(NORTH COURSE)

NORTH STONINGTON, CONNECTICUT

Gamblers are familiar with a stunning complex on a beautiful tract of New England land, where the Foxwoods Resort Casino has been located since 1992. The country-club set also knows about this place, where the South Course at Lake of Isles sits as a private-golf gem in the Nutmeg State.

So what does this have to do with us public-access types? Well, we also received a piece of the pie because the property also includes the eighteen-hole North Course — a purely public place to play. It isn't often that private and public tracks sit side by side, but the unusual neighbors mesh well at Lake of Isles. The arrangement allows the facilities to market themselves to two distinct groups, but more importantly to the public-access player, it offers a fantastic place to play on the same property where country-clubbers pay membership dues. It's a rare arrangement, and both categories of Lake Isles' golfers seem satisfied with the situation.

The Mashantucket Pequot Tribal Nation owns the casino and both courses, and the North surrounds a ninety-acre lake as it meanders through 900 acres of rich, wooded countryside. Both golf courses are carved into rugged, rocky land, which made for a challenge when Robert Trent Jones, Sr., was plotting the holes.

This region of Connecticut features far more rocks than

topsoil, which can make for a beautiful finished product, but it's not such an easy task to bring a golf course to fruition on this terrain. Jones said he had a "spectacular piece of ground" with which to work, and knew there would be some extra headaches in completing the project on such rocky land. The private-club members were happy Jones stuck to his guns when the South Course opened in April, 2005, and the public-access players were equally grateful when they got a place to play one month later.

The arrangement is working well, and it is a particularly ironic scenario in Connecticut. Several private clubs in the state carry outstanding reputations, but until the past decade or so, quality public-access courses were limited. Since 2000, many public tracks have been added to a state full of golfers hungering for them, and the public-private ratio of quality courses is becoming more balanced.

What better picture of balance than having a public and a private on the same property? The private South course is a couple hundred yards longer than its public neighbor, but the North actually is rated tougher. Jones was forced to use an extensive amount of dynamite during the North's construction, but the course still seems to fit naturally into the land.

CHIP SHOTS

Course contact info:
(888) 475-3746,
www.lakeofisles.com

Par: 72
Yardage: 7,252 yards

Rating: 75.8
Slope: 143
Notable: Lake of Isles Golf Shop has been named one of the "100 Best Golf Shops in America" by *Golf World* magazine several times. The 1,800-square-foot shop features equipment from top manufacturers and the atmosphere and creative displays make it a fun shop to visit.

On the green
○○ $120

The North fairways offer a wide welcome, and their gentle roll makes proper placement imperative. The holes follow a path through acres and acres of enormous trees, and the deeper a player gets into the course, the more the round feels like a hike through the woods. But, keep your guard up: the greens are challenging and often two-tiered, and are usually surrounded by rock outcroppings, bunkers, and mounds.

Each hole literally follows the banks of the pre-existing man-made lake, and players travel over wooded bridges that connect the front and back nines. Nature is a part of the round from start to finish, but because of the tricky and testing golf holes, Lake of Isles North — public as it may be — is definitely no walk in the park.

AFTER YOUR ROUND

A sly fox would … : Smart visitors start their day with a round of golf and then take a walk through the enormous Foxwoods Casino. There's much more to do than gamble. There are shops specializing in golf clubs, toys, clothing, and a variety of other items. Also in the casino are concert halls and a nightclub. Luciano Pavarotti, Sophia Loren, Paul Anka, and Jackie Chan have performed at various grand openings in the resort.

SCORECARD

Hole	1	2	3	4	5	6	7	8	9	out	
Yardage	593	216	356	457	530	469	204	369	459	3,653	
Par	5	3	4	4	5	4	3	4	4	36	

Hole	10	11	12	13	14	15	16	17	18	in	total
Yardage	429	196	525	370	462	574	200	384	459	3,599	7,252
Par	4	3	5	4	4	5	3	4	4	36	72

OTHER PUBLIC COURSES IN CONNECTICUT WORTH A VISIT
• Fox Hopyard GC, East Haddam
• Richter Park GC, Danbury

CONNECTICUT

LYMAN ORCHARDS GOLF CLUB
(JONES/PLAYER COURSES)
MIDDLEFIELD, CONNECTICUT

Often, when a property is the home to two courses, one takes a back seat. That's not the case at Lyman Orchards. Both the Jones Course and the Player Course are considered to be among Connecticut's top public-access layouts, and as such, will receive equal attention in this chapter.

The Jones Course (named after course designer Robert Trent Jones, Sr.) has been rated as high as No. 6 and the Player Course (named after the legendary golfer and course designer Gary Player) once reached No. 3 in the *Golf Digest* ranking of public courses.

Robert Trent Jones, Sr., crafted Lyman Orchards' first course in 1969 among the gentle green hills and white pines of the Connecticut countryside, and the course sat alone on the property for fifteen years. Jones's design was a difficult act to follow, but Player answered the call when he created a next-door neighbor in 1994.

The Player Course doesn't feature as many pines, but it does have one of the more unique tree features anywhere in golf. The layout winds through an apple orchard, which gives the round a country feel and might afford an autumn player a quick snack along the way.

Golf has been part of the Lyman Orchards experience for thirty years or so, but the orchards themselves predated golf by 228 years. Visitors have been coming to the orchards for more than two centuries, stocking bushel baskets with pears, peaches, apples, raspberries, and blueberries.

Pumpkins also have been a staple at Lyman Orchards, providing settlers a chance to improve upon the 2,000-year-old European tradition of carving jack-o-lanterns. Until the settlers reached the shores of the colonies, they carved gourds and placed candles in them as part of the holiday All Hallows' Eve. They found pumpkins to be easier to carve, and in 1741 Lyman Orchards was one of the first to offer pumpkins to customers.

Now that golf has become a fixture at the orchards, many visit the place strictly to play their game of choice. But it's almost impossible to avoid the produce of the orchards, or Connecticut's best apple pie, as voted by readers of *Connecticut Magazine*.

There is a dual allure, to be sure, but golf is why we're here. Pumpkins and apples can wait a while. Let's rejoin the Jones and the Player, where two legends of the game have combined to create a fruitful site to play.

The Jones Course is an aquatic adventure in golf. Players are faced with direct carries over water hazards on ten holes, so the prospect of adding strokes to the scorecard is fairly certain. Out of ten ponds, almost every public player should figure to find himself in the drop area at least once.

Risk-reward is a staple of virtually all Jones's layouts, and he stayed the course at Lyman Orchards. No. 3 is a perfect example of this. It's a par-4, 408-yard hole from the back tees. This is short by today's standards, and would seem to make this green easily reachable in two. But a bunker at about 230 yards at this dogleg right poses a problem if you try to cut the corner.

You face risk by trying to cut the corner, reward by making it work. Classic Robert Trent Jones, Sr.

The Player Course doesn't require quite as many risk-reward decisions as its predecessor, but it calls for precision and patience. The par-3s on the Player Course might also require an aspirin because they can be headache-inducing monsters. No. 4 plays 198 yards from the back tee, No. 11 is 219 yards, the 13th plays to 217 and the 16th is the baby at 196.

All four are fairly brutal lengths for the average player, so it might be advisable for the double-digit handicapper to swallow his pride and move up to one of the more manageable tees. But if you'd rather make bogey than make that concession, it's all about options at Lyman Orchards.

CHIP SHOTS

Course contact info:
(860) 349-6031,
www.lymangolf.com

Par: Jones 72; Player 71
Yardage: Jones 7,011 yards; Player 6,725 yards

Rating: Jones 73.2; Player 73.1
Slope: Jones 129; Player 134
Notable: The Jones Course is the Monday qualifying site for the PGA Tour's Travelers Championship, even though the Player Course is considered to be more difficult.

On the green
$35

AFTER YOUR ROUND

Collectors' cornucopia: Middlefield is a small town, and as you might expect, it offers small-town fun. Antique seekers

The Player Course joined the Jones Course at Lyman Orchards in 1994, and parts of the course meander through apple orchards. Many other trees pose a problem on No. 18, not to mention a foreboding swamp to the right of the fairway.

have more than a dozen options, so there are enough after-the-round opportunities to fill the entire day searching for the perfect piece. Art galleries, coin shops, postcard specialists, and memorabilia outlets will keep you browsing — and buying. For a more modern yet just as unique shopping experience, flea markets are also part of the Middlefield landscape.

SCORECARD - JONES COURSE

Hole	1	2	3	4	5	6	7	8	9	out	
Yardage	435	195	408	571	407	366	197	391	572	3,542	
Par	4	3	4	5	4	4	3	4	5	36	
Hole	10	11	12	13	14	15	16	17	18	in	total
Yardage	412	167	516	390	407	402	428	180	567	3,469	7,011
Par	4	3	5	4	4	4	4	3	5	36	72

SCORECARD - PLAYER COURSE

Hole	1	2	3	4	5	6	7	8	9	out	
Yardage	408	378	395	198	397	357	228	592	388	3,341	
Par	4	4	4	3	4	4	3	5	4	35	
Hole	10	11	12	13	14	15	16	17	18	in	total
Yardage	386	219	437	217	493	346	206	536	544	3,384	6,725
Par	4	3	4	3	5	4	3	5	5	36	71

The 9th green at Wintonbury Hills affords little sympathy if a player misses the putting surface on the approach. Pete Dye may have built the course for a buck, but he didn't scrimp on the sand budget.

CONNECTICUT

WINTONBURY HILLS GOLF COURSE
BLOOMFIELD, CONNECTICUT

City officials in Bloomfield, Connecticut, had been considering building a municipal course off and on for nearly forty years. But, as is true for virtually all municipalities, money was a prime consideration when the idea came up of investing in what some residents felt was a luxury.

So when legendary course architect Pete Dye came calling with a special offer, Bloomfield was all ears. In 2002, Dye decided to build five public courses in various parts of the country for a dollar apiece. Dye's motivation was to serve players who loved the game but couldn't afford a country club, and Bloomfield was one of the fortunate beneficiaries. Taxpayers had to foot the bill for construction

costs, of course, but Dye's labor was just one dollar. Public-access golf may never have received such a gift.

Capitalizing on golf's equivalent to manna from heaven, the folks at Wintonbury Hills have made sure to take advantage of Dye's benevolence. It's all about golf at Wintonbury Hills. No skiing in the winter, no tanning beaches in the summer, no hayrides in the fall, no spa treatments in the spring. The staffers here concentrate solely on providing outstanding public golf.

This exclusive focus results in a true treat for anyone living near or visiting Bloomfield. General Manager Doug Juhasz knows he has a beauty. The *Golfweek* and *Golf Magazine* distinctions mentioned in the "Chip Shots" section, on the next page, were earned in 2008. This course can't call on ancient history to prove its excellence, but it is certain to endure. Pete Dye's layouts stand the test of time.

Tim Liddy helped Dye build the course, and the fact that two designers pitched in might explain the dichotomous nature of the layout. It's almost as if they split the holes up and decided: OK, you play it your way and I'll play it mine.

Several holes feature forests and wetlands that a player might expect to face in the Northeast. In fact, ninety-one acres of wetlands are protected areas, so if you hit your ball into one, don't go looking for it. Take your punishment and take a drop. The flipside of Wintonbury Hills is the links-style holes, where slopes, deep bunkers, native grasses, and large, undulating greens are the highlights.

It's an interesting mix that keeps a player on his toes, because he never really knows what's coming next. One of the unexpected highlights is the unique 408-yard 16th hole. Elevated areas on either side of the fairway form a half-tunnel that guides balls to the center. There's a bunker on the right side, but it's 240 yards away. Avoid the bunker, and you've got a chance at par on one of the most distinctive holes in Connecticut.

Wintonbury Hills, like every public course in America, charges no membership fees. But what sets this Billy Casper Golf facility apart from other public tracks is its customer service. No, you're not in a country club, but the first-class treatment and sparkling conditions make you pinch yourself to check that you're actually playing a public-access course.

CHIP SHOTS

Course contact info:
(860) 242-1401,
www.wintonburyhills.com

Par: 70
Yardage: 6,711 yards

Rating: 72.3
Slope: 130
Notable: Wintonbury Hills has been part of the Connecticut landscape a relatively short time, and yet the Pete Dye layout has been drawing attention since it opened in 2003. This public facility was named "The No. 2 Public Course in Connecticut," both by *Golfweek* and *Golf Magazine*.

On the green
○ $49

It shouldn't be a surprise that a course managed by Billy Casper Golf is one of the best in its region. The national management company runs many public courses throughout the country that are known for being among the tops in their respective areas.

What is definitely rare, however, is the fact that such a quality place to play is a taxpayer-owned course. Even more rare is that a legendary golf course architect like Pete Dye designed a municipal beauty.

And all for a buck.

AFTER YOUR ROUND

Ample aesthetics: What else would you expect from a city named Bloomfield? There are bloom-filled sights throughout the town, and other aesthetic touches that add to the quiet, friendly haven that is Bloomfield. Penwood State Park and Talcott Mountain State Park give visitors an opportunity to see more of nature's show-off spots.

Learning lessons: The local 4-H farm seeks to educate the pubic on environmental and other agricultural issues. After your lessons, you can pick apples and raspberries, depending on the season. Another educational opportunity is the Bloomfield Historical Society, where you can explore artifacts and literature about a town that was incorporated in 1835.

SCORECARD

Hole	1	2	3	4	5	6	7	8	9	out	
Yardage	377	365	163	526	333	430	255	564	190	3,203	
Par	4	4	3	5	4	4	3	5	3	35	
Hole	10	11	12	13	14	15	16	17	18	in	total
Yardage	412	443	178	551	445	427	408	230	414	3,508	6,711
Par	4	4	3	5	4	4	4	3	4	35	70

DELAWARE

BACK CREEK GOLF CLUB
MIDDLETOWN, DELAWARE

It's been more than a decade since Back Creek Golf Club opened and immediately established itself as a contender in the realm of Delaware public golf. In fact, as years have passed, the course — situated on property that was once a farm owned by Delaware's first governor, Joshua Clayton — has risen to the rank of heavyweight champion.

Back Creek is ranked in the "Top 100 Modern Golf Courses in America" by *Golfweek*, and few would argue that it is among the top public courses in Delaware. The *Golfweek* modern list includes courses built after 1960 — both public and private. This means that no one who visits or lives in Delaware will be excluded from playing a course that can hold its own with the top private clubs in the country.

Courses judged to be top-notch tracks generally stick to designs that are near and dear to golf purists' hearts. But convention gets tossed aside at various points as a player makes his way around Back Creek. There are moments of quirkiness, and the course contains features that make it difficult to label.

Fifteen holes are completely bereft of trees, which might lead a player to believe that Back Creek identifies itself as a links-type course. But houses surround the layout, and even though they're set far enough back so as not to be a nuisance, it takes away from the linksy feel.

Add to this mix the fact that ponds come into play on six holes, and the identity crisis deepens. Not enough trees to be a parkland course; too many ponds to be links. Luckily, it doesn't seem to matter what you call Back Creek. Just make sure you play it if you get the chance.

There is plenty to love at this Middletown gem, providing, of course, you avoid the waist-high brush that serves as rough on many of the holes. Good luck finding your ball in this mess, let alone hitting out of it. In other words, stay straight.

Another continuing menace is sand. Bunker after bunker — nearly ninety in all — are there to penalize shots even if they happen to avoid the tangled rough. You get the idea: if you watch out for the ponds, stay out of the weeds, and don't go bunker diving, you're in for a delightful round at Back Creek.

The layouts are simple, with each nine looping in opposite directions, keeping those who haven't played the course from being confused about where the next tee is located. The design keeps tees from criss-crossing, and the fairways are individualized as well. Only twice do you experience the "up-and-back" feel where holes run parallel to one another.

The greens at Back Creek are either a great highlight or a hindrance, depending on your point of view. There is plenty of undulation, and those who like conventional golf might say the slopes go too far. Whether you think the greens are tricked-up or just tricky enough to be fun, there is no doubt that taking out the flat stick at Back Creek is definitely an adventure.

In fact, adventure is the word of the day as you make your way around the course. There are no hole descriptions on the scorecard, nor are there signs at the tee boxes showing the hole's design. It is strongly advised to bring a local along, or at least confer with someone who knows the course. Otherwise, there are times when guessing becomes an unwanted part of the game.

Hey, but you wanted a challenge, right? Waist-high fescue, holes of mystery, and roller-coaster greens are just part of the adventure at Back Creek. Remember, it's among the top 100 courses in America.

Come along for the ride.

CHIP SHOTS

Course contact info:
(302) 378-6499,
www.backcreekgc.com

Par: 71
Yardage: 7,003 yards

Rating: 74.2
Slope: 134
Notable: Back Creek has been among the elite courses in Delaware since it opened in 1997, and the club keeps getting better. Several renovations to the golf course have been conducted over the past few years, and a new clubhouse has been opened. Hunt Cottage has pushed Back Creek into the world of full-service, first-class golf.

On the green
$45

Dark skies cast an ominous look at Back Creek's 8th hole.

AFTER YOUR ROUND

Premier is here: Several brands of cultural entertainment can be found under one roof at the Premier Centre for the Arts. The Premier Centre features fourteen art studios, a theater, music studios, and an art gallery. It's worth a browse.

Bowl me over: If you have the kids in tow, the Mid-County Bowling & Entertainment Center offers more than just alleys and pins. In addition to bowling, the center features

Family Fun Galaxy — a potpourri of amusement that includes arcade games, laser tag, bumper cars, skee ball, Frog Hopper, and other activities and prizes.

OTHER COURSES IN DELAWARE WORTH A VISIT
- Bayside Resort GC, Selbyville
- Bear Trap Dunes GC, Ocean View
- Three Little Bakers GC, Wilmington

SCORECARD											
Hole	1	2	3	4	5	6	7	8	9	out	
Yardage	417	201	450	355	541	341	433	156	460	3,354	
Par	4	3	4	4	5	4	4	3	4	35	
Hole	10	11	12	13	14	15	16	17	18	in	total
Yardage	460	530	446	462	191	413	551	170	437	3,660	7,014
Par	4	5	4	4	3	4	5	3	4	36	71

The scenery around the 18th is breathtaking, with the flower-lined cart path and stately clubhouse overlooking the green.

DELAWARE

BAYWOOD GREENS
(LONG NECK COURSE)
LONG NECK, DELAWARE

Sometimes, you don't have to look far to find the perfect description of an immaculate golf course that's open to everyone. At Baywood Greens, their slogan is: "An exclusively public championship course."

You can't say it any better than that.

The bent grass greens, tees, and fairways are incredibly maintained, and the snack bar is adjacent to the Baywood Greens swimming pool. The clubhouse includes a 240-guest banquet room, a bar and grill, locker rooms and the pro shop. All of this at a public course?

More features that elicit the words "breathtaking beauty" are the woods, water, wildlife, timber bridges, and acres and acres of ponds that are just as much a part of the landscape as the tees and greens. Countless flowers, plants, shrubs, and trees add to an experience that becomes far more than golf as you move through the round.

Horticulturist Warren Golde says the course is beautified with "an unlimited budget" from owner Rob Tunnell. Baywood Greens is built on a 750-acre tract of land in Long Neck that is loaded with pines, oaks, maples, and hickory trees. Open flatland provides ample space for the golf course, which works its way through the woods and around protected wetlands.

Baywood Greens has many unique golf features that make it worth a visit, but there are groups who come to the course who have never picked up a golf club. Local garden clubs have come calling over the years, and Golde sends them out on golf carts to view the hundreds of thousands of flowers that line fairways and fill tee boxes. Flower lovers find plenty to enjoy here, but the main reason to roam the grounds is golf, which is often the highlight of the day for those who come visiting.

The artistic design of the golf course combines cosmetic wonders with golf holes that command keen awareness and strategy.

The journey begins as players tunnel their way through

twelve holes surrounded by hardwood forest, which provides a cocoon-like canopy for the first two-thirds of the round. However this description should not be misconstrued as an account of claustrophobic, straightforward golf holes.

The fairways are varied, made of manicured bent grass, and the layout is laden with lakes that constantly come into play. Because the holes cut through the woods, any errant shot is likely to find serious trouble. If you're not hitting it straight, the first dozen holes will cause you some pain.

Just about the time it seems you'll never escape from the woods, the golf course opens right before your eyes. Nos. 13 through 18 feature wider fairways on flat land that is a welcome relief for the crooked hitters. This doesn't mean you can hack away; there is still plenty of danger in the man-made lakes and natural wetlands.

The 14th is a prime example of risk-reward peril. It is both the signature hole of the course and one of the more intriguing challenges. The 425-yard par 4 gives the option of driving to an emerald island fairway that results in a huge shortcut to the hole. It is a risk to try for the island, however, and a bailout area allows the safer players to find a haven.

The finishing hole is another highlight, and it is appropriate that one of the most scenic holes of the course leads into the warm and welcoming clubhouse. The tee boxes on No. 18 are mini-islands in a picturesque lake, decorated with flowers and making for one of the more unique driving spots in golf.

AFTER YOUR ROUND

Club camping: After a day on the bent grass, maybe a night of tent and grass is what you seek. OK, maybe a camper. The Holly Lake Campsite is down the road from Baywood Greens. There's a swimming pool, camp store, game room, nature trails, hayrides, and more.

Sizing it down: If the kids are with you, you could follow a day of big-guy golf with a round of miniature golf at the local little course in nearby Millsboro.

CHIP SHOTS

Course contact info:
(302) 947-9800,
www.baywoodgreens.com

Par: 72
Yardage: 6,983 yards

Rating: 73.4
Slope: 135
Notable: Baywood Greens has received awards from all directions. *Pros n' Hackers* offered accolades for its course conditions and golf experience in 2008, and the course was also recognized in the same year by the *Zagat Survey*, *Golf Digest*, and *Golf Link*.

On the green
◎ ◎ $90

SCORECARD											
Hole	1	2	3	4	5	6	7	8	9	out	
Yardage	375	365	435	462	603	223	538	161	392	3,554	
Par	4	4	4	4	5	3	5	3	4	36	
Hole	10	11	12	13	14	15	16	17	18	in	total
Yardage	410	190	320	534	425	195	515	415	425	3,429	6,983
Par	4	3	4	5	4	3	5	4	4	36	72

The Wanamaker Course at PGA Village, as displayed by the 5th hole, has a primitive feel, using wetlands, native marsh plants, and palmetto trees.

FLORIDA

PGA VILLAGE
(RYDER/WANAMAKER/DYE COURSES)
PORT ST. LUCIE, FLORIDA

There are three fine golf courses at PGA Village designed by a couple of legends in golf-course architecture, but it's impossible to talk about the village without making the extraordinary, thirty-five-acre learning center the focus of the conversation.

Pete Dye and Tom Fazio created enough good golf to keep visitors happy, but at PGA Village, it's practice, practice, practice. Every golfer has been to the local driving range or practice facilities at golf courses in their towns. Now, take that experience and multiply it ... by about 1,000.

The learning center features a massive horseshoe tee that allows for shots into any wind direction. The short-game area is the best in the country, giving players the chance to practice bump-and-runs, flop shots, and everything in between.

Practice bunkers offer different varieties of sand and run the gamut from deep, greenside pits to low-slung fairway bunkers. The best deal in Florida golf just might be the daylong pass at the learning center — $15 for the individual golfer, $5 for spouses.

It's what you would expect from a village set up for PGA of America pros — active or retired. The surprise for the public at large might be that they are welcome too. But even though this feels for all the world like a country club, anyone who loves the game will be happy to know that every aspect of PGA Village is pure public golf.

Throw in a short course for beginners, and consider the PGA Historical Center — an 83,000-square-foot facility that showcases rows and rows of vintage books and various other memorabilia — and the public-access experience is a golf extravaganza.

Let's not forget about the golf courses, where everyone can play at an affordable rate. The Ryder Course and the Wanamaker Course were built by Tom Fazio, and Pete Dye designed the Dye Course. The courses aren't the toughest challenges a player will ever face, but neither are they cupcakes. All three were extensively renovated in 2006 and 2007. Variety is a plus, and the knowledge that the rounds of golf are part of the entire village adds to the experience.

The Ryder Course has an inland Carolinas feel to it, in large part because of pine trees that adorn the modestly rolling holes. Both nines wrap counter-clockwise, with real estate on the perimeter.

The Wanamaker Course has a more primitive feel, acquired through deployment of wetlands, native marsh plants, and palmetto trees. There is

CHIP SHOTS

Course contact info:
(866) 742-2582,
www.pgavillage.com

Par: Ryder - 72; Wanamaker - 71; Dye - 72
Yardage: Ryder - 7,150 yards; Wanamaker - 7,087 yards; Dye - 6,680 yards

Rating: Ryder - 73.8; Wanamaker - 72.9; Dye - 71.8
Slope: Ryder - 133; Wanamaker - 132; Dye - 133
Notable: This is the site of the biennial PGA Teaching and Coaching Summit, which typically draws more than 1,000 PGA teaching pros from nearly every state and as many as 12 countries.

On the green
$56

also more elevation, which affords the occasional heightened view and sense of drama to the holes.

The Wanamaker's holes are more varied than those of its northern counterpart, with Fazio indulging himself and the golfer by including quirkier angles, more crumpled landing areas, and whimsical hazards. The 545-yard, par-5 13th might be the greatest example, with an onslaught of bunkers, including a dunes-like cross hazard ninety yards short of the green.

The Dye Course passes for links golf in Florida. It is virtually flat, wide open, and windswept, and there's only scant evidence of real estate. It's not exactly links golf, more links-like.

The non-returning nines wrap around a ninety-acre marsh called "Big Mamu" that sneaks occasionally into play. After the course opened in 1999, Dye said that he was thrilled to be part of the PGA Village because of what the PGA of America teaching pros have meant to the game. This course is like a gift to people who deserve it so much.

AFTER YOUR ROUND

Elbow room: Port St. Lucie is far enough away from the hustle and bustle of some of Florida's bigger cities to be peaceful. Yet there's enough going on to keep you entertained. Several waterways offer boat rides, fishing, and kayaking. I've taken in a few New York Mets preseason games and had a good time even though I'm a Tigers fan. If you visit in the spring, catching a game at Tradition Field is a great way to spend an afternoon.

SCORECARD - RYDER COURSE

Hole	1	2	3	4	5	6	7	8	9	out	
Yardage	375	455	190	365	520	165	575	395	450	3,490	
Par	4	4	3	4	5	3	5	4	4	36	
Hole	10	11	12	13	14	15	16	17	18	in	total
Yardage	540	430	340	200	405	480	225	565	475	3,660	7,150
Par	5	4	4	3	4	4	3	5	4	36	72

SCORECARD - WANAMAKER COURSE

Hole	1	2	3	4	5	6	7	8	9	out	
Yardage	548	461	414	222	404	178	535	370	449	3,581	
Par	4	4	4	3	4	3	5	4	4	35	
Hole	10	11	12	13	14	15	16	17	18	in	total
Yardage	365	199	401	545	463	356	507	228	442	3,506	7,087
Par	4	3	4	5	4	4	5	3	4	36	71

SCORECARD - DYE COURSE

Hole	1	2	3	4	5	6	7	8	9	out	
Yardage	340	455	160	350	495	155	535	370	410	3,270	
Par	4	4	3	4	5	3	5	4	4	36	
Hole	10	11	12	13	14	15	16	17	18	in	total
Yardage	510	385	330	175	405	440	195	530	440	3,410	6,680
Par	5	4	4	3	4	4	3	5	4	36	72

OTHER PUBLIC COURSES IN FLORIDA WORTH A VISIT

- Doral Resort & Spa (Blue Course), Miami
- El Diablo G&CC, Citrus Springs
- Lake Jovita G&CC (South Course), Dade City
- PGA National Resort & Spa (Champion Course), Palm Beach Gardens
- TPC Sawgrass (Stadium Course), Ponte Vedra Beach
- World Woods GC (Pine Barrens Course), Brooksville

TPC OF TAMPA BAY
TAMPA, FLORIDA

When the first three words of a course are Tournament Players Club, there is no doubt a special golf experience awaits. And when a player doesn't have to pay extravagant membership fees to play a TPC course, he definitely should take advantage of the opportunity.

Several TPC courses are private, requiring that members live in a home on the property or pay dues to join the club. Not so at TPC of Tampa Bay – the course is open to the public year-round. And when we say year-round, we mean it. Remember, this is Florida, where the golf season never ends.

PGA Tour players play a role in the design and architecture of all TPC clubs, which are scattered throughout the United States and Mexico. Some players are the actual designers, but in the case of the TPC of Tampa Bay, the course was designed by Bobby Weed with Chi Chi Rodriguez serving as the player consultant.

One of the highlights of Florida courses is that the wildlife and natural surroundings give players something to survey as they're waiting on the tee. Weed recognized this immediately, and he didn't shy away from the wetlands, cypress heads, and numerous ponds and lagoons. Instead, he and Rodriguez viewed the natural features as opportunities to add beauty to their layout.

Wildlife was abundant when Weed took his first look at the property, and he built the course so that the natural inhabitants were not disturbed. Weed was on horseback during his first tour of the land in 1990, and he has kept the wetlands and flats of native grasses intact. Armadillos, egrets, deer, fox, blue heron, alligators, and otters are just a few of the playing partners you might find. And if you keep your eyes peeled, a bald eagle might just soar overhead. The course's designation as an Audubon Sanctuary is important to those involved with TPC of Tampa Bay.

Weed had his work cut out for him as he preserved the natural elements and added ingredients of his own. He moved thousands of tons of dirt to build the course, which opened in 1991. It took some time for the new ground to mix with the old, but after nearly two decades of maturation, the golf course now blends perfectly with the oaks and pines and cypress trees. Bunkers and wetlands seem to go hand-in-hand.

The key to a good round here is to avoid the water, which comes into play on fifteen holes. Don't be fooled early in your round, because the true test comes on the back nine. The three finishing holes can put crooked numbers on your card that will give you a TPC-sized dose of reality.

The 16th and the 18th aren't long for par-4 holes, but they require precision on every shot. No. 16 is 430 yards, which might sound like a straightforward hole, but it's anything but straight. The dogleg left requires a tee shot on the right side of the fairway in order to have a chance at reaching the green in regulation. The putting surface is tucked into a cocoon of trees that allow little room for error. The 18th is an average-length par-4 at 456 yards, but it does a 180-degree turn from its partner two holes earlier. It doglegs right and features a pond down the ride side of the fairway from tee to green.

CHIP SHOTS

Course contact info:
(813) 949-0090,
www.tpctampabay.com

Par: 71
Yardage: 6,898 yards

Rating: 73.4
Slope: 130
Notable: *Golf World* has ranked the TPC of Tampa Bay No. 18 in the nation among public golf courses, and the course is one of two in the Tampa area designated as an Audubon Cooperative Sanctuary.

On the green
◔◔ $119

No. 17, tucked between the two doglegs, is a long par 3 that forces a carry over trees and water. The faint of heart can bail out to a landing area on the right, but remember, this is a par 3. You're supposed to aim for the green, which, unfortunately, you can't see from the tee box.

It isn't just the finishing holes that present golf challenges at Tampa Bay's TPC. Those three letters signify not only a connection with the PGA Tour, but also guarantee that this is an excellent place to play.

In 2008, TPC courses were used for ten events related to the PGA Tour — actual tournaments, playoffs, featured events, fall series, or skins games. TPC courses represent some of the top venues for professional players, let alone those of us who play the game on nothing but public-access courses. When there's a chance to mix the labels TPC and public access, it is a treat.

The 18th hole at TPC of Tampa Bay, where the slogan is "Where the pros play."

AFTER YOUR ROUND

Kids for a day: No matter how old you might be, there are plenty of opportunities to enjoy activities that might just take you on a visit back to your youth. If you have your children along, they will be in their element.

There's the roller-coaster world of Busch Gardens amusement park, the Lowry Park Zoo, Busch Gardens

Africa, and the Florida Aquarium.

My personal favorite beach site is about thirty minutes west of Tampa. I lived in the Orlando area for seven years, and the Gulf of Mexico was my family's favorite spot. Clearwater was declared the Barr family's No. 1 beach.

SCORECARD

Hole	1	2	3	4	5	6	7	8	9	out	
Yardage	395	191	425	427	332	144	541	414	472	3,341	
Par	4	3	4	4	4	3	5	4	4	35	
Hole	10	11	12	13	14	15	16	17	18	in	total
Yardage	395	179	495	345	588	452	430	217	456	3,557	6,898
Par	4	3	5	4	5	4	4	3	4	36	71

This is Disney? The peace and tranquility at Osprey Ridge includes decorative fountains, expansive ponds, and Carolina pines.

FLORIDA

WALT DISNEY WORLD GOLF COMPLEX
(OSPREY RIDGE)
ORLANDO, FLORIDA

To immerse yourself into any of the ninety-nine holes of golf on the Walt Disney World Resort is to play sleight-of-hand with your imagination. In a place known for flooding the senses with neon lights, bands, cartoon characters, and fireworks, the golf experience is surprisingly serene.

Sometimes, when playing the Tom Fazio-designed Osprey Ridge course that opened in 1992, it's hard to imagine how close you are to all the activity. You get out on the course, and it's a complete world of its own. The golf is great, and Osprey Ridge is the most unique and peaceful of the courses at Disney. It is pure parkland in the middle of Florida, with enough trees to make you think you're playing in a Carolina forest.

One of the overlooked features of Osprey Ridge and

the other courses at Disney is that all are public facilities. No memberships are necessary (or are even possible), and you don't have to be a guest of the resort.

The dramatic Osprey Ridge layout winds through heavy vegetation and oak forests, with rolling terrain and several high ridges uncharacteristic of Florida. Wildlife abounds, and that's no accident. There are eight nesting platforms atop tall poles for ospreys, alongside ponds stocked with fish. There are hand-built boardwalks, instead of asphalt cart paths, winding through wetlands.

The constant at Osprey Ridge is fine golf. But each Disney layout has its own personality, mainly because there were four designers — Fazio, Pete Dye, Joe Lee, and Ron Garl.

There are pointers that help optimize the golfing experience at Osprey Ridge.

The daily greens fees on the eighteen-hole courses are all pretty pricey, ranging from $125-$170 for resort guests during the January through April peak season.

What time of day to play is an important factor to

consider. The course is crowded in the morning, and pace of play can be very sluggish. But the course thins out after 2:00 p.m., and crisp rounds are possible in mid-afternoon virtually any time of year. The afternoon is an ideal time to play if you can stand the heat. Some people can't, particularly in July and August, but if you can tolerate the warm temperatures you will be surprised how fast you can get in eighteen holes in the afternoon. Many players consider the heat worth the trade-off for a nice, smooth round with no waiting.

Another good thing to know is that there are complimentary taxi vouchers (through Yellow Cab) provided for Disney resort guests who are coming to play any of the courses. The valet desk or bell services will call a cab for guests, and pro shop personnel at the golf course will assist guests in returning to their hotels.

The entire golf experience is covered at Disney, and with a little planning you can beat the crowds and save a couple bucks. As Disney's ninety-nine holes of golf prove, especially the eighteen at Osprey Ridge, you'll find that all the magic at this kingdom isn't just for kids.

AFTER YOUR ROUND

Mouse in the house: You've just finished a round on a golf course on Disney property, for goodness' sake. It isn't much trouble to head over to the Magic Kingdom to visit Mickey with the kids, or maybe Animal Kingdom, or perhaps Typhoon Lagoon. You get the idea. There is family fun in every direction.

More than Mickey: Disney might be Orlando's big-ticket draw, but it's not the only cowboy in this Central Florida rodeo. I lived in Orlando for seven years and my family and I discovered Universal Studios Theme Park, and its neighbor, Islands of Adventure, are every bit as fun-filled as Disney's theme parks. And if you get a chance to stay at the Portofino Bay Hotel at Universal Studios, take it. It's made to look and feel like Venice, and it does a pretty convincing job.

CHIP SHOTS

Course contact info:
(407)938-4653,
www.disneyworld.com,
search "Osprey Ridge"

Par: 72
Yardage: 7,101 yards

Rating: 74.4
Slope: 131
Notable: Disney annually plays host to a PGA Tour event, but it is held at the Magnolia and Palms courses. Osprey Ridge is considered the best course on the Disney property, but the other two courses have far fewer trees and far more places for the gallery to view the action.

On the green
◐◐◐ $145

SCORECARD											
Hole	1	2	3	4	5	6	7	8	9	out	
Yardage	353	406	193	439	222	409	582	434	510	3,548	
Par	4	4	3	4	3	4	5	4	5	36	
Hole	10	11	12	13	14	15	16	17	18	in	total
Yardage	431	375	546	179	453	357	542	216	454	3,553	7,101
Par	4	4	5	3	4	4	5	3	4	36	72

COBBLESTONE GOLF COURSE
MARIETTA, GEORGIA

Cobblestone Golf Course celebrated its fifteenth year of operation in 2008, and the accolades just don't stop coming. Neither do the golfers.

The course, adjacent to scenic Lake Acworth, gets a near-unanimous nod as the top public course in Georgia. *Golf Magazine* and *Golfweek* each have rated Cobblestone as one the premier public courses in the nation. So there's no doubt of its credibility in the realm of excellent public golf.

It might be even more impressive to consider that *Golfweek*, in a ranking that includes private clubs, has named Cobblestone among the "Top 10 Courses in Georgia." This list includes a club of which you may have heard: Augusta National, home of The Masters.

Cobblestone is about thirty minutes north of Atlanta, and its proximity to the city brings a flood of rounds every year. The greenskeepers at Cobblestone understand the course is a popular place to play, and they manage to keep the greens manicured and the fairways lush despite the heavy traffic.

The Ken Dye layout uses Lake Acworth to perfection. Several of the holes run along the lake, which is a natural beauty.

The course is superlative in its quality, and the affordable rates make it one of the best bargains in golf. Already reasonable, the prices are even better with the purchase of a "Cobblestone Card." Card prices range anywhere from $19 to $249, depending on where you live and the savings package you seek. The savings with the card include $20 off greens fees Monday through Thursday, twilight rate savings, 10 percent off golf lessons, and more.

The course is affordable, but don't think you are in for a cheap round. The Cobblestone challenge is pretty steep. There are bunkers galore, and the narrow and undulating fairways run through thick and beautiful Georgia woods. The rough is indeed rough and multi-level greens give a clear indication that the Cobblestone test is no bargain.

Cobblestone's highlights are diverse – some bring out the best in a player, some offer the best of the course, and others feature both.

No. 16 is a fun little par 3, just 133 yards. It's not the difficulty that will stay in your memory, but the scenery. Sure, there are bunkers to contend with around the green, and other trouble if you don't hit pay dirt, but it's a pretty straightforward hole. However, with the lake running all the way down the fairway on the left and the woods as a backdrop, it's 133 yards of sweet spot.

The No. 1 handicap hole on the course hits you in the face as soon as you leave the first green. The second hole is a brutal 472-yard par 4 that requires a straight-down-the-middle tee shot or there is some nasty trouble to be found.

A harrowing ditch to the left, and a steep, thatchy slope to the right bring legitimate fright off the No. 2 tee. Even if you hit the fairway, there could be challenges. If you land too far to the right on the fairway, trees block an approach shot to the green.

The toughest hole on the course is near the beginning of the round, but Dye comes full circle by offering the easiest hole near the finish. No. 17 is a 316-yard, downhill par 4 from the back tees. It's just 280 from the front tees, so if a player is feeling gutsy and the wind is right, a tee shot to the green is not out of the question.

The price is right, the challenges are diverse, and you can customize each to your liking. You can pick a savings package, and choose what tees to play. At classy Cobblestone, you can do it your way.

CHIP SHOTS

Course contact info:
(707) 917-5152,
www.cobblestonegolf.com

Par: 71
Yardage: 6,759 yards

Rating: 73.1
Slope: 140
Notable: Qualifiers annually compete on Cobblestone for a spot in the PGA Tour's BellSouth Classic, held at the TPC of Sugarloaf in nearby Duluth.

On the green
$60

AFTER YOUR ROUND

Roller coaster of a day: Marietta isn't the biggest city around, but it has plenty of attractions to entertain its approximately 60,000 residents, not to mention visitors to the city. Six Flags amusement park is right in town, and if the dips and undulations at Cobblestone aren't enough, you can roller coaster to your heart's content after your round.

A forgiving slope offers Cobblestone players who miss the 12th green to the right or long left a chance to roll onto the putting surface in regulation. But bunkers wait for those who miss short left.

No wait to get wet: White Water Park is another in-town experience that is a contrast to the tranquility of Cobblestone, with water slides, rides, attractions, and a ninety-foot free-fall slide. There are lounge chairs available to get your heart started again. A special area for small children gives everyone in the family a chance to get in on the fun.

OTHER PUBLIC COURSES IN GEORGIA WORTH A VISIT

- Achasta GC, Dahlonega
- Barnsley Gardens Resort (The General Course), Adairsville
- Harbor Club G&CC, Greensboro
- Sea Island GC (Seaside Course), St. Simons Island
- Sea Island GC (Plantation Course), St. Simons Island

SCORECARD

Hole	1	2	3	4	5	6	7	8	9	out	
Yardage	526	472	197	313	157	403	523	240	570	3,401	
Par	4	4	3	4	3	4	5	3	5	35	
Hole	10	11	12	13	14	15	16	17	18	in	total
Yardage	398	436	422	209	461	542	133	316	441	3,358	6,759
Par	4	4	4	3	4	5	3	4	4	36	71

GEORGIA

REYNOLDS PLANTATION
(THE NATIONAL COURSE)
GREENSBORO, GEORGIA

Reynolds Plantation is not one of the places you go to play golf and then leave to visit the other hot spots in town. First of all, the Plantation is seventy-five minutes east of Atlanta in the middle of wilderness and farmland, so you'd have to go a pretty fair piece to find a hot spot. Secondly, with a luxurious Ritz-Carlton Lodge and ninety-nine holes of nature-filled, first-rate golf, there really isn't much reason to leave.

There are five courses on the property, all with their own reason to play, but many choose The National. Others prefer the Great Waters Course, but this author goes with The National. The Tom Fazio design comprises the nine-hole Ridge, Bluff, and Cove courses, and the Bluff/Cove is the route featured in the "chip shots" and scorecard on these two pages.

Twenty-seven holes may be an additional draw at The National, but it isn't the primary reason to play this splendid track. At this course, you get quantity, but it's quality that really counts.

Situated on scenic Lake Oconee — Georgia's second-largest body of water — The National lets players escape for a few hours, no matter how busy the lives they lead. Reynolds Plantation is an hour from Hartsfield International Airport, which is the closest point of hubbub.

In addition to the scenery, ambience, and sumptuous food in the clubhouse, outstanding golf is the course of the day.

The National opened with eighteen holes in 1998, then added nine more in 2000. The other four layouts on Reynolds Plantation are the Plantation Course (1987), Great Waters Course (1993), and Oconee Course (2002). The number of courses has steadily added to a golf experience rich in variety and excellence, and the cream of the crop is the National.

The course sits on the former Port Armor Golf Club, a 1985 Bob Cupp design that once was rated the No. 2 golf course in Georgia. Port Armor had fallen into serious disrepair, and Reynolds Plantation acquired the property and promptly pumped $2 million into rebuilding the course. A total of $1 million was spent on a new irrigation system to keep the course from flooding, which was the main reason for its disrepair.

Not only did the new owners rebuild what was once a fine golf course, but by most accounts exceeded the quality of the original design.

As good as the golf is, they didn't forget about the experience before and after the round. The clubhouse is spacious, classy, and filled with the latest technology. And the food? Some of Georgia's best.

Back to golf, although that food is difficult to forget. The National is the class act of the property. The twenty-seven holes feature twenty to sixty feet of elevation change on many holes and offers character, variety, and personality.

It's tough to design twenty-seven holes and have them all be so distinct, but that's exactly what Tom Fazio managed to do. The world-famous golf architect knew he had a great piece of property on his hands, but carving a one-of-a-kind layout when there were other courses nearby seemed like a dicey proposition.

Fazio conquered the challenge, creating a golf course that requires both grace and power from its players.

CHIP SHOTS

Course contact info:
(888) 298-3119,
www.reynoldsplantation.com

Par: 72
Yardage: 6,698 yards

Rating: 73.8
Slope: 138
Notable: There is a top-notch golf academy adaptable to all levels. It covers 16 acres and it is considered one of the top teaching centers in Georgia. And there is tradition in this state. Augusta National, home of the Masters, is but an hour away. Call ahead to reserve a room at the Ritz-Carlton and get public access to any of the three courses.

On the green
◯◯ $115

AFTER YOUR ROUND

Tradition time: If you prefer a little touch of yesterday, as opposed to modern tourist towns and strip malls, then Greensboro is your kind of place. Greene County, in which Greensboro sits, was formed by a Georgia Legislative Act on February 3, 1786. Greensboro is a puppy by comparison; it's only been around since 1803. A walk through the downtown streets is a great way to spend a couple of hours after your round, no matter how many days you're in town.

Park it: A.H. Stephens Historic Park was named for Alexander Stephens, who served as Georgia's governor

The 5th hole on the Great Waters Course shows why it's a tough choice for players. The National Course was this author's choice.

and vice president of the Confederate States during the Civil War. In the park, visit the Confederate Museum, Liberty Hall, and experience activities such as boating, fishing, and both walking and horseback-riding trails. A campground is within the park.

One fine diner: In a time when restaurants open and close like a Charles Barkley golf swing, there's a diner in Greensboro that has been around since the early days of American golf. The appropriately named Yesterday Café was part of historic Greensboro's downtown landscape when hungry customers arrived by horse and buggy. The original golden cash register is on display, and the walls are lined with historic photos. Piano music played on a baby grand adds a touch of class.

SCORECARD

Hole	1	2	3	4	5	6	7	8	9	out	
Yardage	379	356	149	383	562	400	553	179	564	3,525	
Par	4	4	3	4	5	4	5	3	5	37	
Hole	10	11	12	13	14	15	16	17	18	in	total
Yardage	474	185	413	345	421	167	495	179	494	3,173	6,698
Par	4	3	4	4	4	3	5	3	5	35	72

Waterfalls, palms, and hibiscus beautify Ko Olina's 12th, and they are also part of the landscape throughout the course.

HAWAII

KO OLINA GOLF CLUB
HONOLULU, HAWAII

On an island filled with incomparable beauty in virtually every direction, it would be easy for golf to become an afterthought. On a visit to Oahu, however, it would be advisable to bring your clubs.

Yes, the beauty is undeniable. Mountain ranges reach the clouds, mixing magically with rainbows and crashing Pacific waves. In Oahu, you can walk through rainbows just as surely as you can bury your feet in the sand.

There might be a prettier place to play, but the search for such a place would take some time. Here, there is quality golf, with beauty and simplicity tossed in. An added bonus: a golf consortium on Oahu has been formed that allows a

player to have reduced greens fees on other courses in the consortium once he has played one.

Ko Olina Golf Club is the premier course in the consortium, and if you have time for just one round, this is the pick. Pairing it with sister courses makes for a real bargain, and it's advised that you leave time for at least two rounds.

A walk onto Ko Olina is like finding yourself in a magical realm. The beauty of this course isn't magic, it's real, and standing on this combination of God's and man's handiwork is an awe-inspiring experience you won't want to miss.

Ko Olina is a about a half hour away from Honolulu on the west coast of Oahu, and offers the best view of the ocean of any course on the island. Yes, this is paradise. But you pay a price if you don't pay attention to your game. No. 1 is a par 5 with out-of-bounds on the left side and several bunkers on the right. That's followed by the most difficult par 4 on the course, once again with out-of-bounds and bunkers. No. 2 also includes a water hazard and a multi-leveled green. Two testers to start your round. So much for Aloha.

Ted Robinson designed Ko Olina, and while he did some wonderful work, the raw material gave him a pretty good head start. Within the panorama, Robinson created water features that are as attractive as they are hazardous.

But the landing areas are large, so as to attract the golfer who may never hit a par round in his life. But with its multi-tiered greens and 6,698-yard distance from the back tees, it also can be challenging if you decide to play the tips.

AFTER YOUR ROUND

Well, this is Hawaii: Tourists from all over the world come just to look around, and it's not too difficult to find great things to see: black sand beaches, mountains, volcanoes, and the ultra-beach experience that is Waikiki.

Cultural contrast: If you stay in the heart of Honolulu, it's a picture of hustle-bustle, big-city tourism on the front side of a myriad of businesses, and Waikiki beach out the back. I'm not much of a shopping guy, but when I visited there were enough intriguing shops to maintain my interest for quite a while. And I was relieved to find out that when I tired of all the browsing, I could walk through the shops, leaving city streets behind to wiggle my toes in the sand.

OTHER PUBLIC COURSES IN HAWAII WORTH A VISIT
- Big Island CC (Big Island Course), Kailua Kona
- The Challenge at Manele Bay, Lanai
- Hawaii Prince GC, Ewa Beach
- Kauai Lagoons GC (Kiele Course), Kauai
- Poipu Bay GC, Kauai
- Princeville at Hanalei (Prince Course), Princeville

SCORECARD

Hole	1	2	3	4	5	6	7	8	9	out	
Yardage	487	387	345	184	508	357	412	165	409	3,254	
Par	5	4	4	3	5	4	4	3	4	36	
Hole	10	11	12	13	14	15	16	17	18	in	total
Yardage	393	355	166	500	498	340	205	338	403	3,198	6,452
Par	4	4	3	5	5	4	3	4	4	36	72

HAWAII

MAUNA KEA GOLF COURSE
KOHALA COAST, HAWAII

When most tourists set their sites on Hawaii, they think of Oahu, and those who bring their clubs will most likely play Ala Wai Golf Course, a municipal course that is the most-played course in America. Maui is another highly desirable destination spot.

Ala Wai is no secret, and Oahu and Maui are not hidden destinations.

The island of Oahu, especially Waikiki and Honolulu, is overcrowded. Maui's got a lot of great golf, but it is also awash with tourists.

Hawaii's Big Island has just what a player is looking for — a quiet atmosphere and some great golf. Those who really want to experience some breathtaking Hawaiian golf should take a jaunt over to the Big Island. There is a line of gems along the Pacific coast that many golfers are not aware of — courses that are hidden beauties to say the least.

The Big Island is big indeed. It covers 4,028 square miles. Maui is the next largest Hawaiian island at 727 square miles. The entire Big Island has a population of approximately 150,000 — compared with 800,000 in the city of Honolulu alone — so there is plenty of room to roam . . . and play golf.

There is an array of natural beauty throughout the Big Island, but golfers can find rich splendor along the Kohala Coast, where seven courses sit aligned just north of the Kona Airport. Just fly into Honolulu International Airport, then jump onto either an Aloha Airlines or Hawaiian Airlines shuttle plane for the forty-five-minute flight to Kona. One left turn out of the Kona airport, and you are seven miles from the southern tip of the Kohala Coast golf.

The courses include the Waikoloa Beach Kings' and Beach courses; the more-forgiving Hapuna Beach Course; the Koala Course; and more. All of the courses are beauties in their own right, but the one to play is the Big Island's Mauna Kea Golf Course.

The Mauna Kea course was designed by Robert Trent Jones, Sr.; it always was an outstanding layout and it got better after Robert Trent Jones, Jr., was called in to renovate it. The new-look course features 120 bunkers, dramatic elevation changes, rugged lava beds, and countless views of the crystal-blue Pacific.

Robert Trent Jones, Jr., didn't do much in the way of alterations to the course's highlights: No. 6, with its elevated tee; the par-3 11th; the 16th, with its oceanside green; and the par-3 3rd, which features a tee shot that must carry a jutting finger of the ocean and is said to be one of the most photographed holes in the world.

The rates, as might be expected, are pretty high, but they vary by the season.

On the financial front, one positive aspect is that those who stay in the resort have reduced greens fees not only at Mauna Kea, but also at Hapuna Beach right next store. If players are planning to visit Maui or Oahu, the reduced rates also apply at the Maui Prince Hotel course and the Prince Hole Course in Waikiki.

AFTER YOUR ROUND

Wherever you turn: You don't have to do too much, other than open your eyes, to find splendor here. Mountains, ocean, and colorful flowers are everywhere, and there are special wonders to seek out. Macadamia nuts and orchids are among the island's top-selling goods. Astronauts once trained in Volcanoes National Park because the rocky ground so closely resembles the moon. During winter near the city of Hilo, it is possible to lie in the sun on the beach and peek at the snowy peaks of the Mauna Kea Mountains.

Variety of viewing: There are countless ways to get up-close and personal to the Big Island's beauty. I went horseback riding on the beach to view my first Hawaiian sunset, then the next day took a helicopter ride over the rain forest. Walking trails through black lava, and bike riding are among the island's recreational options.

The scenic 3rd hole at Mauna Kea is said to be one of the most photographed holes in the world.

Island fare: There are high-end restaurants in the resorts that dot the Kona Coast that offer tasty, but pricey food. For those in the regular-guy club — to which I happen to belong — there are several bistro-style eateries the further inland you go. This is where you can find authentic Hawaiian food that is out of this world. I tried huli-huli chicken, even though I really didn't know what it was. I discovered in a hurry what I'd been missing the previous forty-two years of my life. The chicken is barbecued in huli-huli sauce made of Hawaiian brown sugar cane along with soy sauce and fresh ginger. I topped off this delicious meal with haupia, a traditional Hawaiian coconut-flavored desert that those on the island refer to as "stiff pudding." Not sure what that means, but it sure was good.

SCORECARD

Hole	1	2	3	4	5	6	7	8	9	out	
Yardage	383	394	261	413	593	344	204	530	427	3,549	
Par	4	4	3	4	5	4	3	5	4	36	
Hole	10	11	12	13	14	15	16	17	18	in	total
Yardage	554	247	387	409	413	201	422	555	428	3,616	7,165
Par	5	3	4	4	4	3	4	5	4	36	72

HAWAII

WAIKOLOA BEACH RESORT
(KINGS' COURSE)
KOHALA COAST

Black lava, endless mountains, sunsets you'd pay to see again and again, beaches, luaus, and beautiful flowers that grow naturally in areas where we'd expect weeds. These are givens in America's fiftieth state and its No. 1 tourist attraction.

Now, let's play a little golf.

The paradise of Hawaii's Big Island offers splendid choices when playing our game of choice. And one of the most intriguing is the Waikoloa Beach Resort, where sister courses intertwine mystical Hawaiian tradition with magical Hawaiian golf.

It is somehow fitting that there are two courses — the Kings' and the Beach — that seem to fit together so seamlessly at Waikoloa, just as the Waikoloa logo itself displays a matched pair: two sturdy naupaka plants intertwined as one. Of the two kinds of naupaka, one grows near the sea and the other in the mountains. Each bears what appears to be half a blossom, and only when placed together do they form a perfectly circular flower.

Warmth and wind form another natural pair that is a virtual constant at Waikoloa Beach. The two courses are affected in one way or another by the wind, and the warmth enriches the golfer's experience.

The Beach Course, measuring a modest 6,594 yards and playing to a par 70, provides a leisurely round for most players. Robert Trent Jones, Jr., designed the Beach Course in 1981 not as a stern and demanding test, but to supply a breath of fresh air. The course can be tricky, but for the most part it provides brilliant conditions and a soothing "walk-in-the-park" atmosphere. But don't forget your clubs.

The Beach Course sat solo on the Waikoloa property — much like a lone naupaka plant — for nine years before Tom Weiskopf and Jay Morrish teamed to design the Kings' Course in 1990. It can be stretched to more than 7,000 yards from the back tees, but it remains playable for resort guests who choose a more forgiving tee box.

The Kings' Course is a fairly demanding track that forces concentration along the way. It doesn't take the wisdom of King Solomon, mind you, but it is definitely a thinking-player's course.

The Weiskopf-Morrish design is a solid layout that plays inland from the Pacific. No. 5, which some Waikoloa staffers label the course's signature hole, is one example of the need for strategy at the Kings'. It is a very short par 4 at 327 yards, but it is not short on risk-reward.

The 5th usually plays with the ocean breeze at your back, and depending on the strength of the wind, the temptation on the tee may be to let the shaft out and take a shot at the green. If you make it, you're putting for eagle. If you miss, you could be in a huge, difficult-to-escape bunker short of the green. Boulders and lava are also heavy out

CHIP SHOTS

Course contact info:
(877) 924-5656
www.waikoloabeachgolf.com

Par: 72
Yardage: 7,074 yards

Rating: 73.4
Slope: 135
Notable: Somehow, course designers Tom Weiskopf and Jay Morrish found a way to give a Scottish feeling to the Kings' Course, even on the Kohala Coast. A couple of double greens, pot bunkers, and open fairways do the trick.

On the green
◯ ◯ $105 (Stay and Play rate)

Waikoloa Beach Resort is home to two golf courses, fields of black lava, and more palm trees than you can count.

respects the surrounding Hawaiian culture. Another is the Mamalahoa Trail, a thirty-two-mile horse path said to be used by Hawaiian kings, that was carved through black lava in the mid-nineteenth century and remains intact and protected today. It meanders throughout the Waikoloa property.

The Hawaiian government takes the islands' history and culture seriously, and so do the golf courses sprinkled throughout paradise. Course designers have been careful not to infringe on the natural beauty of the area. In fact, Waikoloa Beach, as well as many other Hawaiian layouts, actually enhances an already-sparkling picture.

AFTER YOUR ROUND

Surprises and secrets abound here: Believe it or not, the Big Island features all five climate groups — tropical, dry, temperate, continental, and polar. That's right, polar. Some mountain peaks on the island reach 10,500 feet and snow is visible on a clear day (which, of course, is virtually every day). I recommend visiting Mauna Kea, the world's largest sea mountain and a spectacular dormant volcano that soars to 13,796 feet above sea level and more than 33,000 feet from the ocean floor. The Kilauea rainforest can be found deep in the heart of the region, away from the highway that circles the island. Keep driving and you'll reach the Ka'u Desert, an area so arid you will be stunned to find it on an island so rich with vegetation. I did my share of playing golf, eating, and visiting the touristy areas in town, but a simple drive around the island offered the most glorious sights of all.

front, so if you land short all brands of danger lurk. This is where you begin ruing the bravado you displayed a few minutes before.

If you take it easy on your drive, opting to play to the right side of the fairway, you obviously forgo a shot at eagle. But a short chip awaits and, if executed, offers a decent birdie opportunity and an excellent chance at par.

The 5th is just one example of great golf design that

SCORECARD

Hole	1	2	3	4	5	6	7	8	9	out	
Yardage	379	562	232	513	327	465	184	426	434	3,522	
Par	4	5	3	5	4	4	3	4	4	36	
Hole	10	11	12	13	14	15	16	17	18	in	total
Yardage	453	188	460	332	601	163	442	412	501	3,552	7,074
Par	4	4	4	3	5	5	4	3	4	36	72

The 17th hole at Circling Raven features mounds on both sides that will keep balls in the fairway, but sand is a problem down the right side.

IDAHO

CIRCLING RAVEN GOLF CLUB
WORLEY, IDAHO

If there is any question about the ideas that inspired Circling Raven Golf Club, you need look no further than the principles of the Coeur d'Alene Tribe. They read, in part: "Reverence for the past. Perseverance in the present. Protection of the Tribe in the future. Through innovation, motivation and cooperation, the Coeur d'Alene Tribe will continue to perpetuate a way of life that focuses upon family, community and protection of the Tribal homelands."

Such dedication to heritage and purity of the land is evident at Circling Raven, which is built on Tribal property adjacent to the Coeur d'Alene Casino. Yes, the Tribe is made up of businessmen, but it also considers its land sacred. The bar was set high in order for Circling Raven to fit into land

so esteemed, and judging by the reaction of the pundits and public, the course lives up to the high standard established.

In August, 2008, *Native American Casino Magazine* named Circling Raven "The Best Native American Casino Golf Course" in the nation, the second time Circling Raven has been so honored. The recognition is particularly prestigious when considering the other outstanding facilities that fit into the category: Barona Creek Golf Club in Lakeside, California; Shenendoah Golf Club at Turning Stone in Verona, New York; and Dancing Rabbit Golf Club in Choctaw, Mississippi, are just a few.

There are approximately seventy tribal golf courses in the United States, and the category is quickly becoming the golf industry's fastest-growing niche. In a time when golf-course construction has reached a plateau, tribal golf courses are being developed at a brisk pace.

Circling Raven is becoming well known in the Idaho area. Area residents as well as tourists understand that this course is something special. Celebrities have been seen playing the course, so you never know whom you might meet. Among those who have played Circling Raven are Hall of Fame baseball player Joe Morgan, Dennis Franz of *NYPD Blue*, former Super Bowl MVP Mark Rypien, talk show host Maury Povich, NBA Hall of Famer Bill Russell, Detroit Lions placekicker Jason Hansen, Seattle Seahawk tackle Cortez Kennedy, football coach Dennis Erickson, and World Series perfect-game pitcher Don Larsen. Often, when such big names play a course, you can be sure that in-the-sky greens fees will follow. Not so at Circling Raven. This course is open to the public, and its prices are reasonable. It's not often you can get on a course of this quality for less than $100, but that's the case at Circling Raven.

Players can be sure they're getting their money's worth and more. The golf course was built in woodlands, and it winds through 620 acres of natural grasses and protected wetlands. Only 100 acres were disturbed during the building of the golf course, which is an indication of just how natural this golf course plays.

Natural setting sometimes brings with it unwanted visitors. Most of the wildlife that appear on the course are pleasant surprises — moose, elk, and deer, among them. But there is also the occasional black bear, so it's important to keep your eyes open for more than just your golf ball.

CHIP SHOTS

Course contact info:
(800) 523-2464,
www.circlingraven.com

Par: 72
Yardage: 7,189 yards

Rating: 74.5
Slope: 140
Notable: *Golfweek* named Circling Raven "The No. 11 Casino Course in America," and just in case you're wondering, casino course translates into public course. In 2008, *Golf Digest* and *Golf Magazine* each included Circling Raven among "The 10 Best New Courses in the Country." No dues, no membership fees, and not an extraordinary cost to play. The inexpensive greens fees will give you plenty of change left over to gamble, if you choose.

On the green
◐◐ $85

Circling Raven is a links-style course, but more American links than Scottish. In Scotland, players from most other holes are clearly visible due to the open spaces and the general flatness of the land. At Circling Raven, however, the holes play linksy, but the surrounding mounds and trees belie that feeling. It makes for a difficult round, but there is a payoff: players on other holes are not visible, so it gives you a great feeling of peace. The Coeur d'Alene Tribe wouldn't have it any other way.

AFTER YOUR ROUND

Worth a gamble: You won't have to go far to try your luck, if you play your cards right. I enjoy a little blackjack, and I find the tables an exciting spot after an all-aces round of golf. The Circling Raven is located adjacent to the Coeur d'Alene Casino, so you can chip to the green then cash in some chips.

Bustling buffet: Coeur d'Alene Casino features a staple of gambling establishments: the morning-noon-and-night buffet. When I got in line, I was told to expect gourmet food without the gourmet price. Sounded like a mouthwatering deal, and my expectations were exceeded. Made-to-order omelets, lunch offerings of all kinds, prime rib, and Friday night seafood buffets are among the highlights. I didn't sample every dish, but it sure felt like I did. Believe me, it will fill you up.

SCORECARD

Hole	1	2	3	4	5	6	7	8	9	out	
Yardage	513	395	217	406	574	387	212	386	474	3,564	
Par	5	4	3	4	5	4	3	4	4	36	
Hole	10	11	12	13	14	15	16	17	18	in	total
Yardage	336	446	581	253	397	426	192	559	435	3,625	7,189
Par	4	4	5	3	4	4	3	5	4	36	72

OTHER PUBLIC COURSES IN IDAHO WORTH A VISIT
- BanBury GC, Eagle
- Falcon Crest GC, Kuna
- Sun Valley GC, Sun Valley

IDAHO

COEUR D'ALENE RESORT GOLF COURSE
COEUR D'ALENE, IDAHO

"One-of-a-kind" has become a cliché, and "unique" is often misused altogether. But there is a feature at Coeur d'Alene Golf Course in which both descriptions fit exactly, for there is nothing like it anywhere on the planet.

The par-3 14th at Coeur d'Alene features a picturesque island green that requires players to strike an absolutely precise tee shot. You've seen island greens, you say? Of course you have. The most famous is the 17th hole at TPC Sawgrass, a Pete Dye design in Ponte Vedra, Florida, that is the annual site of the PGA Tour's TPC Championship.

Since the introduction of the TPC innovation — which, by the way, isn't quite an island; there's a thin isthmus of land in the back of the green that allows players entry — island greens have popped up all over the country.

But, there are two items that distinguish the island green at Coeur d'Alene's 14th: The island green is movable, and a ferry picks you up after you strike your tee shot to take you to the green.

The 14th green comprises 15,000 square feet of stunning, emerald turf, four trees, two bunkers and a small staircase to walk to the putting surface after disembarking from the custom-designed, hand-crafted Honduran mahogany water

taxi. According to the staffers at Coeur d'Alene, the floating green weighs up to 5,000,000 pounds, depending on moisture content. Playable yardage can change from 100 to 175 yards, and the computer-controlled distance from the tee is altered every day.

Designer Scott Miller went to town on his drawing board when he conjured up this beauty, and the rest of the course is also a picture in golf excellence. The other holes may not be one-of-a-kind, but they back up the notion that Coeur d'Alene is no one-hit wonder.

The golf course sits on property that was an operating sawmill from 1916 to the early 1970s, first known as the Rutledge Timber Company and later as the Potlatch Lumber Company. After the site sat vacant for several years, the Hagadone Corporation bought the land in 1988 and hired Miller to devise the golf course. Thanks to his creative genius, the property went from floating logs to a floating green and seventeen other beautiful holes.

The par-5 9th might have been the signature hole at Coeur d'Alene if it weren't for No. 14. The hole measures more than 600 yards, and it offers you a chance to take out the big stick and let 'er rip off the tee. Length is obviously important, but accuracy also is a must.

Players should be aware of strategically placed bunkers on the right side of the 9th fairway, but if you go too far left, you have no angle to reach the green, which is tucked to the left and protected by bunkers.

The 5th hole also is a highlight. It is a short par-3 at less than 150 yards, but there is no green grass from tee to putting surface. The entire length of the hole is one enormous bunker, and there are two more large bunkers that virtually surround the green. This resembles another kind of island green — ensconced in sand rather than water.

Coeur d'Alene encompasses 200 pristine acres of land, with mountain views on every hole. Speaking of views, each hole is surrounded by contours so you never see golfers on other holes no matter where you are on the course.

Tees, greens, and fairways all are bent grass, which makes the fairways at Coeur d'Alene as smooth as the greens at most other courses. Estimates of the amount of flowers at Coeur d'Alene make the course a horticultural heaven. It is beautified with 1,500 wild flowers, 4,000 petunias, 25,000 junipers, and 30,000 geraniums.

Sparkling beauty, and a golf landmark not found anywhere else in the world. These are just two of the reasons to visit Coeur d'Alene. If you make the trip yourself, you will find so many more.

CHIP SHOTS

Course contact info:
(800) 935-6283,
www.cdaresort.com

Par: 71
Yardage: 6,803 yards

Rating: 71.1
Slope: 119
Notable: Chip Beck, PGA Tour Player and winner of the 1992 Merrill Lynch Shootout at Coeur d'Alene, called the Idaho course one of the finest he has ever seen. Awards have poured in since the former sawmill property was purchased in 1988 and developed into a golf course shortly thereafter. *Golf Digest, Golf Magazine, Golfweek, GolfWorld,* and *Golf Odyssey* are among the publications that have recognized Coeur d'Alene for its beauty, for being a fun place to play, and as one of the top courses in the country. It has attributes that are better than those found at most private clubs, but this public facility allows everyone to play.

On the green
◎◎ $99

The par-3 14th hole at Coeur d'Alene is the world's only floating island green. Its length is changed daily.

AFTER YOUR ROUND

Pure Coeur d'Alene: A masseuse would be a great person to see to start your activities after the golf is done and before the evening begins. A full-service spa at Coeur d'Alene Resort is available, and, believe me, it's worth a stop. The experts loosened the unwelcome kink in my right shoulder that bothers me about one out of every three times I play.

Entertainment time: Silverwood Theme Park is located twenty miles north of Coeur d'Alene. Don't forget the wine tours, antique shops, summer theater, symphony, and art galleries nearby. Bowling, casinos, rock climbing, carriage rides, and bike rentals are a few more activities to fill your visit. I wasn't able to get to all of them during my enjoyable stay at Coeur d'Alene, but if you've got any energy left after your round of golf and a massage, I would recommend the bikes. The trails cut through the woods, and reminded me of some of the chase scenes from *Jurassic Park*.

SCORECARD

Hole	1	2	3	4	5	6	7	8	9	out	
Yardage	540	479	155	322	148	169	435	437	601	3,286	
Par	5	4	3	4	3	3	4	4	5	35	
Hole	10	11	12	13	14	15	16	17	18	in	total
Yardage	469	538	249	368	218	495	429	269	482	3,517	6,803
Par	4	5	3	4	3	5	4	4	4	36	71

No. 18 at Cog Hill is a supreme test in accuracy, offering but a thin strip of entrance between pond and bunker to the green.

ILLINOIS

COG HILL GOLF & COUNTRY CLUB
(DUBSDREAD COURSE)
LEMONT, ILLINOIS

Watch the PGA Tour's Western Open, and try to remember what you see. It might give you some help if you are ever fortunate enough to play Cog Hill's Dubsdread Course. The course is home to the Western Open, and it's also available for everyday public play.

There is the intrigue of knowing you are walking the same fairways as the best in the game, but you'll also be able to actually compare a shot you make with one made by a touring pro in the very same position. You might hit it perfectly and come up with the same result.

There's a chance. Not a very good one, but a chance.

Jeff Sluman's tournament-record 63 was a round to behold in 1992, and will be a difficult standard to match. Perhaps you could hope for 83 or 93, but at least you'll have a chance to get on the course.

There are four courses at Cog Hill, and Dubsdread is in a class of its own. The other courses — Nos. 1, 2, and 3 — are in the $50 range, and Dubsdread greens fees are more than $100. It's a high-end public course, but it's a golf bargain if you want to compare your game with the superstars of golf who've played Dubsdread — a rare and enjoyable treat.

The Dubsdread Course has an old-fashioned feel to it, and it continues to be upgraded by designer Joe Jemsek. Nationally ranked since it opened in 1964, Dubsdread is known for its stringent shot-making requirements and incredible scenery.

One of the classic, and toughest, holes on the course is the par-4 16th. Even Tom Watson, who won the Western Open three times, said this was one of two lay-up holes on the course. Hitting the green in regulation is a serious risk-reward. Many players, including the world's best, opt for safety.

The 16th checks in at 456 yards, and almost every year of the tournament, it plays to an average score of more than 4.0. And these are the pros. It isn't the length, it's the angles and the thought behind them.

The 8th hole is considered to be another lay-up hole, but it is generally thought to be less of a challenge than No. 16. Also, the 16th sets up the finish of your round, so success is vital.

No. 16 is a dogleg left, with a large bunker running parallel to the right side of the fairway where your ball would land off the tee. The natural instinct is to stay away from the bunker, but if you hit the drive too far left, you're in thick trees that virtually eliminate your chance to reach the green in less than 4.

Tiger Woods, after playing Dubsdread in 2003, said it was one of his favorite layouts on the PGA Tour and that's why he makes it a point to play the Western Open every year. Davis Love III says it "excites me to come back" to Cog Hill, and Phil Mickelson called the wind one of the greatest challenges on Dubsdread.

The pros aren't the only top-notch golfers who face Nos. 8, 16, and the other sixteen Dubsdread toughies. The course has been host to four U.S. Golf Association championships, most recently the 1997 U.S. Amateur.

Tight landing areas, tons of bunkers, and sloping greens make this course difficult no matter what your handicap. As proven year in and year out, pros, top amateurs, and public-course players all have a chance for a world-class round at Cog Hill.

AFTER YOUR ROUND

History lesson: Lemont was settled in 1836 and incorporated in 1873, and is one of the oldest communities in Illinois. It is a peaceful and traditional escape from the rest of the Chicago area. The Old Stone Church (built in 1861), the Lemont Area Historical Society & Museum, and the Lemont Genealogy Library are worth taking half a day to explore. The SS. Cyril and Methodius Parish, and the Hindu Temple of Greater Chicago are religious landmarks. If, like me, you are into old cemeteries, the St. James Catholic Cemetery has readable gravestones that date back to the mid-1800s.

Back to today: It's not all hindsight in Lemont. If you'd rather think about a little real-time fun, there are six miles of trails along the historic I&M (Illinois and Michigan) Canal. Bikers, walkers, joggers, and in-line skaters are afforded plenty of room to do their thing.

CHIP SHOTS

Course contact info:
(630) 257-5872,
www.coghillgolf.com

Par: 72
Yardage: 7,554 yards

Rating: 77
Slope: 142
Notable: Home to the PGA Tour's Western Open since 1991, the Dubsdread Course has been given five stars by *Golf Digest*, and is annually among *Golfweek's* "Top Public Courses in the Country."

On the green
○○○ $150

OTHER PUBLIC COURSES IN ILLINOIS WORTH A VISIT
- Cantigny Golf, Wheaton
- Eagle Ridge Resort & Spa (The General Course), Galena
- The Glen Club, Glenview, Glenview
- Harborside International GC (Portside Course), Chicago
- Kokopelli GC, Marion
- TPC Deere Run, Silvas
- Pine Meadow GC, Mundelein
- ThunderHawk GC, Beach Park
- WeaverRidge GC, Peoria

SCORECARD

Hole	1	2	3	4	5	6	7	8	9	out	
Yardage	458	224	443	462	507	240	431	379	613	3,757	
Par	4	3	4	4	5	3	4	4	5	36	
Hole	10	11	12	13	14	15	16	17	18	in	total
Yardage	383	607	216	480	215	523	456	423	494	3,797	7,554
Par	4	5	3	4	3	5	4	4	4	36	72

GOLF CLUB AT EAGLEWOOD
ITASCA, ILLINOIS

The Golf Club at Eaglewood has a storied tradition in an area loaded with golf courses of lore. The 1928 design is just thirty-five miles west of Chicago, known both as the Second City and as a first-rate locale for storybook courses.

Eaglewood is a short course at 6,017, but it is long on legacy. More than eight decades of comfortable but challenging golf has attracted many guests to the resort. Even older than the golf are some of the oak trees on the property. Many are more than 100 years old and provide a stately surrounding to a classy course.

Knowledgeable golfers staying in Chicago have no qualms about making the drive to play a round at Eaglewood. The extremely reasonable price is one of the major draws. The greens fees don't come close to $100, and this includes carts and first-rate service. Prices are even cheaper for those who stay at the resort.

Another reason to play Eaglewood goes all the way back to the course's roots. Charles Maddox and Frank P. MacDonald, who designed the layout, were leading golf course architects in the 1920s who spent a considerable amount of time in Illinois. Maddox created several well-known private courses in Illinois, such as Stonehenge Golf Club in Barrington, and Forest Hills Country Club in Rockford. MacDonald teamed with Maddox on other Illinois projects, including Highlands in Elgin.

Present-day Eaglewood doesn't rely solely on history, however. A 2006 renovation that cost in excess of $1 million kept the original feel of the course, but modernized several facets to keep up with Chicagoland standards.

Seventy bunkers were redesigned and many were moved, making the hazards more a part of the green complexes. The irrigation system was also replaced to improve turf conditions and enhance enjoyment. Rolling green fairways, majestic trees, and sparkling lakes are part of the Eaglewood backdrop.

And don't be fooled by the 6,017-yard length, which is modest by today's yardstick. This is a resort course, designed to be forgiving to the golfer who may play occasionally at public-access courses. But the sloping greens have earned Eaglewood the nickname "The Little Green Menace," not the brand of moniker applied to a push-over course.

One of the toughest challenges is the 201-yard 6th. Going against the Eaglewood norm, the yardage is substantial for a par-3 hole. Another little tidbit? The 6th features an island green that requires both length and pinpoint accuracy.

The 106-acre Eaglewood property provides a relaxing escape for golfers, but even those who don't play will find plenty to do while other family members complete the eighteen-hole circuit. Frank Lloyd Wright's former home and studio is in nearby Oak Park, and it's worth a visit, especially because the famed architect's work inspired the Eaglewood resort's building design.

Fireplaces were a staple of Wright structures, and the Eaglewood lobby features one that's particularly dramatic. Burnham's restaurant, just off the lobby, also includes a wood-burning fireplace.

There is no need to travel off the property to find activities that might surprise visitors. There is an Olympic-size indoor swimming pool, a six-lane bowling alley, pool tables, and dartboards. If you want to take a short jaunt, the Eaglewood concierge can help you plan a trip to a nearby water park.

If you happen to make a winter visit, you obviously will miss out on playing golf. But cross-country skiing, snowshoeing, ice-skating, and sleigh rides are available to those who don't mind braving the cold.

Summertime is the best time to visit, however, if you or your party love the links. If you are by yourself, Eaglewood is a wonderful place for peaceful solitude. And even if you're on a convention, there's fun to be had. Eaglewood staffers will organize a Business Group 9-Hole Tournament for groups between forty-eight and seventy-two players.

CHIP SHOTS

Course contact info:
(877) 285-6150,
www.eaglewoodresort.com

Par: 72
Yardage: 6,017 yards

Rating: 67.9
Slope: 115
Notable: Chicago is so full of history-rich courses that *Golfweek* once named it "The Top Golf City in America, " devoting nearly half of a special issue to the town's golf courses and tradition.

On the green
$45

Stately trees lining fairways, and even the occasional semi-blind shot to the green, add to the beauty and challenge at Eaglewood.

AFTER YOUR ROUND

Sports, comedy, and blues: Golf is far from the only sport in Chicago, just thirty-five minutes from Itasca. Baseball lovers can catch a Cubs or White Sox game, while gridiron fans opt for the Bears. Second City — the comedy club where Bill Murray, John Belushi, and other famous comedians got their start — is available for those in the mood to laugh.

Bossman's Blues, Blue Chicago, and Buddy Guy's Legends are first-class spots to hear blues tunes.

Closer to the course: If you don't feel like making the half-hour hike to Chicago, in-town options include the Itasca Historical Depot Museum, Overshadowed Theatrical Productions, and Itasca Caribbean Water Park.

SCORECARD

Hole	1	2	3	4	5	6	7	8	9	out	
Yardage	366	336	365	337	318	201	476	194	272	2,865	
Par	4	4	4	4	4	3	5	3	4	35	
Hole	10	11	12	13	14	15	16	17	18	in	total
Yardage	538	172	515	91	336	293	311	421	475	3,152	6,017
Par	4	4	4	3	5	5	4	4	4	37	72

Harrison Hills staffers have designated No. 15 as the signature hole. Missing the green on the right side is not advised or your scorecard will be autographed with a big number.

INDIANA

HARRISON HILLS GOLF AND COUNTRY CLUB
ATTICA, INDIANA

If you're looking for the prototypical small-town Midwestern public golf course — quiet, well maintained, affordable, and with plenty of elbow room — then Harrison Hills Golf and Country Club is the place to play. But don't be mistaken. This might be a small town, but there are plenty of big-time Indiana state tournaments that prove Harrison Hills is a course with force.

Indiana's PGA Assistants Championship, the state's Father/Son Championship, and the Public Links Championship have all been held at Harrison Hills, a 200-acre layout with rolling undulations and ultra-sharp bent grass. It has been an Indiana Open Qualifying site several times and is also a Chicago Open qualifier.

Harrison Hills is 6,820 yards long, which is a fairly standard length for a par-72 layout, but there is nothing customary or even-keeled about how it gets there. Six of the ten par 4s measure less than 400 yards and one of them — No. 11 — is barely more than 300. Doglegs and hazards keep players honest, but length has nothing to do with the challenges of the par 4s.

Let's look at the 306-yard 11th hole. There's a good chance at par, and maybe even birdie, but neither score is automatic. A pond protects the left side of the short fairway and the right side is made troublesome by a thicket of trees. If you hit it long and straight, and you're feeling brave, you might feel like going for the green in one. It's doable, and the green slopes from back to front, making it a tantalizing target. Don't celebrate too early, even if you rest on the putting surface after one or two strokes. The slope might be welcoming on approach shots, but that same undulation makes it a severe test once the flat stick comes out.

The par 5s are another story, providing the aforementioned contrasts at Harrison Hills. Three holes' yardages are in the mid-500s and the other — No. 7 — is a "you gotta be kidding me" 646 yards. You expect a yardage difference between par 4s and par 5s, but the range between the shortest 4 and the longest 5 at the Attica, Indiana, course is a mind-boggling 340 yards.

Players standing on the No. 7 tee might look at the generous landing area and think they're in store for a long but straightforward hole all the way down the 600-plus-yard fairway. That's true for the fairway, but the green is a different story. Subtle elevation deviations can give players fits, especially those who are weary from the long trek from tee box to putting surface. For many reasons, length being foremost, players should be very proud if they accomplish a par at No. 7.

The outcome at the 7th hole might be an uncertain venture for many, but virtually every player has one sure thing in store. They'll walk away from the Harrison Hills experience anticipating their next visit.

CHIP SHOTS

Course contact info:
(765) 762-1135,
www.harrisonhills.com

Par: 72
Yardage: 6,820 yards

Rating: 73.9
Slope: 132
Notable: Harrison Hills is a perfect fit to be featured in a book that includes many inexpensive public courses that some might otherwise overlook. The course's slogan is "Indiana's Hidden Golf Gem."

On the green
⊙ $45

AFTER YOUR ROUND

Saving history: An old-time marquee in Attica's quaint downtown alerts visitors to the historic, one-screen Devon Theater that has been refurbished to reflect its original glory. A traditional fruit farm is also worth a visit and a couple of decent campgrounds are available if you don't mind roughing it a bit.

Sweet shop: Wolf's Homemade Candies on S. Council Street is a staple for Attica-area residents and a must-see for visitors. Think I'm kidding? When a former co-worker returned from the "sweetery," I had a few samplings from his tasty stop. My taste buds had a party when I ate the dark chocolate raspberry creams, chocolate covered toffee, and peanut butter fudge. Our office usually was a group of mild-mannered folks, but the break-room battle for the candy got pretty intense.

OTHER PUBLIC COURSES IN INDIANA WORTH A VISIT

- Bear Slide GC, Cicero
- Brickyard Crossing, Speedway
- Fort GC, Indianapolis
- Heartland Crossing Golf Links, Cambry
- Otter Creek GC, Columbus
- The Trophy Club, Lebanon
- Prairie View GC, Carmel
- Purgatory GC, Noblesville

SCORECARD

Hole	1	2	3	4	5	6	7	8	9	out	
Yardage	394	195	354	432	522	372	646	218	435	3,568	
Par	4	3	4	4	5	4	5	3	4	36	
Hole	10	11	12	13	14	15	16	17	18	in	total
Yardage	432	306	195	523	321	356	411	151	557	3,252	6,820
Par	4	4	3	5	4	4	4	3	5	36	72

No. 10 is a perfect bridge to the inward nine.

INDIANA

WARREN GOLF COURSE AT NOTRE DAME
SOUTH BEND, INDIANA

In the shadow of the Golden Dome, among the legends of Knute Rockne and the Gipper, there is a new song being sung at the University of Notre Dame, "Hail, hail to public golf." The Fighting Irish are waking up to the echoes of those who love to play a great course without having to pay private-club fees. Warren Golf Course at Notre Dame has played host to all who wish to play since opening in 1999.

Public-access players have been walking the fairways at Notre Dame for years, and there is further proof that Warren Golf Course is a place where public golf is first and foremost. The United States Golf Association named Warren Golf Course the site of the 2010 U.S. Women's Amateur Public Links Championship, one of the top USGA

amateur tournaments in the nation. The tournament is held annually on a public course, and only visits the top U.S. venues.

The William K. Warren family, who made public golf possible at Notre Dame, sought to provide affordable public-access excellence at the course and, as it matured, its reputation grew.

"One of the visions Mr. Warren had when he endowed the course to the university was that it serve as the host of premier amateur golf tournaments," said John Foster, general manager and head golf pro at Warren Golf Course. "The Women's Amateur Public Links Championship is definitely the most prestigious event [to visit Warren]."

The USGA lays down rigid standards when selecting a WAPL site, and when it picked Warren it was testament to the course's difficulty, beauty, and top-notch public-golf experience.

This isn't the first amateur tournament Warren has hosted, but it is the most high-profile event held at the course. Three U.S. Amateur qualifiers, one USGA Senior Amateur qualifier, and the 2005 NCAA Men's Regional Golf Championship were staged at the Bill Coore-Ben Crenshaw layout.

Crenshaw and Coore sought to make the course playable for everyone who visited, offering wide fairways so players could stand at the tee without worry. As exemplified by the amount of amateur tournaments that have been held at Warren, however, the course is no cakewalk. The rough is tough, and bunkers have been carved out of natural ground in spots that prove troublesome on both tee shots and approaches to the green. The putting surfaces are small by most standards, and they are curvaceous enough to force you to use a keen eye. Putting is perhaps the most crucial facet of the game at Warren, and usually it's a determining factor in tournament standings.

The holes are straightforward with no tricks, but they demand accuracy to avoid the thick rough. The monster of the layout is No. 11, a par 3 that plays to a gargantuan 245 yards from the championship tees. It is an extra-long par 3, and length isn't the only challenge. Bunkers line the fairways and border the green to catch shots that fall short, right or left. The one break on No. 11 is an expansive green

CHIP SHOTS

Course contact info:
(574) 631-4653,
www.warrengolfcourse.com

Par: 71
Yardage: 7,020 yards

Rating: 74.6
Slope: 135
Notable: Those offering a welcome at Notre Dame's golf facility do a pretty good job: "[The course] is a glimpse back to a time when golf was played for the pleasure of walking the links ... when you were more refreshed upon completion of your round than you were when you began . . . . " After a pitch like that, how can you resist?

On the green
◎ $56

whose contours will hold a low runner, which is often necessary on such a long tee shot.

Media attention is not always directed at public courses until they have been open for some time, but the Warren layout, which opened in 1999, immediately grabbed pundits' attention. Various national publications have placed the facility among the nation's best in categories that include public courses, affordable courses, and daily-fee courses.

The Warren family's vision has been realized, and public-access golfers who visit or live near "Old Notre Dame" are definitely the ones who benefit.

AFTER YOUR ROUND

Campus cordiality: You're already on the campus, so take some time to walk around one of the most beautiful examples of college life this country has to offer. Tradition lives and breathes at Notre Dame, and you can almost feel it on your skin as you visit the Basilica of the Sacred Heart, the famous "Touchdown Jesus" statue, the "Golden Dome" athletic complex, and the historic structures that serve as classroom and administration buildings. On my last visit to Notre Dame, I couldn't decide whether the trip around the golf course or the tour of the campus was my favorite walk of the day. Call it a toss-up.

SCORECARD

Hole	1	2	3	4	5	6	7	8	9	out	
Yardage	372	462	410	143	518	473	407	441	185	3,411	
Par	4	4	4	3	5	4	4	4	3	35	
Hole	10	11	12	13	14	15	16	17	18	in	total
Yardage	495	245	443	433	210	418	345	565	455	3,609	7,020
Par	5	3	4	4	3	4	4	5	4	36	71

IOWA

THE HARVESTER GOLF CLUB
RHODES, IOWA

There is no shortage of length at The Harvester Golf Club. In fact, length is its strength, not to mention an isolated prairie-land feel that brings peace to what might otherwise be a tumultuous test.

The Harvester, at 7,340 yards from the back tees, will challenge the best players around. Reality trumps machismo at The Harvester. A low-handicapper faces a test he might enjoy, but a double-digit player would be smart to move up to a tee box more suitable for his game.

The Harvester also is long on customer service. It is a high-end facility that offers a pricey round for a public-course player, but its staffers roll out the red carpet to those forking over the greens fees. This is the kind of service that will bring players back.

Perhaps even more gleaming than The Harvester welcome is the condition of the course. Pristine from tee to green, tough from fairway to rough, this course is a picture in lush challenge. Course architect Keith Foster did it right when he created this 2000 design. His vision perfectly meshed with the Iowa terrain, and he did his best not to disturb the natural ambience.

When Iowa State graduate Dickson Jensen wanted to convert the 300 acres of prairie land he owned into a prime-time golf course, he took one look at Foster's résumé and chose his man. Foster has lent his hand to some outstanding courses, including Arizona's Sun Ridge Canyon, and two eye-catching tracks in Texas — The Tradition and The Quarry.

There are some courses that require tons of earthmoving, bulldozing, and the importing of many features not native to the area. Sometimes this method works well, but it almost never feels natural. Many of the notable courses in the world are set in areas where they are allowed to become integrated into their environment. Disturbance of the surrounding landscape is minimal at The Harvester.

The expansive course is awash with fescue and native grasses, and a sixty-acre lake and several ponds come into play on many holes. The water hazards are at once cosmetic and arduous. More evidence of Foster's natural-is-better philosophy include untouched wetlands and dense woods.

Bent grass makes up the tees, fairways, and greens. Foster called for bluegrass in the rough, and the thicker,

coarser grass grabs golf balls and presents a surprisingly different feel as players try to dig their way out.

The course's reputation in and around Rhodes has resulted in a steady stream of tournaments and special events. While these are often a course's bread and butter — a chance to make good money in one fell swoop — the maintenance staff doesn't save its best performance for the big days.

It is the consistency of conditions evident throughout the season that keeps daily-fee players coming back — and selecting The Harvester when it's time for their group to hold an outing.

It doesn't take long for The Harvester to make an impression, though the 1st hole isn't quite as welcoming as the staff's greeting in the clubhouse. It's a beautiful hole, and it appears to be a 425-yard, straightforward par 4. But the view from the tee box is a bit deceptive, giving new guests cause for alarm.

The first drive of the day must be hit just a little bit left of center, and first-time visitors often miss the subtlety of this requirement. The penalty is a second shot out of deep rough that virtually eliminates the chance of reaching the green in

The Harvester clubhouse, perched on the most elevated spot on the property, overlooks virtually very hole on the course, including No. 6 (foreground).

CHIP SHOTS

Course contact info:
(641) 227-4653,
www.harvestergolf.com

Par: 72
Yardage: 7,340 yards

Rating: 76
Slope: 140
Notable: Because of The Harvester's emphasis on the preservation of the natural surroundings, wildlife have not deserted the property. The beverage server might not be your only visitor as you make your way around The Harvester. A deer, an owl, or maybe a woodchuck might join you for a while.

On the green
○ $64

regulation. Making a bogey on the 1st hole isn't much of a start, but playing catch-up isn't so bad on a place as sweet as The Harvester.

AFTER YOUR ROUND

Slim pickings: In the 2000 census, the population of Rhodes came in at a whopping 294. Perhaps it's cracked the 300 mark by now, but in a town that encompasses exactly one square mile, the recreational opportunities are virtually nil. You might want to play 36 at The Harvester, and then do some work on the practice range until nightfall.

Aim for Ames: The closest city to Rhodes with a population of at least 50,000 is Ames, just a touch more than a forty-minute drive away. The Ames Community Arts Council stages local theater productions, concerts, dance, comedy, and art shows. And the Ames Farmers' Market is a favorite stop.

SCORECARD											
Hole	1	2	3	4	5	6	7	8	9	out	
Yardage	425	360	195	575	370	560	405	225	465	3,580	
Par	4	4	3	5	4	5	4	3	4	36	
Hole	10	11	12	13	14	15	16	17	18	in	total
Yardage	470	385	410	390	230	650	480	180	565	3,760	7,340
Par	4	4	4	4	3	5	4	3	5	36	72

OTHER PUBLIC COURSES IN IOWA WORTH A VISIT
- Amana Colonies GC, Amana
- Legacy GC, Norwalk
- Spencer G&CC, Spencer
- Spirit Hollow GC, Burlington

KANSAS

BUFFALO DUNES GOLF COURSE
GARDEN CITY, KANSAS

It isn't often that a municipal golf course finds its way into the realm of outstanding venues to play the game. But Buffalo Dunes Golf Course, owned and operated by Garden City, Kansas, proves that municipal golf doesn't mean sacrificing excellence for affordability. Those in charge at Buffalo Dunes have come up with a way to offer both.

Even in a sometimes-difficult, wind-swept environment, the course maintenance staff presents a splendid oasis in the middle of Kansas prairieland. This brand of conditioning usually is reserved for private clubs, or at least high-end public courses. The dedication of the Buffalo Dunes maintenance staff, along with the municipality's close eye on spending, have allowed low prices and high quality to find common ground.

Garden City chose a parcel seven miles south of its city limits when it first conceptualized its course. After designer Frank Hummel brought the dream alive, golfers in the area realized they had a treat. The excellence has not degraded one iota since Buffalo Dunes opened in 1976.

CHIP SHOTS

Course contact info:
(620) 276-1210,
www.buffalodunes.net

Par: 72
Yardage: 6,767 yards

Rating: 72.8
Slope: 128
Notable: Buffalo Dunes has received awards from *Golf Digest* for quality golf every year since 2000. Just as impressive is the price at Buffalo Dunes. It has been chosen by *Golf Magazine* as one of "The Top 50 Bangs for the Buck" in public golf, and has also been recognized by *Maximum Golf* magazine for being a top-notch bargain.

On the green
⚪ $55

As might be expected in the flatlands and winds of Kansas, the course is a replica of Scottish links. The deep, native-grass rough lining the fairways adds to the feel that you are in the birthplace of golf. The fairways are well maintained, the greens are of average size, the bunkers are deep, and three water hazards provide peril.

There isn't a course in western Kansas that can match the level set by Buffalo Dunes, and only a handful of municipal courses throughout the country achieve its standard of quality. The only real knocks on Buffalo Dunes are beyond the staff's control, and even those have their up-sides. What are they? Well, the course is situated in a pretty isolated area, so you have to do some driving to get there. It takes a while to reach the 1st tee, but the peace and quiet is worth the effort. No traffic, no real estate, no distractions. Just beautiful golf.

Another obstacle facing Buffalo Dunes is the wind. Gusts of 20 mph are fairly common, and some players call this a negative. But course management likes to take the glass-half-full approach, saying the wind adds to the challenge and creates more decisions. Strategy, after all, is an enjoyable part of the game.

Equally as likable is the staff — not only for its performance, but also its attitude. There is a very laid-back atmosphere at Buffalo Dunes, from the folks in the clubhouse, to the marshals, to the beverage servers, to the guys who offer to clean your clubs.

Even the staff at the practice range is friendly. You hit from grass on the range, and there's a chipping green and a practice bunker. No one will rush you; just take your time and improve your game.

The golf course's condition may have a ritzy, country club look, but the employees are there to make you feel welcome. You don't get any "you're lucky to be playing our club" snobbery. Their gracious attitude is just one more reason to make Buffalo Dunes your Kansas pick.

AFTER YOUR ROUND

Wild times: The 3,670-acre Finney Game Refuge is just south of Garden City and is home to the oldest publicly owned bison herd in Kansas. The herd began with a gift of one bull and two cows in 1924. The refuge is also home to box turtles, pheasants, quail, rabbit, deer, squirrel, doves, and many other Kansas creatures.

We're not in Kansas anymore: Siamang gibbons, red pandas, snow leopards, snow monkeys, sun bears, and Bactrian camels? This is not a mirage in the middle of the plains of Kansas, it's the Lee Richardson Zoo. The zoo is filled with hundreds of animals and it's open all year round. Free admission for walkers, and $3 to drive through.

Native grasses make for a prairieland-feel at Buffalo Dunes, including behind the 400-yard 6th.

OTHER PUBLIC COURSES IN KANSAS WORTH A VISIT
- Auburn Hills GC, Wichita
- Colbert Hills GC, Manhattan
- Prairie Highlands GC, Olathe
- Sand Creek Station GC, Newton

SCORECARD

Hole	1	2	3	4	5	6	7	8	9	out	
Yardage	548	339	389	195	539	400	357	189	392	3,348	
Par	5	4	4	3	5	4	4	3	4	36	
Hole	10	11	12	13	14	15	16	17	18	in	total
Yardage	391	423	198	515	413	398	564	160	357	3,419	6,767
Par	4	4	3	5	4	4	5	3	4	36	72

KENTUCKY

CHERRY BLOSSOM GOLF COURSE & COUNTRY CLUB
GEORGETOWN, KENTUCKY

OK, we get it. Cherry Blossom Golf Course & Country Club is the finest public golf course in Kentucky. It seems the national pundits want to hammer us over the head with the fact that Cherry Blossom holds the public bragging rights in the Bluegrass State. *Golfweek* has placed Cherry Blossom on the top of its public list for five consecutive years.

All it took was one lone visit for me to wish that I lived in one of the homes in Cherry Blossom Village, the master-planned community in which the 178-acre bluegrass golf course is situated. The 427-acre village will one day accommodate more than 500-single family homes and upwards of 400 upscale townhomes. The value of the homes already built at the village range from $200,000 to more than $500,000.

Cherry Blossom Golf Course is named for the native cherry trees that are prevalent throughout the property. After surveying the former farmland on the outskirts of Georgetown, developers decided not only to build a golf course, but a golf-course community. Such developments can often be a bit pricey, but this isn't the case at Cherry Blossom. Even though the course is challenging, well maintained, and features perhaps the slickest greens in Kentucky, you can play for under $50 on weekdays.

The course is minutes away from Lexington, the most revered thoroughbred-breeding region in the country. Many living in the Cherry Blossom area think an awful lot about horses, and golf course architects Clyde Johnson and Danny McQueen knew it would take quite a golf course to buck the trend. Johnson's pairing with McQueen isn't his first collaboration. He teamed with John Daly in 1995 to design Wicked Stick Golf Links in Myrtle Beach, South Carolina. It was Daly's first signature course. The tee shots aren't quite as long as Daly's "grip it and rip it" distances he's made famous on the PGA Tour and brought to the design of Wicked Stick.

Johnson and McQueen, however, hit a home run at Cherry Blossom, ensuring that those immersing themselves in the course will undoubtedly forget about horse racing (at least temporarily) and virtually everything else when traversing the eighteen glorious holes.

The extra scenic touches are visible from the start of the round. A stream meanders behind the 1st green, making its way through the practice range, past the 10th tee and winding to a conclusion at the 11th green.

Twelve ponds are situated throughout the course, and they are placed to be both scenic and hazardous. The largest water feature is a huge pond that forces a carry off the 14th tee, protects the rear of the 17th green, and encompasses the entire right side of the 18th, almost engulfing its green. That's one pond involved in the strategy of three holes.

Also adjacent to the oversized water hazard is the Restaurant & Bar at Cherry Blossom. A casual atmosphere makes a perfect place to enjoy a beverage or a home-style favorite served by folks looking to offer a sumptuous finale to a round on the golf course. Even if you didn't have a particularly good round, the restaurant's menu will leave you feeling good. Everything from salads, sandwiches, steaks, stir-fry, and pastas are prepared to please.

AFTER YOUR ROUND

Hoofin' it: The Kentucky Derby may be up the road a piece in Louisville, but Lexington offers more than its share of race courses. Horses are the name of the game at no fewer than ten locations in the Lexington metropolitan area, so if you're feeling lucky there are plenty of options for you to put a few dollars on your favorite pony.

Kentucky kernels: Some of the traditional and modern Kentucky specialties include Cayce corn bread, sweet potatoes casserole, Appalachian ginger bread, chocolate nut pie, and Kentucky hot brown. Of course, there are the standard restaurants throughout the town, but search hard enough and you'll find plenty of pure Kentucky.

CHIP SHOTS

Course contact info:
(502) 570-9849,
www.cherryblossomgolf.com

Par: 72
Yardage: 6,842 yards

Rating: 72.6
Slope: 136
Notable: Officials for the NGA Hooters Tour, a developmental circuit for players hoping to someday play in the PGA Tour, thought enough of Cherry Blossom to hold tournaments at the course in mid-May of both 2008 and 2009.

On the green
$35

A late right-hand curl at the 18th gives one final twist to a round at Cherry Blossom.

OTHER PUBLIC COURSES IN KENTUCKY WORTH A VISIT
- Kearney Hill Golf Links, Lexington
- Lassing Pointe GC, Union
- Old Silo GC, Mount Sterling
- Wasioto Winds GC, Pineville

SCORECARD

Hole	1	2	3	4	5	6	7	8	9	out	
Yardage	398	179	385	207	533	405	406	375	526	3,414	
Par	4	3	4	3	5	4	4	4	5	36	
Hole	10	11	12	13	14	15	16	17	18	in	total
Yardage	407	372	138	424	572	357	201	519	438	3,428	6,842
Par	4	4	3	4	5	4	3	5	4	36	72

KENTUCKY

QUAIL CHASE GOLF CLUB
(WEST/EAST COURSES)
LOUISVILLE, KENTUCKY

In the thoroughbred capital of the world, some don't think about Kentucky when it comes to picking a premium location in which to take a few swings of the golf clubs. But players who saddle up for a round at Quail Chase Golf Club in Louisville are sure find the track to their liking.

It's a great course on which to play the game, and even if you're visiting Louisville for the Kentucky Derby, you should leave a day open to take the short drive to Quail Chase. Don't expect to play on Kentucky bluegrass — Quail Chase opts for Bermuda grass fairways and bent grass greens that are in tremendous condition. Locals say the conditions are consistent no matter what time of year you play.

Besides the green grass and the smooth putting greens, there is another kind of green that plays into the experience at Quail Chase, Louisville's only twenty-seven-hole complex. The bang for the buck is perhaps the best in Kentucky. Greens fees at Quail Chase are comparable to municipal courses in the area, and the conditions stand up to many of Kentucky's private clubs.

Throw in the fact that there are three nines from which to choose, and you have a variety of top-notch combinations available that will quench your thirst for great golf while not drying up your wallet. Since 1989, Quail Chase has done a splendid job of finding the niche between the sometimes less-than-par conditions of municipal courses and the outlandish prices of ritzy clubs.

Architect David Pfaff built the original eighteen — the South and the West Courses — and added the East Course in 1991. The most recent addition is about 200 yards longer than the original two nines, and as such, is the most difficult challenge of the three.

The fairways offer different looks off the tee, which makes a player think before digging into his bag for the big stick. The driver is the play on many holes, but there are also several featuring pinched fairways where the 3-wood might be the wiser choice.

The highlights of the West Course are the two longest holes. The par-5 3rd plays even longer than its 516 yards because of the uphill fairway off the tee. The rising slope is followed by a severe drop-off to the left, giving a roller-coaster effect to a fairly long hole. The approach shot is no picnic either, forcing near perfection as you aim for a tiny

green. If you miss left, out-of-bounds will be the penalty; an errant shot to the right means contending with a large maple tree.

The 5th is even longer than No. 3, and the 561-yarder also starts with an uphill tee shot. Mirroring the 3rd, it's back downhill on No. 5's second and third shots. Another small green waits on the approach, and there's more sand with which to contend.

The two par 5s on the West are memorable for their challenge, but after finishing the westward nine, the real highlights come on the newest nine holes at Quail Chase. Almost every hole on the East Course could be considered a signature. It's hard to choose a category that stands out because equity of excellence carries from No. 1 to the finisher. Pfaff set a high standard with the original eighteen, and he raised the bar with the East. Like its predecessors, the course meanders through rolling Kentucky countryside, but the distinction on the East is that there's more attention to

This shot of Quail Chase East No. 6 is the over-the-water view from the 8th fairway.

CHIP SHOTS

Course contact info:
(877) 239-2110,
www.quailchase.com

Par: 72
Yardage: 6,760 yards

Rating: 73.3
Slope: 128
Notable: *Golfweek* rated Quail Chase as "The No. 2 Public Course in Kentucky," but it is the most affordable in the state and the top public layout in the Louisville area.

On the green
⚫ $42

layout detail, creating more strategic options.

It doesn't take long to discover that the East is the stiffest challenge of the three layouts. The par-4 1st hole is a long, uphill test at 461 yards, and Quail Chase personnel say the 4th is the hole that's most discussed (out of all 27) when players come in for a post-round beverage in the comfortable clubhouse.

AFTER YOUR ROUND

Horses, of course: Many of those who come to Quail Chase do so as a secondary activity during their visit to see another Kentucky highlight. Rounds pick up dramatically just before and after the Kentucky Derby, one of the biggest sports-related spectator parties in the country that supersedes the race itself. The horses are the attraction, but many of the 100,000 who frolic in the infield can't even see the race. But virtually everyone who attends calls it a people-watcher's paradise. Parasols, party dresses, bow ties, and mint juleps are as much an attraction as jockeys and silks.

SCORECARD - WEST NINE

Hole	1	2	3	4	5	6	7	8	9	out	
Yardage	367	199	516	386	561	367	390	380	352	3,280	
Par	4	3	5	4	4	5	3	4	4	36	

SCORECARD - EAST NINE

Hole	1	2	3	4	5	6	7	8	9	out	
Yardage	461	391	507	158	423	190	433	536	381	3,480	6,760
Par	4	4	5	3	4	3	4	5	4	36	72

LOUISIANA

GRAY PLANTATION GOLF COURSE
LAKE CHARLES, LOUISANA

For those craving a genuine peek at Cajun life, mixed with the chance to play a handful of outstanding golf courses along the way, Shreveport is the starting point for a spicy, twelve-course tour of western Louisiana. The Audubon Golf Trail was the brainstorm of Louisiana state tourism officials in 2001, and it combined a half-dozen, top-of-the-line courses in a bit of golf-marketing brilliance.

Six more courses have joined the trail since that first year, but none have surpassed Gray Plantation Golf Course, in Lake Charles, as the top crawfish in the boil. Gray Plantation is an example of one of the state's great golf secrets, and it's a wonder it took those down on the bayou so long to figure out how many excellent tracks lay in Louisiana.

Marketing efforts such as the Audubon Golf Trail are common in established golf destinations, but Louisiana had not been in that category until it combined the grouping of Gray Plantation and five other courses. Gray's eleven trail partners include Audubon Park, Black Bear, Carter Plantation, Cypress Bend, Oakwing, Olde Oaks, Tamahka Trails, The Island, TPC of Louisiana, The Atchafalaya at Idlewild, and The Wetlands.

Courses on the trail have doubled since that first year in 2001, and by all accounts the marketing venture has been a huge success. Louisiana, which was not considered much of a golf destination prior to the establishment of the Audubon Golf Trail, experienced a 10 percent increase in golf tourism in the first year of the $1.2 million campaign. And as the members of the consortium increase, so do the golf tourists.

There is more competition to become the trail's

A watery fairway waits for players on Gray Plantation's 213-yard par-3 13th.

unofficial leader, but Gray Plantation is holding its own. Designed by Rocky Roquemore, the course is a scenic picture of bayou country. Sixty acres of lakes are within the course's boundaries, and they come into play on twelve holes. Toss in the fact that the course is situated on the Calcasieu waterway, and you know you need to keep your shots straight to avoid a soaking-wet round.

But don't concentrate solely on avoiding the water because you might forget about the sand and the trees. Towering pines pinch the fairways and ninety-four bunkers are there to keep you honest. This a genuine ace of a layout, accentuated to the fullest by four brilliant par 3s — two of which feature island greens.

The powers that be at Gray Plantation call No. 6, one of the island-green jaw-droppers, the course's signature hole. The 6th borders the Calcasieu and requires a dead-on tee shot over 168 yards of water to hit the smallest green on the course. There's no doubt this is a great golf hole, but there are several that could qualify as signatures.

Among the contenders is No. 17, the other par-3 island. This scenic, 165-yarder not only requires the same over-the-water carry as No. 6, but even if you hit the green you still might not make par. The putting surface has three tiers, and if you're not on the same level as the pin, it's 50-50 you'll three-putt for bogey.

CHIP SHOTS

Course contact info:
(337) 562-1663,
www.graywoodllc.com,
click on "golf course"

Par: 72
Yardage: 7,233 yards

Rating: 73.6
Slope: 138
Notable: Rarely does the outcome of a poll provide a pure consensus, but the experts seem convinced that Gray Plantation is the best public-access course in Louisiana. *Golf Digest*, the *Zagat Survey*, and other national publications have named it the state's top choice. It also annually ranks among the top 100 public courses in America on several national rankings.

On the green
$50

The lucky golfers in Louisiana aren't the only players taking notice of Gray Plantation. Thousands of tourists flock to the course each year, and accolades are pouring in. It's one thing to be recognized by a publication in your own state, but Gray Plantation has taken it one step further. Texas Golfer Media selected the course as "Best Golf Community" in their "Neighboring State Division."

Now that's what we call being a good neighbor. It turns out bayou hospitality, particularly on the Audubon Golf Trail, is as common as crawfish.

AFTER YOUR ROUND

Golf and gambling: Louisiana's Audubon Golf Trail is a marketing tool for golf, but it also could be called the Casino Trail. There are a variety of casinos on the trail, and the Horseshoe Casino in Bossier City proved to be one of the best. That doesn't mean I walked out with any money, but objectivity allows me to impart the casino's benefits. In other words, I didn't win but you might.

OTHER PUBLIC COURSES IN LOUISIANA WORTH A VISIT
- The Atchafalaya Golf Course at Idlewild, Patterson
- Bluffs CC, St. Francisville
- Carter Plantation, Springfield

SCORECARD

Hole	1	2	3	4	5	6	7	8	9	out	
Yardage	540	418	430	473	403	168	589	145	439	3,605	
Par	5	4	4	4	4	3	5	3	4	36	

Hole	10	11	12	13	14	15	16	17	18	in	total
Yardage	586	370	468	213	390	583	379	165	474	3,628	7,233
Par	5	4	4	3	4	5	4	3	4	36	72

LOUISIANA

TPC LOUISIANA
AVONDALE, LOUISIANA

Like so much of the Louisiana Gulf Coast area, TPC Louisiana suffered extensive damage on August 29, 2005, when Hurricane Katrina took a rampaging route of devastation. And just like their strong-willed neighbors, officials at the year-old golf course refused to concede defeat to the storm.

When Katrina hit, playing golf was far from the minds of those affected. TPC Louisiana was closed for more than a year during the clean-up and rebuilding process. As work progressed on the course, recreation increasingly became an important part of the healing process for people in the state.

After a year's absence, the New Orleans Saints returned to the Superdome, which many thought might not be possible. When TPC Louisiana reopened, golfers were ready to get back to the game and they weren't disappointed with the renovations: the results were magnificent.

The course was backed by the PGA Tour, as all TPC courses are. This guarantees a quality layout, and in most cases, a chance to host a PGA Tour event. The Zurich Classic of New Orleans was played at the course in 2005, just before Katrina hit. The 2006 event wasn't held at TPC Louisiana because it was still under repair, but the tournament returned in 2007.

That is a testament to the job Pete Dye and PGA Tour players Steve Elkington and Louisiana native Kelly Gibson performed when piecing the track back together. It isn't only the PGA Tour players who receive the privilege of enjoying the lengthy layout. Public-access players can walk the fairways as well — as spectators during the week the tournament visits, and as appreciative players the rest of the year.

It's a bear of a course if you play the TPC tees at more than 7,500 yards, but if you want to see what it's like to play in a PGA Tour event, go ahead and take your chances. It might be best to shelve brute strength on this visit, however, and let logic take over. That choice will result in a more enjoyable, not to mention a quicker, round.

If you shorten up the course by playing one of the more lenient sets of tees, you will find that it is a pretty playable layout. The fairways are fairly generous, and you might be surprised how well you can score if you're hitting it straight. It doesn't take many off-center hits, however, to find massive waste bunkers that make for scratchy and difficult shots to the green.

Those greens are TPC-slick, but if you're approaching from the fairways you are allowed some room for error. As a general rule, there aren't an abundance of bunkers near the putting surfaces, so if your pitching wedge is working you can miss a green or two. No. 18 is an exception and is not a green that can be missed without penalty.

The course has a distinct Southern Louisiana feel. Drainage canals surround the layout, and there are plenty of wetlands and cypress trees. One other natural feature of which to be aware: alligators aren't shy about making the occasional appearance.

The 18th is the picture of the place, and it is preceded by two beauties that make for an exciting and testing trio of finishers. No. 16 is a par 4 with an expansive waste bunker to the right, and a perfectly placed — yet irksome — water hazard to the left. Don't forget that the swamp is home to a twelve-foot gator to the back left of the green.

No. 17 is a long par 3 at 230 yards, and it can cripple you on the way to the signature 18th if you allow it. The finisher at TPC Louisiana is a 583-yard dogleg right with water all the way down the right side — which prevents all but the bravest players from attempting to cut the turn. But shying away from the water forces you to the left and makes the hole play more than 600 yards.

Modifications on TPC Louisiana's par-5 18th include a new tee box, the addition of two pot bunkers, and widening of the fairway.

It takes patience and determination to score at TPC Louisiana. But, as exemplified by the work and energy of the people of this city during disaster, those two qualities aren't in short supply here. You'll be in excellent company.

AFTER YOUR ROUND

Party, Mardi Gras: If you time your golf visit with the annual zaniness of Mardi Gras (the last week of February), you'll find plenty of action on your trip. TPC Louisiana is just twenty minutes from downtown New Orleans, which

features all the nightlife anyone can handle. But be careful; you don't want to miss that morning tee time.

Spice is nice: You don't have to be in town at Mardi Gras time to enjoy some of the country's most distinctive food. To visit New Orleans and not visit the dozens of restaurants featuring Louisiana specialties would be a culinary crime. Cajun spices practically ooze into the streets of New Orleans. Creole, gumbo, jambalaya, crawfish, Cajun deer steak, Cajun meatloaf, corn and crabmeat soup, and barbecued shrimp are some of the best dishes in the world.

SCORECARD

Hole	1	2	3	4	5	6	7	8	9	out	
Yardage	398	550	224	483	442	494	580	380	200	3,751	
Par	4	5	3	4	4	4	5	4	3	36	
Hole	10	11	12	13	14	15	16	17	18	in	total
Yardage	399	573	495	371	220	469	428	230	583	3,768	7,519
Par	4	5	4	4	3	4	4	3	5	36	72

A common green shared by Nos. 9 and 18 at Belgrade Lakes is rare in the United States, and is a throwback to the origins of the game.

MAINE

BELGRADE LAKES GOLF CLUB
BELGRADE, MAINE

Maine probably isn't near the top of most destination lists when considering a golf vacation, and if quantity were the only factor considered, it might be justified. At last count there were just a few more than 125 public golf courses in a state covering 30,862 square miles with 17 million acres of forest and 3,500 miles of coastline. That isn't much public golf, even compared to states with similar climate and length of golf season.

Michigan, for instance, is another state whose season runs from May to October. It comprises approximately three times the square miles that Maine does at 96,810; about the same amount of lakefront miles (3,222) as Maine has coastline; and 1 million more acres of forestland. Yet Michigan, with more than 825 public golf courses, has about seven times as many as Maine.

Fortunately for those who play golf in The Pine Tree State, quantity is not the lone indicator of a golf destination's value. Quality also comes into play, and while the numbers might be limited, there are a handful of outstanding public tracks. Chief among them is Belgrade Lakes Golf Club, about twenty miles north of the state capital of Augusta.

The statistics with which Belgrade Lakes players are concerned have nothing to do with statewide trends. Those lucky enough to tread the Belgrade fairways are focusing solely on hole distances, and par 3s, 4s, and 5s.

They also better pay attention to the number of boulders on the course, which are a story in themselves. When Clive Clark began digging out the fairways, before the course opened in 1998, he unearthed tons and tons of glacial rock. Clark turned what could have been an unexpected problem into a glorious plus. He simply pushed the rocks and boulders to the outside of each fairway, forming a quasi-bowling-alley approach to many of the holes. Instead of gutters or even rough, however, the holes are lined with piles of rock. It gives a fantastically unique look to a course that never had this in its plans.

Forget the numbers. This is a rocky splendor of a place to play.

These glacial rocks are not limited to the cosmetic. They come into play on several holes, and this is never more evident than on No. 3. This par 5 would be challenging enough, but the fact that the entire 475 yards is lined with piles of rocks on the right side doesn't make things any easier.

The Belgrade Lakes scorecard includes perhaps the most unnecessary warning in the history of golf, reading simply: "Stay out of the rocks." You think I'm scaling a wall of granite for a golf ball? I think I'll just reach into my bag for another, thank you very much. The boulders look really cool from a distance, but proximity brings with it a clear picture of potentially jagged torture.

The glacial leftovers are not the only eye-catcher. Nos. 9 and 18 share a huge green, a rare throwback to the days of the game's origin. You find far more of this in Scotland, where courses hundreds of years old stick to the original layout.

CHIP SHOTS

Course contact info:
(207) 495-4653,
www.belgradelakesgolf.com

Par: 71
Yardage: 6,723 yards

Rating: 72.2
Slope: 135
Notable: Belgrade Lakes was one of the 12 courses in the country to receive *Golf Digest*'s 5-star ranking in their "Places to Play" issue in 2002. Other courses on that list included Pebble Beach Golf Links and Pinehurst No. 2, not bad company.

On the green
◐ ◐ $125

The putting surface provides a wonderful finishing touch to both the outward and inward nines, but it's far from the most fascinating feature. And please take that rock warning seriously. Fred Flintstone, you're not.

AFTER YOUR ROUND

Capital ideas: Located less than twenty minutes north of Augusta, Maine's capital since 1827, an educational experience awaits. History lessons are a given in an area that was explored by English settlers as early as 1607, and Wabanaki Indians were in the area long before then. Capital attractions include the Maine State House, the Maine State Museum, Old Fort Western, the Pine Tree State Arboretum, the Children's Discovery Museum, and Blaine House — designated as the governor's mansion in 1919. Bicycling, shopping, and theater are also nearby.

OTHER COURSES IN MAINE WORTH A VISIT
- Fox Ridge, Auburn
- Kebo Valley GC, Bar Harbor
- The Ledges GC, York
- Sunday River GC, Newry

SCORECARD

Hole	1	2	3	4	5	6	7	8	9	out	
Yardage	435	168	475	443	174	510	409	207	439	3,260	
Par	4	3	5	4	3	5	4	3	4	35	
Hole	10	11	12	13	14	15	16	17	18	in	total
Yardage	377	433	585	229	358	334	558	189	400	3,463	6,723
Par	4	4	5	3	4	4	5	3	4	36	71

MAINE

SUGARLOAF GOLF CLUB
CARRABASSETT VALLEY, MAINE

It's not quite as tough as playing golf wearing a pair of ski boots or going skiing with a golf bag strapped to your back, but Sugarloaf Golf Club is one polar bear of a golf course.

Sugarloaf is nestled into rugged mountains that have made the resort — and the region — a popular place for those seeking snowy slopes. But not all the outdoor recreation at Sugarloaf is restricted to the frigid winter of central Maine.

The season is on the short side, but golf is a stronghold in the area. Robert Trent Jones, Jr., who has never been afraid to put teeth into his designs, conceptualized Sugarloaf in 1985. The legendary course architect pulled no punches, instilling enough bite into the beautiful mountain layout to make it downright ferocious.

The challenge may be a bit on the frightening side for some, but isn't that what makes the game so much fun? The nation's golf course experts have not been scared off by the mountainside lies and rocky hazards. Sugarloaf has consistently been named the No. 1 public golf course in Maine by virtually every national magazine that make such rankings, and it's on many lists as one of the country's top 100 courses you can play.

It is a spectacular place, but visions of a low score are far more rare than scenic topography. If you can remove scorecard thoughts for one round, you are guaranteed one of the most enjoyable rounds of your life. But if you're looking for low numbers, you'll have to ascend to the peak of your game to pull it off.

CHIP SHOTS

Course contact info:
(207) 237-2000,
www.sugarloaf.com

Par: 72
Yardage: 6,910 yards

Rating: 74.4
Slope: 151

Notable: *Golfweek* has rated Sugarloaf "The Top Public Course in Maine." *Golf Digest* has rated it as "The No. 1 Golf Course in Maine" every year since 1985, and the *New England Journal of Golf* ranks Sugarloaf at the top of its "Top 100 Must-Play Courses." Need any more convincing?

On the green
◐◐ $80

With an extremely high rating/slope combination of 74.4 / 151, this is beauty and the beast in its purest form.

The price can be another highlight, if you time your visit correctly. In off-peak weeks, the cost isn't nearly as steep as the challenge of the mountains. Sugarloaf has plenty to offer: challenge, beauty, and periodic price breaks.

The resort is about 40 miles from the Canadian border and more than 150 miles from the nearest major airport, but the well-rounded golf experience makes it worth the effort it takes to get there.

Without question, the quintessential Sugarloaf stretch runs parallel to the Carrabassett River. Labeled the String of Pearls, the six-hole sequence makes you feel lucky that we are in the digital age of photography. The technology saves the trouble of changing rolls of film, which undoubtedly would be an urge on the ultra-picturesque String of Pearls.

The first of the pearls is No. 10, a 334-yard par-4 that cascades downward, plummeting to a pristine fairway, then to a green surrounded by imposing bunkers. Another elevated tee waits at No. 11, and this time there is a bonus. It's a one-shot effort to the green on this 216-yard par-3, and you can get a panoramic view of your ball sailing into the valley.

The String of Pearls finales are Nos. 14 and 15, which require frightening carries over the Carrabassett River. The holes wrap up a lengthy stretch that is breathtaking in two ways: the scenery will leave you gaping, and the challenge will have you gasping.

Sure, this is ski country, but golf has found a home in a gorgeous piece of the great northeast. The dual-season attractions might make a trip to Maine a semiannual event.

AFTER YOUR ROUND

Flying high: Outstanding fly-fishing in the Carrabassett River is among the plethora of outdoor activities available in and around Sugarloaf. Hiking, biking, and canoeing provide more outdoor fun just when you thought the wicked-tough golf satiated your sense of adventure.

A walk in the park: The Carrabassett Valley Town Park is located behind the Town Office on Carriage Road, featuring highlights such as a playground for kids and a pool for swimmers of all ages. Other area attractions include the Narrow Gauge Pathway and Poplar Stream Falls.

This aerial view of Sugarloaf's 11th, which provides a picture-perfect view of a clear autumn day in Maine, was taken from the hole's elevated tee.

SCORECARD

Hole	1	2	3	4	5	6	7	8	9	out	
Yardage	421	563	217	530	403	402	384	187	417	3,524	
Par	4	5	3	5	4	4	4	3	4	36	
Hole	10	11	12	13	14	15	16	17	18	in	total
Yardage	334	216	542	401	401	178	525	382	407	3,386	6,910
Par	4	3	5	4	4	3	5	4	4	36	72

MARYLAND

BULLE ROCK
HAVRE DE GRACE, MARYLAND

The name itself signifies strength and grace. Bulle Rock, named after the first thoroughbred horse brought to the United States, combines the need for power and finesse. It is a mix brought to life for players looking to play the finest Maryland has to offer in public golf.

What else would you expect from legendary golf course architect Pete Dye, who took the land and turned it into a golf paradise. Bulle Rock is one of three Dye designs within 100 miles of Washington D.C., and it is the place to play if you happen to be visiting the nation's capital. Take a break from sightseeing for a day on the course.

Bulle Rock has received plaudits from publications throughout the country, but one of the best descriptions of the course comes from a publication in its own backyard. The *Baltimore Sun* said this about the best public-access course in the state: "[Bulle Rock] is an ambitious mission with the kind of amenities previously offered by only the elite of country clubs."

Bulle Rock owner Ed Abel was like many golfers before he opened the club in 1998. He was frustrated that many of the great golf courses in the country had a steel gate around the entrance and the word "private" painted on a stone wall. He sought to present players with an elite course that replaced that word with "welcome."

Abel has not only provided the word on the wall, he has produced the feeling throughout the grounds at Bulle Rock. The experience begins as you take the winding road to the clubhouse. There is a perfect view of the lush and manicured course, and the clubhouse sits on the horizon.

And what of the clubhouse? The country-club feel continues before players reach the first tee. Locker room attendants see to your every need, providing locker and towel. They'll even shine your shoes for a nominal fee. Caddies, who aren't often seen at public courses, are also an option.

Once on the course, the special treatment continues. This time it doesn't come from staffers or attendants; the course itself is the treat.

What a way to finish the outward nine. This rock-lined water hazard and several bunkers on the right of the 9th fairway keep a player honest on the way to the clubhouse.

Bulle Rock is a traditional golf course with bent grass, but there are eighteen distinctive holes. There are no "up-and-back" holes that are often a staple at public courses forced to compress a layout on a small tract of land. Dye had 235 acres to work with and he took full advantage of the area. Even if the course is crowded, the space between the holes does not allow players to see golfers on other holes — a solitary and welcome experience even when the course is at peak usage.

As might be expected at a course where the pros play, Bulle Rock can be quite a challenge. Played from the tips, the course measures more than 7,000 yards, including the monstrous, 665-yard par 5 11th. The length on No. 11 can intimidate the best of players, and it provides evidence that high handicappers might want to swallow their pride and move up to the medium-range tees. You have to be an exceptional player to enjoy a round from the back tees, and you can be assured that there are no "tricked-up" or gimmick holes.

CHIP SHOTS

Course contact info:
(410) 939-8887,
www.bullerock.com

Par: 72
Yardage: 7,375 yards

Rating: 76.4
Slope: 147
Notable: The McDonald's LPGA Championship — one of four LPGA major championships — had been held at Bulle Rock for several years until changing venues after the 2009 tournament. Hosting a professional event is a coup for any course, and latching onto such a major tournament put Bulle Rock in even more elite company.

On the green
◍ ◍ ◍ $150

Bulle Rock is both hospitable and challenging, and its location is also a highlight. It's a short drive from Baltimore, certainly reachable from Washington, D.C., and it's worth the one-and-a-half hour drive from Philadelphia. Regardless of your starting point, if the destination is Bulle Rock, you'll be glad you came.

AFTER YOUR ROUND

Quack attack: If you feel like laughing and learning, experience Baltimore sightseeing from a duck's point of view — take a ride on the Ride the Ducks adventure through town. Tourists are given a duck call, and they travel on land and water in one amazing vehicle that is both amphibious and road-safe. The vehicle stops at many local attractions, including a splash into the famous Inner Harbor.

Ducking the duck: Landlubbers can enjoy more conventional experiences, such as Harborplace & The Gallery, Fort McHenry National Monument, the Baltimore Museum of Art, the Baltimore Opera Company, and the Senator Theatre.

OTHER PUBLIC COURSES IN MARYLAND WORTH A VISIT
- Beechtree GC, Aberdeen
- Hyatt Regency Chesapeake Bay Golf Resort, Spa & Marina (River Marsh Course), Cambridge
- Greystone GC, White Hall,
- The Links at Lighthouse Sound, Ocean City
- Maryland National GC, Middletown
- Musket Ridge GC, Myersville
- Whiskey Creek GC, Urbana
- Worthington Manor GC, Urbana

SCORECARD

Hole	1	2	3	4	5	6	7	8	9	out	
Yardage	358	572	177	417	483	413	202	546	478	3,646	
Par	4	5	3	4	4	4	3	5	4	36	

Hole	10	11	12	13	14	15	16	17	18	in	total
Yardage	393	665	190	476	372	529	425	194	485	3,729	7,375
Par	4	5	3	4	4	5	4	3	4	36	72

MARYLAND

QUEENSTOWN HARBOR GOLF LINKS
(RIVER COURSE)
QUEENSTOWN, MARYLAND

When *Washington Golf Monthly* named the River Course at Queenstown Harbor the best public golf course within a ninety-minute drive of Washington D.C., chances increased for public players to run into some politicos as they made their way around a beautiful layout.

Sure, Washington, D.C.'s VIPs who play the game often are members or get invited to play the premium private courses in the area. But when they get a break from the busy life of national politics, they have been spotted on the River Course.

And why wouldn't congressmen and senators play the River? When it comes to satisfying your appetite for tasty golf, Queenstown Harbor's River Course earns high marks. In fact, the River was awarded the prestigious four-star rating from *Golf Digest*, and it allows public players an outstanding venue on which to play.

The River Course isn't the only layout on the Queenstown property to attain this sought-after rating. The Lakes Course, on the same tract of land as the River, is also a four-star course.

The Lakes is a splendid place to play, but it doesn't present nearly the same challenge as its partner course. It is more forgiving and offers the high-handicapper an enjoyable venue, but better players should take on the River. That's where the true test lies.

The Chesapeake Bay is visible from both courses, which adds scenic views to the challenge. Area players are hearing more and more about the River, so it is advised to plan ahead for a tee time. And though locals have long known of its impressive features, this public beauty has not been overly familiar to Washington, D.C. visitors. But that's changing. The River has been rated as high as "The No. 2 Best Public Golf Course in Maryland" by *Golf Digest*, and it has been ranked as "The Top Public Course" by three Maryland regional publications. No wonder the word is spreading.

Queenstown Harbor Golf Links opened nearly twenty years ago, but the history of the land dates back to the 1600s when Lord Baltimore, Cecilius Calvert, gave the land to businessman Henry Coursey as a reward for his support in colonial politics. Coursey called Queenstown Harbor "My Lord's Gift," and that label has stuck with the land for more than four hundred years.

The property was untouched until it was purchased to be developed into Queenstown Harbor Golf Links, which opened in July, 1991. Residents and visitors who play the game are grateful for the transformation. The developers have been environmentally conscious, maintaining a respect for both the history and the beauty of the land. Chesapeake Wildlife Heritage of Maryland has recognized Queenstown Harbor as a safe haven for wildlife to thrive.

Golfers must also respect Queenstown Harbor Golf Links, particularly the River Course, which demands precise golf shots. For some, the course is more than they expect and too much to handle. But while the River is a difficult course, it isn't an unfair challenge. You'll just need to be on your toes. Water is part of the course from No. 1 to No. 18, and is more hazard than cosmetic. Ponds and creeks come into play on fourteen holes, and can ruin a player's scorecard in a hurry.

Make sure to play the River if you have a chance. It's within a chip shot of Washington D.C., and for the public player it offers a capital place to play.

AFTER YOUR ROUND

Capital attractions: Places to visit in the nation's capital present opportunities to view historic icons and gather knowledge of this country. It is advised, if not required, to put the golf clubs away for a day to view the sights of Washington, D.C. When I played Queenstown Harbor, it was my third visit to the nation's capital, but somehow the experience never grows old. It was my daughter's first visit, and watching her at the foot of the Lincoln Memorial was a precious moment that any father would remember. The trip was nearly ten years ago and she still talks about it.

CHIP SHOTS

Course contact info:
(800) 827-5257,
www.qhgolf.com

Par: 72
Yardage: 7,110 yards

Rating: 74.2
Slope: 138
Notable: Forecaddies, a rarity in public golf, are available at Queenstown. For those not familiar with the concept, the forecaddie is not your usual brand of caddie. Rather than walk beside you and carry your bag, he positions himself in the place your shot is supposed to land. Forecaddies are extremely familiar with the course and can offer expert advice on course management and the lay of the land.

On the green
$75

The weeping willow trees are plentiful and expansive at Queenstown Harbor, but this one doesn't block the view from the 15th fairway to the 14th green.

Hole	1	2	3	4	5	6	7	8	9	out	
Yardage	404	155	444	401	551	374	538	204	427	3,498	
Par	4	3	4	4	5	4	5	3	4	36	
Hole	10	11	12	13	14	15	16	17	18	in	total
Yardage	478	569	400	148	419	445	196	372	585	3,612	7,110
Par	4	5	4	3	4	4	3	4	5	36	72

MASSACHUSETTS

CRUMPIN-FOX CLUB
BERNARDSTON, MASSACHUSETTS

We're all familiar with that patience-is-a-virtue thing, but the old saying was put to a severe test after David Berelson envisioned a championship golf course as the centerpiece of his 600-acre property in Bernardston.

The dream began in 1969, when Berelson hired Roger Rulewich to build a course that was to be modeled after the famed Pine Valley. That was just the beginning of a process that took twenty-one years to complete. The project stalled more than once, due in large part to two ownership changes. Nine holes were built in 1977 and Berelson's dream finally came to fruition in 1990. It may have been Berelson's idea but he had long since sold the property.

It was a long and winding road to the completion of the golf course, to be sure, but these New Englanders can be a patient lot. It doesn't seem to matter how long it took to build the course. Locals and visitors alike are just glad it got done.

Crumpin-Fox Club has a genuine ambience, mostly because it is tucked in an isolated part of Massachusetts. There are no major cities within thirty minutes of the course, and the locale offers a feeling of peace that otherwise would not be possible. You might have to drive a while, and then do a little extra searching to find the place, but thoughts of logistics fade quickly as you step to the first tee.

The path ahead is so alluring, you might find it a chore to concentrate on that first drive. A walk down the 1st fairway is a joy, because each step carries you further into an isolated world of picturesque golf — complete with a potpourri of natural

A simple touch of Americana in the distance on the 8th hole at Crumpin-Fox.

features, crystal clear visions of pristine conditioning, and imaginative holes to keep challenge a steady companion.

No doubt, the property was beautiful when Rulewich conceptualized the course, but he had some distinct handicaps to overcome. First, there was no topsoil on the site. The entire course was covered with sand and the holes had to be staked out on the sandy areas.

Still, Rulewich understood he had a chance to build something wonderful. He wasn't bothered by the hindrance of a lack of dirt. He allowed his imagination to take over and the outcome was striking. No consecutive holes run parallel or in the same direction, there are gently climbing holes, and sharp-dropping par-3s. The par-5s are the most memorable features at Crumpin-Fox, with the signature 8th leading the way.

The 592-yarder is both the longest and the most difficult hole on the course. The tee stands high above the

CHIP SHOTS

Course contact info:
(800) 943-1901,
www.golfthefox.com

Par: 72
Yardage: 7,007 yards

Rating: 73.8
Slope: 141
Notable: The course drew its name from the Bernardston-based Crump Soda Company that was sold in 1853 to Eli Fox. This became the Crump & Fox Soda Company and the golf course — opened 137 years later — followed suit with a twist to come up with Crumpin-Fox.

On the green
⬤ $36

The green is huge, but unless you're willing to bail to the right and chip up on your 4th shot, carrying the water is your only play. The putting surface abuts the lake, so anything short of the green puts you in the drink. One large bunker and two smaller traps crowd the backside, so there is really no room for error.

No. 8 is a long hole, a tough hole, and a scenic hole. It takes plenty of patience to succeed on this beauty. Patience. It's been a Crumpin-Fox staple from the very beginning.

AFTER YOUR ROUND

Stick around: The closest big cities to Bernardston are Springfield (forty-five minutes to the south) and Boston (two hours east), so unless you leave some time for a drive, the Bernardston area is the ticket. One stop that will make you "shutter" is the Hallmark Museum of Contemporary Photography. Meadowedge Art for Children is another visit worth taking if you have the kids along. Last but not least is the Songline Emu Farm. Don't know what an emu is? Time to go farming.

OTHER PUBLIC COURSES IN MASSACHUSETTS WORTH A VISIT

- Cape Cod National GC, Brewster
- Farm Neck GC, Martha's Vineyard
- George Wright Municipal GC, Boston
- Pinehills (Rees Jones Course), Plymouth
- Pinehills (Nicklaus Course), Plymouth
- Red Tail GC, Devens
- Waverly Oaks GC, Plymouth

fairway, deep into a chute surrounded by thick forestland. A huge lake runs the entire length of the hole on the left side of the fairway. Woods impose all the way down the right side, and the fairway makes a horseshoe left turn at the very end, forcing the approach to fly the aforementioned lake.

SCORECARD

Hole	1	2	3	4	5	6	7	8	9	out	
Yardage	414	362	193	392	528	448	387	592	188	3,504	
Par	4	4	3	4	5	4	4	5	3	36	
Hole	10	11	12	13	14	15	16	17	18	in	total
Yardage	424	161	388	393	527	175	457	565	413	3,503	7,007
Par	4	3	4	4	5	3	4	5	4	36	72

MASSACHUSETTS

HIGHLAND LINKS GOLF COURSE
NORTH TRURO, MASSACHUSETTS

The contrasts of Cape Cod golf are as striking as the waves that crash into the Northeastern Atlantic coast. This peninsula, discovered in 1602 by English captain Bartholomew Gosnold, is home to more than forty courses. Some are so private that having a familiar name is as much a requirement of membership as the six-figure annual dues. Others are municipal layouts where informality is the order of the day.

Highland Links Golf Course is one of those municipal layouts, and you probably would never play it if you only look at the course for the physical attributes. From tee to green, it isn't spectacular, but it has so much personality, so much history, that you can't help but get caught up in the rich character of the place.

The course has nine greens and eighteen tees, much like old layouts in Scotland, the birthplace of golf. Highland Links, at the tip of the Cape in North Truro, was founded in 1892 and is the oldest track on the peninsula.

The original nine-hole course has no fairway irrigation. It was built on bluffs that rise 100 feet or so above the Atlantic and has views of the famed Cape Cod Lighthouse. You think Highland Links doesn't abound with golf history? Francis Ouimet, the 1913 U.S. Open champion and a Massachusetts native, played an exhibition match here nearly a century ago.

Highland Links became a resort course in the early 1900s and became a part of the National Park Service when the Cape Cod National Seashore was established during the John F. Kennedy administration. Today, a former hotel is the Truro Historical Museum, and the town of Truro manages Highland Links. It is a municipal course like no other. Erosion has forced the move of the working lighthouse from the 7th green to a spot closer to the tee, but the history and spirit of golf have not faded one iota.

The 1st hole is a straightforward par-4 that is fairly well drivable at 250 yards. At 460 yards, the 2nd hole is a short par-5 by today's standards, but it has a few more complications than No. 1.

Highland Links' draw is its history and rustic look, but there is also natural beauty, including here at No. 2.

After driving from an elevated tee, you watch your ball disappear into a valley on No. 2, and then you face a dogleg left. You can try to cut it to get to the green, or play it safe and layup for a chip to the green on your third shot.

The hole is an interesting play, but even more intriguing is the sight as you head toward the green. Off in the distance are several domes that were once the site of World War II surveillance stations.

The course isn't manicured, or lush, but the rugged feel only adds to the historical ambience that saturates the grounds. Shaggy greens are slower than you might be used to, and the bunkers are not without tufts of grass growing through the sand. The rates are extremely modest, so it's easy to look at it as an entrance fee to a museum.

But where else can you see cart paths lined with crushed clam and oyster shells? The occasional whale or dolphin can be spotted off the coast, and the famous lighthouse shines brightly as the winds blow into your face.

The layout is meant as much for sightseers as for serious golfers. It is steeped in history and has fantastic views,

CHIP SHOTS

Course contact info:
(508) 487-9201, www.truro-ma.gov, search "Highland Links"

Par: 70
Yardage: 5,299 yards

Rating: 65.0
Slope: 105
Notable: If you play Highland Links during the off-season, from mid-fall to mid-spring when the clubhouse is closed, you are asked to slip your modest green fee under the door before heading off for your round. At this course, "you have the honors" takes on a whole new meaning.

On the green
○ $45

and many people come just to ogle. Those are the people that go away satisfied. If you come strictly for the golf, you might not leave so happy.

But at Highland Links, today's round should take a back seat to what's really important. This nine-hole track gives you a rare chance to take a walk flush into the game's rich history.

AFTER YOUR ROUND

Shoreline tradition: Highland Links is near the northern tip of Cape Cod, home of the Cape Cod Museum of Natural History, the New England Fire and History Museum, and the Stony Brook Grist Mill. Also on the Cape are the Sandwich Glass Museum, Heritage Museums and Gardens, Green Briar Nature Center and Jam Kitchen, and Yesteryears Doll Museum. You get the idea: history, history, and more history.

Sea what I mean: Seafood all over the Cape, and it is as fresh as this morning. The restaurants are authentic, with fishing nets, lighthouse pieces, buoys, and maps lining the walls. Lobsters, scallops, and swordfish are just the beginning of the seafood edibles that abound just down the road from Highland Links.

SCORECARD

Hole	1	2	3	4	5	6	7	8	9	out	
Yardage	250	460	160	346	380	464	171	353	136	2,720	
Par	4	5	3	4	4	5	3	4	3	35	
Hole	10	11	12	13	14	15	16	17	18	in	total
Yardage	242	377	118	415	361	453	159	349	105	2,579	5,299
Par	4	4	3	5	4	5	3	4	3	35	70

MASSACHUSETTS

SHAKER HILLS GOLF CLUB
HARVARD, MASSACHUSETTS

A mid-iron away from Boston, Shaker Hills Golf Club requires just a thirty-five-mile westward drive from the city to reach what many consider the finest public golf course in Massachusetts. The layout is elite, a word often associated with Northeastern private clubs.

But Shaker Hills is purely public, and the public is purely grateful. Five of the bent grass fairways are doglegs and all of them are tree-lined to provide a risk-reward approach to the greens. Water comes into play on eight holes. The putting services are multi-tiered, varying in size and shape, and they are well protected by several bunkers per hole.

The accolades have come pouring in since Shaker Hills opened its doors in 1993. It's received recognition from *Golf Digest* reviewers and other nationally known pundits: "Eighth-Best in Massachusetts" (including private and public clubs), one of the "Top Public Courses in America," one of the "Top Seventy-Five Affordable Courses in the Nation," and "The Best Public Course in the State."

Even though Shaker Hills has established itself as a public-course force, the staff continues to provide players with service that compares favorably to private clubs in the region. If you live near Boston and can't afford a private club, Shaker Hills is the place to play. In fact, even if you belong to a private club, it would be worth a day away from the club to mix it up with the players at Shaker Hills. It wouldn't be a downgrade from the course to which you are accustomed. Shaker Hills is right around the corner from Stow Acres Country Club, so course architects Brian Silva and Mark Mungeam knew they had to take their best shot to fit in.

By all indications, the design duo's goal has been realized.

The aim-to-please attitude displayed by the staff at Shaker Hills helps set players up for their round. But if the golf didn't measure up, all the good service in the world would be irrelevant. The 3rd, 4th, and 5th holes are prime examples of the golf at hand. Many golf pundits in the region call this stretch the toughest consecutive three holes in Massachusetts.

The 3rd is a 210-yard par-3 with water along the left and front of the green, No. 4 is a 466-yard par-4 with a slight dogleg left, and the 5th is a 606-yard par-5 with a tight fairway that doglegs right. When you wrap up this par-12, 1,282-yard combination of sweet, rugged golf, you will have played the most difficult trio that Massachusetts has to offer.

Perhaps the most interesting hole on the course is the 14th. It is an extremely short par-4 at 315 yards, but the layout is a strategist's dream. The tee shot must be right down the middle, as the fairway bends left to the green. You can't get too close to the green because of a ledge outcropping that will swallow your ball. Two large bunkers protect a small plateau green, so even though this hole is short, you have to be extremely careful to escape with par.

Another beauty comes at the end of the round. Standing on the 18th tee, you know you're almost home but there's still a little work to be done. The 460-yard, par-4 forces a drive over a large waste area, then the approach must be shaped around an outcropping of ledge that splits the fairway. Make it home in two, and you've earned your par.

AFTER YOUR ROUND

History, culture, and sport: The Fruitlands Museum comprises four separate art museums; the Village Theatre project offers first-rate drama in Harvard. A thirty-minute drive to Boston offers a plethora of sightseeing opportunities, from the Seaport World Trade Center, Swan Boats of Boston, the popular bar named Cheers, many historic

---

CHIP SHOTS

Course contact info:
(978) 772-9900,
www.shakerhills.com

Par: 71
Yardage: 6,850 yards

Rating: 74.0
Slope: 137
Notable: The folks at Shaker Hills are adept at letting people know they have a beautiful golf course on their hands. When asked about the course designers, Shaker Hills personnel have been known to answer: "Brian Silva and Mark Mungeam, with considerable cooperation from the Creator."

On the green
⬤ $75

No. 8 at Shaker Hills is a long par 4 that features a lake front and left of the tee with an extremely difficult second shot up the hill to a tree-lined green. Par is a good score here.

churches, and — depending on the season — a chance to catch the Red Sox, Bruins, Celtics, or Patriots.

Apples and more: If you happen to hit the season, the local apple orchard in Harvard features autumn treats and a pleasant place to eat. Next door to Boston in Cambridge,

Harvard Square is packed full of flavors from around the world. Restaurant specialties include Asian, Italian, Thai, Vietnamese, Middle Eastern, Greek, French, and Indian. If it's international flavors you crave, Harvard Square is the place to go.

SCORECARD

Hole	1	2	3	4	5	6	7	8	9	out	
Yardage	386	535	210	466	606	185	373	416	372	3,549	
Par	4	5	3	4	5	3	4	4	4	36	
Hole	10	11	12	13	14	15	16	17	18	in	total
Yardage	412	410	395	164	315	563	230	352	460	3,301	6,850
Par	4	4	4	3	4	5	3	4	4	35	71

MICHIGAN

FOREST DUNES GOLF CLUB
ROSCOMMON, MICHIGAN

Northern Michigan, or "Up North" to those in the mitten state, has become renown for far more than Traverse City cherries, Boyne Mountain skiing, and legendary stately pines that reach to the sky. Golf is now a firmly entrenched part of the landscape, so much so that the region is known as "Michigan's Golf Mecca."

One of the northern residents is Forest Dunes Golf Club, located in Roscommon, a few miles down I-75 from the cluster of fantastic courses in Gaylord. Gaylord formerly was the only destination that came to mind when Michigan golfers headed north. But, thanks to Forest Dunes, they can cut a few miles off their trip if they choose.

Gaylord's Treetops Resort is still a great place to play, but Forest Dunes has created a worthy stop in Roscommon. And here's a little secret: Forest Dunes may go private if it sells enough memberships. It's a semi-private facility now, which means it is still open to the public at large. So you public-access players still have time to enjoy a course that may be private someday.

As of now, Forest Dunes mixes members with Joe and Jane Public, and it seems to be working well. Just as the course features a tale of two players, it also offers a story of two layouts. Several holes present contrasting design styles, giving players a variety of distinct experiences as they play the Tom Weiskopf design.

Half the holes play through the thick, upper Michigan woods of pine, bracken, and wildflowers surrounding Huron National Forest; and the others feature more open spaces with sand, brush, and dunes of glacial sand. It is a vexing, yet intriguing contrast.

The 15,000-square-foot clubhouse is another point of intrigue. The Adirondack lodge-style structure includes locker rooms, a spa, a formal dining room, and a more laid-back grill. Forest Dunes is run by Troon Golf, a company that packs plenty of punch in the field of golf-course management.

Forest Dunes unobtrusively blends golf with nature, and has been recognized as being one of the game's top stewards of the environment. The club has been named an Audubon International Certified Golf Signature Sanctuary, one of only sixteen in the world. The forces behind Forest Dunes understand the responsibility of guarding this pristine Great Lakes land.

Weiskopf says Forest Dunes is one of "the top three [courses] with which I have been involved in the United States." That's quite an endorsement when you consider

The split fairway at Forest Dunes' 10th hole offers two options. Which one would you choose?

Weiskopf has designed dozens of layouts throughout the country.

Players can be assured of fairness at Forest Dunes. Weiskopf insists that the fairways be at least thirty-five yards wide, and he made sure that enough trees were cleared to give players an open shot to the greens. It's not an easy course, but it's a playable, enjoyable track.

The features at Forest Dunes range from the conventional to the unusual, from the serene to the exhilarating. The par-4 10th hole, named "Decision," includes a split fairway divided by mounds and sand. The 11th features a 10,000-square-foot, crescent-shaped green.

The course saves its best for two holes near the end of your round. The par-3, 231-yard 16th demands a 200-yard carry over dunes they call "Hell's Acres." The 17th is a cozy, 302-yard par 4 that requires several decisions on the short trek to the green.

The course even offers a 19th hole — a 117-yarder with a postage-stamp green. Almost all who play the course take advantage of the extra hole. After playing Forest Dunes, many say eighteen just wasn't enough.

CHIP SHOTS

Course contact info:
(866) 386-3764,
www.forestdunesgolf.com

Par: 72
Yardage: 7,104 yards

Rating: 74.8
Slope: 142
Notable: Forest Dunes may be a private club one day, but it's earning plenty of accolades as a public-access facility. *Golf Digest* has named it "The No. 3 Best Public-Access Course in Michigan" and *Golfweek* has ranked it No. 2 in the same category.

On the green
◯◯◯ $125

AFTER YOUR ROUND

Inside information: I've lived in lower Michigan for forty years, and I never tire of the four-hour trip up north. Besides the scenery, there are fruit stands everywhere, hiking and biking and lakes and beaches. There are cozy inns, luxury hotels, and lakeside cottages. I've found that the best way to enjoy the region is to just get in the car and go. The ultimate destination, even if it isn't specific when you start out, will undoubtedly leave you pleased.

Lake living: Perch and trout and other fresh Michigan fish are common specialties in Roscommon waterways. Cherry pies are world-class in nearby Traverse City, which touts itself as the "Cherry Capital of the World". If your accommodations include cooking facilities, the roads are lined with stands selling fresh vegetables and fruit. An in-the-cottage meal is a great way to go with some of Michigan's delicious produce.

Water works: A couple of the specific wet wonders in Roscommon are the AuSable River and Big Lake. Grayling and Prudenville are about fifteen miles away, where you can find Houghton Lake and the Grayling Fish Hatchery.

OTHER PUBLIC COURSES IN MICHIGAN WORTH A VISIT
- Angels Crossing GC, Vicksburg
- Arcadia Bluffs GC, Arcadia
- Bay Harbor GC (Links/Quarry nines), Harbor Springs
- Boyne Highlands Resort (Heather Course), Harbor Springs
- Marquette GC (Greywalls Course), Marquette
- The Resorts of Tullymore & St. Ives (Tullymore Course), Stanwood

SCORECARD

Hole	1	2	3	4	5	6	7	8	9	out	
Yardage	399	451	203	402	602	375	531	448	166	3,577	
Par	4	4	3	4	5	4	5	4	3	36	

Hole	10	11	12	13	14	15	16	17	18	in	total
Yardage	439	192	397	373	464	558	231	302	571	3,527	7,104
Par	4	3	4	4	4	5	3	4	5	36	72

MICHIGAN

HIGH POINTE GOLF CLUB
WILLIAMSBURG, MICHIGAN

Tom Doak has become revered as something of a Renaissance man in the world of golf course architecture. His 2001 Pacific Dunes layout in Oregon not only bested the seemingly unmatchable Bandon Dunes on the same property, but it is generally regarded as the finest public golf course in America.

But long before he reached the king-of-the-hill status he now enjoys, Doak was a fledgling in the field. He was thrilled, in fact, to land his first design assignment when it arrived just outside of Traverse City, Michigan — even though the challenge to get noticed would be difficult in northern Michigan, where outstanding public courses abound.

Doak achieved two objectives when he completed High Pointe Golf Club in 1989: he more than met the standards of the competitors in the vicinity, and when his first course was completed it signaled that a golf-course design "star" was born. He was unknown at the time, but his reputation skyrocketed immediately.

His first work earned spots on lists including "Top 100 Courses You Can Play," "One of 100 Greatest Courses in the U.S.," and "America's Best" in such publications as Golf Magazine, Golfweek, Golf Digest, among others. Not bad for a neophyte.

Tough economic conditions forced closure and ownership reorganization of High Pointe in 2009, but Doak's first design is scheduled to reopen in 2010. No changes to the course itself are planned, and officials say the experience at High Pointe will remain a . . . high point.

Variety is one of the key elements to Doak's success at High Pointe. The front nine is linksy — or as close as American designers come to links — with open fairways, rolling land, and plenty of natural grasses. The inward nine has a much more traditional feel, with Michigan woodlands at every periphery, and lush, green fairways throughout.

Players might feel a little more pinched on the back nine, but High Pointe staffers insist that is an illusion. They contend the fairways on the back are nearly as wide as the front, but the surrounding trees make them appear narrower. Illusion or not, the trees are intimidating and prove an inescapable part of High Pointe's challenge. Hitting fairways, as with most courses, is a key to scoring. But the difference on this Williamsburg wonder is the variance in penalty. Deep bunkers await errant shots on the front; thick trees will swallow your ball on the back. Either way, you want to be in the short grass.

If you are hitting it straight, huge greens welcome your approach. Hitting them is not really a problem, but it takes much more than a soft plop to score. Putting surfaces in excess of 5,000 square feet are good targets, but they also can present monstrous putts. Those in the know at High Pointe say landing on the same tier as the hole is hugely important and staying below the hole is as vital as hitting the green.

Locals say most downhill putts are almost as unsinkable as Tom Doak's reputation.

AFTER YOUR ROUND

Fresh water fun: Grand Traverse Bay offers a great way to get in a day of play. Beaches, marinas, water skiing, and fishing are some of the ways to enjoy the Bay. When you're not on the water, the main drag in Traverse City — about twelve miles from Williamsburg — is a delightfully quaint lineup of gift stores, candy stores, and specialty shops.

Brewing ale and a sail: Several original beers are available at the Mackinaw Brewing Co. on Front Street in Traverse City. The Traverse Tall Ship Co. offers a cruise on the Manitou, a 114-foot replica of the cargo schooners commonly found in the Great Lakes in the 1800s.

CHIP SHOTS

Course contact info:
(866)753-7888;
www.highpointegolf.com

Par: 71
Yardage: 6,890 yards

Rating: 73.3
Slope: 136
Notable: The High Pointe Golf Club includes a pace-of-play feature on each hole to keep golfers abreast of where they should be at certain times of a round. There's plenty of time allowed (2 hours, 5 minutes for the front nine, and 4:15 overall), and it's an underused method to prevent backups on the course.

On the green
$55

Even on the occasions when fairways run parallel at High Pointe, golfers on the other side of the thicket of trees are not visible because the fairways were cut from northern Michigan forestland.

SCORECARD

Hole	1	2	3	4	5	6	7	8	9	out	
Yardage	400	360	459	199	396	516	359	451	557	3,697	
Par	4	4	4	3	4	5	4	4	5	37	
Hole	10	11	12	13	14	15	16	17	18	in	total
Yardage	425	168	412	434	396	182	447	217	512	3,193	6,890
Par	4	3	4	4	4	3	4	3	5	34	71

Scenes such as this inspired Robert Trent Jones, Sr., to exploit the forest scenery on every hole he could when designing his course at Treetops.

MICHIGAN

TREETOPS RESORT
(SIGNATURE COURSE)
GAYLORD, MICHIGAN

You may run into trouble when selecting the Gaylord, Michigan, area as a destination for a golf weekend. Not the brand of trouble that includes bunkers, water hazards, and out-of-bounds, but the kind that makes it difficult to narrow your course choices to a number that you can fit into one weekend. The golf is simply too good, and there is simply too much of it.

Over the past few decades, Gaylord has become Michigan's golf mecca. It happened almost accidentally at first: entrepreneurs with a vision began changing this region immensely. There was Everett Kircher, a ski resort mogul who built a golf resort near Boyne Mountain in the 1950s so folks would have a reason to visit in the summer; landowner Harry Melling, who saw golf's potential — even in northern Michigan's short season — and brought in

Robert Trent Jones, Sr., in 1987 to build the first course at Treetops; and rock-quarry businessman David Johnson, who added golf at Bay Harbor in 1994 as an afterthought to help attract potential homebuyers to a development he was undertaking.

Quality courses now abound in northern Michigan. Several resorts near Gaylord are worth visiting, but if you only have one weekend, Treetops is a fine choice. Treetops golf is pure, and it takes but one visit to understand that golf is the total focus — all other amenities are just extras.

OK, so you've narrowed down the resort to Treetops. Now it's time to choose a course, right? Not necessarily. It's customary to pick just one course as a site's best, but the layouts at Treetops are so varied and memorable that you should try to play all five. All the tracks are worth the price of admission. If forced to name the best of the bunch, the Signature Course might get the nod. The most unique is the par-3 Threetops Course.

The five courses — Robert Trent Jones, Sr.'s Master-piece (1987), Tom Fazio's Premier (1992), and Rick Smith's nine-hole, par-3 Threetops (1992), Signature (1993) and Tradition (1996) — offer eighty-one holes that defy visitors to find a weak link.

Smith's Signature Course is a classy track that stands up to any layout in the country. Like all the courses at Treetops, it is a picture of hardwoods, hills, valleys, and great golf holes. The Signature gets the nod when it comes to championship regulation golf at Treetops, but there is another course here that has a certain novelty that stands out, especially in a sport that prides itself on tradition: the par-3 Threetops Course can be played in under two hours and it offers surreal elevation changes that make club selection a mystery and views from the tees remarkable.

Threetops was Smith's first foray into course design, and what at first was considered a "practice run" for future projects is now a real talker in the golf industry. When the course opened, skeptical golfers paid $15 per round and were offered a money-back guarantee. Now, rounds go for $50, and the demand for tee times is fierce. The made-for-television Par-3 Shootout is held every year at Threetops, and has included such royal figures of the game as Jack Nicklaus, Arnold Palmer, Lee Trevino, and Phil Mickelson.

AFTER YOUR ROUND

Away from it all: Treetops is located near downtown Gaylord, which features a quaint Alpine-style shopping district. But nature does the talking here, both during and after your day on the course. Horseback riding and fly-fishing are right down the road, both of which are first-rate and immersed in

the deep woods of upper Michigan. Another great family activity that you may not have thought of is U-Pick strawberries. You can ride bikes on the trails, or play tennis on one of the three courts on Treetops' property. Golf, however, is the focus. I've spent more than forty years living and playing in Michigan, and Treetops is one of my favorite spots in my home state.

CHIP SHOTS

Course contact info:
(888) 873-3867,
www.treetops.com

Par: 70
Yardage: 6,653 yards

Rating: 72.8
Slope: 140
Notable: Treetops has a lodge and inn on-site, and the folks at Treetops put a premium on the stay-and-play concept. Staying on-site greatly reduces greens fees at any of the five courses. The Signature is the top course on the property, but do your best to tear yourself away from it after one round. It would be a shame to play any of these courses more than once and forgo a chance to play one of the other fab four.

On the green
◯◯ $155

SCORECARD											
Hole	1	2	3	4	5	6	7	8	9	out	
Yardage	447	176	467	186	421	512	416	190	411	3,226	
Par	4	3	4	3	4	5	4	3	4	34	
Hole	10	11	12	13	14	15	16	17	18	in	total
Yardage	556	175	423	440	418	485	368	199	363	3,427	6,653
Par	5	3	4	4	4	5	4	3	4	36	70

MINNESOTA

GIANTS RIDGE
(QUARRY/LEGEND COURSES)
BIWABIK, MINNESOTA

It isn't often that a sibling will give up the best bedroom in the house for her little sister. Or just imagine older sis vacating the bathroom on the first knock: "Oh, OK, it's your turn," without a fight. This kind of courtesy might be hard to imagine in most households, but it's akin to what happened at the Legend Course, located at northern Minnesota's Giants Ridge

From 1999 to 2003 or so, the Legend Course owned the public-course rankings in Minnesota. It sat at No. 1 on some public lists, and it also fared pretty well in the ratings that included private courses — ranking as high as No. 3 in the state.

Then along came little sister.

When the Quarry opened in 2004, the Legend took a graceful step back as the new course took over. The statewide and national accolades came pouring in: "No. 1 Public Course," "Best You Can Play," "Golf Development of the Year." Just like that, the Quarry was the state's new golf "beauty queen," but it's not as if the Legend had been bumped from the competition altogether. The Legend still ranks consistently anywhere between No. 3 and No. 5 among Minnesota public courses. Miss Congeniality ain't bad, particularly when you consider the Minnesota golf season is so short and Giants Ridge operates as a ski resort most of the year.

More than a million cubic yards of dirt were moved in the building of the two courses. Maybe that's why architect Jeffrey Brauer waited five years to add the Quarry: he wanted to give the bulldozers a break.

Sculpting the holes was a major effort at Giants Ridge, but it wasn't as if there wasn't plenty of raw material with which to work. The challenging, par-72 Legend Course meanders through huge, glacier-shaped boulders and rock outcroppings, towering pines and handsome hardwoods. These superlative features are all within eyeshot of Superior National Forest. It's as if the course was molded through and around these natural features, with the rugged property touched up with emerald bent-grass fairways and white-sand bunkers to create significant man-made enhancement.

Sometimes "signature hole" is a gimmicky expression, but the term definitely applies to the par-5 3rd at the Legend Course. Not only a signature, but perhaps a legend at the Legend.

There is what appears for all the world to be a humongous, four-toed footprint in the left rough. So the folks at Giants Ridge filled the giant "foot" and the four "toes" with white sand to create a five-bunker complex that is among the most unique in the country. You can try to clear the foot to cut significant distance from the 501-yard hole and give yourself a chance to reach the green in two. Or you can take the safe route to the right of the pinky toe and play conservatively the rest of the way. Either route makes for a really fun golf hole.

The aptly named Quarry Course takes a different approach with similar results. The newer layout has the advantage of being built around deserted mines and an abandoned sand quarry. You can imagine the gulches and caverns and other unique hazards possible at such a site. So could Brauer; and he brought them to life.

Nos. 17 and 18 make for great Quarry finishers. The par-3 17th is one of the most difficult holes on the course. It commands an extremely difficult 200-yard carry over a pond to a huge green. It is very difficult shot, and there really is no bailout area. The 18th is lined by Embarrass Mine Lake on the right side. The highlight here is the approach into the dogleg par 4, which is made difficult by the lake and two bunkers on the right. These are just a couple of the pretty portions of a course that is cosmetically pleasing throughout. But what would you expect from Minnesota golf's "beauty queen?"

CHIP SHOTS

Course contact info:
(800) 688-7669,
www.giantsridge.com

Par: Legend 72; Quarry 72
Yardage: Legend 6,930 yards; Quarry 7,201 yards

Rating: Legend 73.7; Quarry 75.6
Slope: Legend 133; Quarry 146
Notable: Giants Ridge is not only the site of the No. 1 public golf course in Minnesota, it also has been named the state's "No. 1 Ski Resort" by *Ski Magazine*.

On the green
◡◡ $85

The 9th on the Quarry Course is a topsy-turvy ride to paydirt.

AFTER YOUR ROUND

Close to home: Biwabik (population 959, or 954, depending on whether that family down the road has moved yet) has limited options for entertainment, but the Giants Ridge Lodge itself is a fun place to be. There is a spa and salon, an indoor pool and hot tub, a game room, and a fitness center to keep you busy after your round. Doing it all with views of Superior National Forest doesn't hurt either. If you want to take a twenty-minute drive to the U.S. Hockey Hall of Fame Museum — opened in 1973 in Eveleth — you will see exhibits honoring outstanding coaches, players, builders, and administrators who have contributed to the success and promotion of American hockey.

OTHER PUBLIC COURSES IN MINNESOTA WORTH A VISIT
- Chaska Town Course, Chaska
- Madden's on Gull Lake (Classic Course), Brainerd
- Dacotah Ridge GC, Morton
- Deacon's Lodge GC, Brainerd
- Legends GC, Prior Lake
- StoneRidge GC, Stillwater
- The Wilderness at Fortune Bay, Tower
- The Wilds GC, Prior Lake

SCORECARD - LEGEND COURSE

Hole	1	2	3	4	5	6	7	8	9	out	
Yardage	377	165	501	402	412	219	411	456	536	3,479	
Par	4	3	5	4	4	3	4	4	5	36	
Hole	10	11	12	13	14	15	16	17	18	in	total
Yardage	410	157	401	418	510	452	520	226	357	3,451	6,930
Par	4	3	4	4	5	4	5	3	4	36	72

SCORECARD - QUARRY COURSE

Hole	1	2	3	4	5	6	7	8	9	out	
Yardage	433	575	444	269	525	369	189	478	377	3,659	
Par	4	5	4	3	5	4	3	4	4	36	
Hole	10	11	12	13	14	15	16	17	18	in	total
Yardage	362	158	486	323	513	454	558	220	468	3,542	7,201
Par	4	3	4	4	5	4	5	3	4	36	72

MINNESOTA

RUSH CREEK GOLF CLUB
MAPLE GROVE, MINNESOTA

Looking for a rush? Players seeking a spirited game need look no further than Rush Creek Golf Club, a public facility with country-club maintenance. The staff installed new greens before the 2008 season, and the bent grass fairways add distance to your drives. Both features add speed to the game. In other words, Rush Creek is a rush.

But there is no hurry when you tee it up at Rush Creek. The country-club atmosphere, exemplified by expert maintenance personnel, carries through to other facets of the course. A relaxing approach to the game makes for an enjoyable round, but don't be fooled. Players must be ready for a challenge.

The conditions are conducive to good scoring if you're hitting it straight, but the smooth fairways will carry errant shots into that nasty rough. Getting home in regulation is next to impossible if you happen to land in the rough stuff. Somehow, the course seems to be in mid-season condition whether it's just opening in May or winding out the season in the fall. After it hosts a tournament, it is as pristine a place to play as you will find in most public or private facilities.

It didn't take long for the golfers of Minnesota to take notice of Rush Creek after the Maple Grove gem opened in 1996. The pros caught on pretty quickly, too. In each of its first two years of operation, Rush Creek was named among the "Top 14 Places to Play" by *Golf Digest* in a list that included private as well as public courses.

Its reputation has risen even further since those early years, and it is now considered the top public course in Minnesota. Professional tournaments and top amateur events held at Rush Creek have solidified its standing as a public-access venue that is an exhilarating place to play.

Business travelers, vacationers, and residents of the Twin Cities find Rush Creek a stop worth making. Because it is a public facility and is located in a major metropolitan area, if you play your cards right and book a tee time, you can squeeze in a round no matter what your business in Minneapolis or St. Paul.

The course may be close to big cities, but that feeling is forgotten once you make your way onto the course. There are no major streets around the facility, and you won't see homes lining fairways or surrounding greens. Mature trees

along the fairways offer a canopy of peace and quiet. And the staff at Rush Creek does a great job of making you feel like "a member for a day."

The greens at Rush Creek are cunning and curvaceous, and narrow fairways and deep rough only increase the challenge. Water comes into play on thirteen holes, and there are more than fifty bunkers sprinkled throughout the layout.

From the clubhouse, the course does not appear as intimidating as it plays. Part of the reason for this is that the green slopes are undetectable from the clubhouse, and the same is true for the density of woods and rough.

Players are required to be on top of their games from No. 1 to No. 18 at Rush Creek. In fact, the two toughest holes on the course are the 9th and the 18th. Don't be thinking about the hot dog at the turn, or the post-round beverage. It'll cost you on the scorecard.

Even if you're playing Rush Creek by yourself, you won't be alone. Beavers, woodchucks, deer, and several species of birds will be part of the scenery. There is also more company available. Caddie service is offered if you make arrangements forty-eight hours in advance.

Twin bunkers protect the 18th green at Rush Creek, and — depending on conditions — a glass-smooth pond that reflects the blue skies.

include the Underwater Adventures Aquarium, Nickelodeon Universe, and the Minneapolis Institute of Arts. In St. Paul, you can find the Omnitheater-Science Museum and the Minnesota Children's Museum. Here's an unexpected opportunity: take a Mississippi River ride where you might spot bald eagles, herons, egrets, and falcons while traveling on a riverboat from St. Paul's bustling downtown harbor through Mississippi National River and Recreation Area.

AFTER YOUR ROUND

Twin Cities' neighbor: Maple Grove is home to an arboretum, a farmers' market, a small shopping district, and the Angel of Hope statue. Not exactly a bustling metropolis, but perhaps a calm evening fits the bill after a round at Rush Creek. If you choose to take the twenty-mile drive into Minneapolis or St. Paul, you will find all the trappings and activities of the big city. A few options in Minneapolis

CHIP SHOTS

Course contact info:
(763) 494-0400,
www.rushcreek.com

Par: 72
Yardage: 7,000 yards

Rating: 74.8
Slope: 144
Notable: Rush Creek finished as the top public golf course in Minnesota in voting by players in the Twin Cities area. Rush Creek has hosted the Minnesota LPGA Classic, the World Championship of Women's Golf, the Marshall Field's Challenge, and the U.S. Amateur Public Links Championship.

On the green
◐◐ $79

SCORECARD

Hole	1	2	3	4	5	6	7	8	9	out	
Yardage	428	532	196	336	417	340	203	609	452	3,513	
Par	4	5	3	4	4	4	3	5	4	36	
Hole	10	11	12	13	14	15	16	17	18	in	total
Yardage	575	410	186	345	440	169	409	384	569	3,487	7,000
Par	5	4	3	4	4	3	4	4	5	36	72

MISSISSIPPI

FALLEN OAK GOLF CLUB
SAUCIER, MISSISSIPPI

You can play all night at the Beau Rivage casino and all day at its golf course, Fallen Oak Golf Club. The chances you take at the tables are of your own volition, but you don't have to worry about taking a gamble on the quality of the golf here – that's a sure bet.

The Beau Rivage casino is well known in the Gulf Coast as one of Mississippi's classiest destinations, and when the head honchos decided to build a golf course they wanted to match the standards that had been set at the resort. Their first step was a good one: Beau Rivage hired Tom Fazio, the world-famous golf course architect, to design the place. When Beau Rivage held a news conference in May 2006 to announce Fallen Oak's opening, Fazio laid out all the standard quotes – "great place to play," "wonderful opportunity," "one of my favorite pieces of work," among them. But when he spoke in specifics, he revealed intricacies about Fallen Oak that define its character and its unique opportunities.

"Many of the golf holes fit naturally around the existing features of the property, but there were parts of the existing property that were not as abundant in natural charm," Fazio said. "We created dramatic and interesting features where

there once was flat land. The golf course presents a variety of golf strategies in its playable fairways, dramatic bunkers, and gently rolling greens."

In other words, Fazio was given the green light to run free with his vision. His ability to design unique golf courses is why he was hired to create Fallen Oak. When Tom Fazio wants one-of-a-kind, then one-of-a-kind it is. Generous fairways are perfect for those in need of a friendly welcome off the tee. Yet there can be tough shots ahead even if you plop your drive in the middle of the crisply cut fairways.

That's the beauty of Fallen Oak. It plays to your game. You have the option to play conservatively or to take a risk at several holes. The layout is far from straightforward, and it's an often-wonderful guessing game.

The golf course not only adds another selling point to the Beau Rivage property, it adds a highlight to the Mississippi economy, which welcomes the boost. The jobless rate in the Magnolia State has been among the highest in the nation, and Beau Rivage offers employment to hundreds of residents of Saucier, nearby Biloxi, and beyond. Staffers are happy to be employed at a classy place such as Fallen Oak, and it shows in the genuine focus on friendly customer service.

The folks at Fallen Oak call the course "as much an adventure as a work of art." The art here includes nature's canvas of pecan orchards, magnolia groves, huge oak

No. 18 at Fallen Oak has many spots from which to enjoy its beauty, but this isn't one of them if you're at all interested in making par.

trees, and wetlands. These features are not just cosmetic: all come into play on various holes and some can be treacherous – and scorecard-marring – hazards. For example, a huge water oak serves as your target off the 1st tee, but there's a good reason it's called a water oak: streams and a lake border the fairway and green.

You don't have to go far to see what's in store. In fact, the views from the clubhouse include the 9th and 18th fairways – green slopes and terrain that make you eager to pay your fee and get out to the tee.

AFTER YOUR ROUND

Game on: Whether you finish your round at noon or midnight, you can go straight from the 18th green to the Beau Rivage Casino (after changing your shoes, of course). The electric action heats up the day and lights the night, with more than 2,000 slot machines and all of the standard casino table games. You don't necessarily need to be a gambler to enjoy Beau Rivage, although it sure doesn't hurt. Entertainment options include headline musicians, special events, and the Beau Rivage Theatre. Comedians Ron White and Jerry Lewis, and musical acts such as Tony Bennett, Lynyrd Skynyrd, Queen Latifah, Chicago, and the Black Crowes have all lit up the Beau Rivage stage.

Off-site family fun: A twenty-mile drive to Gulfport will take you to the World's Largest Rocking Chair exhibition, and outdoor recreation spots within a thirty-minute radius of Fallen Oak include Airey Lake Recreation Area, Big Biloxi Recreation Area, and Little Biloxi State Wildlife Management Area.

CHIP SHOTS

Course contact info:
(228) 386-7111,
www.fallenoakgolf.com

Par: 72
Yardage: 7,016 yards (non-tournament tees); 7,487 yards (tournament tees)

Rating: 73.8
(non-tournament tees)
Slope: 139
(non-tournament tees)
Notable: Fallen Oak has played host to Mississippi's Governor's Cup, the Captain's Challenge, and has been rated among the country's "Top 50" by *Golf Digest* and the "Top 100" by *Golf Magazine*.

On the green
◉ ◉ ◉ $175 (includes one night lodging in Beau Rivage Hotel & Casino)

OTHER PUBLIC COURSES IN MISSISSIPPI WORTH A VISIT
• Canebrake GC, Hattiesburg
• Dancing Rabbit GC at Pearl River Resort (Azaleas Course), Choctaw
• Dancing Rabbit GC at Pearl River Resort (Oaks Course), Choctaw
• Shell Landing GC, Gautier

SCORECARD

Hole	1	2	3	4	5	6	7	8	9	out	
Yardage	537	455	193	423	426	548	330	176	422	3,510	
Par	5	4	3	4	4	5	4	3	4	36	
Hole	10	11	12	13	14	15	16	17	18	in	total
Yardage	416	396	382	541	161	565	418	198	429	3,506	7,016
Par	5	4	4	4	3	5	4	3	4	36	72

MISSISSIPPI

GRAND BEAR GOLF COURSE
SAUCIER, MISSISSIPPI

As you traipse the 650 acres of gentle slopes amid the looming pines of DeSota National Forest, it is difficult to realize that just a few yards away there are bells, whistles, jingles, and jangles amid a casino's sometimes chaotic atmosphere.

Though the Grand Bear Golf Course may be close in proximity to the Grand Biloxi Casino Resort and Spa, the two locales are light years apart when it comes to ambience. Wetlands and crunchy pine-needle rough are among the elements that provide the beauty of the course, and those inescapable towering pines offer an enveloping shield against the outside world.

Jingles and jangles, you say? Not out here.

Most of the scenery is natural — highlights include two rivers with white-sand banks and several Mississippi marshes — but there are also several touches of man-made additions. "Human help" includes a 6.5-acre, stocked lake; deep, smoothly raked bunkers; and greens featuring the kind of easy-on-the-eyes grooming that you'd expect at a first-class golf course.

The manicuring is an indicator of a top-drawer track. Jack Nicklaus — the Golden Bear — designed Grand Bear and his autograph on a course is a symbolic signature of excellence. This assurance isn't always the case when a former PGA Tour player's name is stamped on a golf course. Often, the famous name is brought in for marquee value and offers minimal input to a design firm. But that's not the case with Nicklaus. He is just as diligent a worker in design as he was in a PGA Tour career that made him one of the great golfers in history.

As fantastic as Nicklaus was, he somehow still relates to the mid-handicapper. He created a layout at Grand Bear that gives the public-access players an opportunity to score, providing they play well. That's precisely the vision Grand Bear management had when it brought in Nicklaus. They wanted a course that was fair to all their guests, one that was not too difficult for the resort golfer to enjoy. But this isn't to say that Grand Bear doesn't have some teeth. You must be long on some holes, such as the 603-yard 5th; and brave on others, including the "I dare you" 17th.

No. 5 features a tighter fairway than most of the other holes on the course, and there is little forgiveness if you venture into the rough. There is some tall grass to slow you down, but thick pines wait if you roll through the tall grass. A creek that cuts through the fairway must be dealt with on your second shot, and the approach enters a green that slopes hard to the right. If the pin is on the left side of the putting surface and your approach lands in the middle of the green, there's no shot of getting close to the pin. Expect two tough putts to make par.

The 17th hole forces a decision. It's a 433-yard par-4, which leaves a very short approach shot if you strike it well off the tee. But here's the catch: a stream runs through the fairway in a spot that will swallow your drive if you don't strike it pure. A powerful tee shot can carry the creek, but there is a risk. Just like in the casino, there are no guarantees.

Grand Bear is a touch pricey for those watching their pennies, but not terribly so. And those lucky enough to have fortune smile on them in the casino can use their winnings to supplement the golf budget.

AFTER YOUR ROUND

More than gaming: The Grand Biloxi Casino is a great option for entertainment, but there's more to explore. For those lookin' for a little muddin', Red Creek Off Road offers rough-and-tumble, mucky ATV rides through the backwoods of Perkinston — fifteen minutes from Grand Bear. Gulfport, twenty miles from Grand Bear, is full of fun. Options include Gulf Islands Water Park, Ship Island Excursions, and First Amusement amusement park.

CHIP SHOTS

Course contact info:
(800) 946-2946,
www.grandcasinobiloxi.com
(click on "Grand Bear Golf Course")

Par: 72
Yardage: 7,202 yards

Rating: 75.5
Slope: 143
Notable: Grand Bear has played host to Shell's Wonderful World of Golf, which staged a match between Jesper Parnevik and Paul Azinger. John Daly's Make a Wish Tournament was also held at Grand Bear, which is among the "Top 21 Casino Courses in the Country," according to *Golfweek*. It's among the top 100 public-access courses on several rankings and also makes virtually every listing of best public-access golf in Mississippi.

On the green
◔ $75

Grand Bear's 17th mirrors the path of the Big Biloxi River, curling left with forest filling the horizon.

MISSOURI

BRANSON CREEK GOLF CLUB
BRANSON, MISSOURI

More than 7 million tourists each year visit Branson, Missouri, a city that tabs itself the "Live Entertainment Capital of the World." With about a dozen public golf courses in the area, you'd think tee times would be difficult to obtain. Fortunately for golfers, most of the visitors come to town to see shows at several of the star-studded theaters here and don't give golf a second thought.

These non-golfing folks are missing one of the classiest acts in town: Branson Creek Golf Club. The Tom Fazio design is an outdoor stage of interactive golf entertainment — swinging clubs, elegant balls, an eighteen-member flag corps, and more.

If you plan on showing off, you'll need to concentrate on the golf and not the views. They don't call Missouri the "Show Me" state for nothing, and Branson Creek fits right into that theme. This facility, with its wonderful layout in the Ozark Mountains, has been named the best public course in Missouri, and that ranking is richly deserved.

The course is situated in the rolling hills of a southern Missouri plateau. Several holes play along rocky ridges and just as scenic are the holes that plummet into the course's valleys. Elevated tees and flower-filled hills surround the fairways, only adding to the cosmetic appeal.

Evergreens and dogwoods complement jagged rock outcroppings, streams, and ponds. There are so many "golf-calendar moments" on this course that you could fill up the next several years with nothing but shots of Branson Creek. Just make sure you're not holding up the foursome behind you when you start snapping the shutter.

Branson Creek relies more on appearance than brute challenge, offering mid-range handicappers a chance to enjoy their rounds. The course measures just more than 7,000 yards from the back tees, so there is some length. But generous fairways and expansive greens offer forgiveness even if you don't strike it on the sweet spot.

Each hole at Branson Creek comes with a nickname, and one of the top holes comes with a fitting and funny name. The 5th honors former Silver Dollar City Mayor Shad Heller. They call the hole "Heller High Water," and they're telling the truth. When you're there, just look to your right and that lake confirms that there's plenty of high water.

Shadows fall on the 17th green at Branson Creek, a club many call the best public course in Missouri.

The par-3 9th is called "Fazio's Vision," but the course designer can't claim it strictly as his own. The views — and they're fantastic — belong to everyone who plays the hole.

Branson Creek is friendly to the resort golfer, but there are some risk-reward shots on a couple of dogleg holes. These strategic moments aren't the only decisions you'll have to make. There is risk-reward of another variety that has nothing to do with club selection.

The facility is open all year, and the winter months can get a bit frosty in the Ozarks. It's a little risky to play a round in January or February, particularly if you have trouble swinging in the cold, but there is a reward. Greens fees are reduced in the winter months, offering one of the great deals in golf. An outstanding, mountain-golf experience is open to the public and can be played for about fifty bucks.

Now, that's a show-stopper.

AFTER YOUR ROUND

Think big: Big-time names provide live entertainment year-round at the Osmond Family Theater. Different members of the Osmond family are frequent performers. Andy Williams also owns a theater in this town that features live entertainment at almost every corner. Variety shows, such as Jim Stafford, Hamner Barber, Grand Jubilee; and vocalists such as Cassandre and Bob Anderson's musical tribute to Sinatra are just a few of the dozens of entertainment options in Branson.

OTHER PUBLIC COURSES IN MISSOURI WORTH A VISIT
- Lodge of Four Seasons Golf Resort & Spa, Lake Ozark
- Old Kinderhook Resort & GC, Camdenton
- Shoal Creek GC, Kansas City
- Winghaven CC, O'Fallon

Ship ahoy: Titanic Branson is a permanent two-story museum attraction shaped like the Titanic herself. This astounding, signature building was built half-scale to the original ship and enables visitors to walk an elegant replica of Titanic's staircase, touch the frozen surface of an "iceberg," stand in the mighty ship's bridge, and then hear the captain's commands. Another large-scale adventure comes at the local IMAX entertainment complex, where movies are shown on an eight-story screen.

CHIP SHOTS

Course contact info:
(800) 946-2946,
(417) 339-4653,
www.bransoncreekgolf.com

Par: 71
Yardage: 7,036 yards

Rating: 73.0
Slope: 133
Notable: Tom Fazio had this to say about Branson Creek: "Every hole out here is a magazine front cover." And, it's not just the course about which PGA Tour players rave. Corey Pavin said, "Your practice facility . . . is one of the best I've seen."

On the green
○ $75

Hole	1	2	3	4	5	6	7	8	9	out	
Yardage	578	471	405	195	449	353	245	524	198	3,418	
Par	5	4	4	3	4	4	3	5	3	35	
Hole	10	11	12	13	14	15	16	17	18	in	total
Yardage	377	158	477	462	615	366	425	165	573	3,618	7,036
Par	4	3	4	4	5	4	4	3	5	36	71

SCORECARD

Bogeys might loom as ominous as the shadows at the Woodlands' par-3, 208-yard 6th. It's green or nothing if you expect a reasonable shot at par.

MISSOURI

TAPAWINGO NATIONAL GOLF CLUB
(WOODLANDS/PRAIRIE COURSES)
SUNSET HILLS, MISSOURI

Gary Player, a guy who knows a thing or two about good golf, was on top of his game when he designed Tapawingo National Golf Club. The Sunset Hills public facility brought out the best in Player, and he, in turn, tips his hat to Tapawingo.

Player has designed more than 100 courses since retiring from his playing days, and he says only four or five pieces of property have stood out as the best of the best. When asked about Tapawingo, Player speaks of the lay of the land, the trees, hills, rolling terrain, and the beauty of the Meramec River. This hall-of-famer knows better than to take credit for the natural beauty.

"God designed the first six holes," Player says. "Player Design helped out with the rest."

Tapawingo's original eighteen — the Woodlands and

Prairie courses — have been open for more than fifteen years, enough time to mature and become one with the terrain of which Player spoke. But there wasn't as much need for maturation as there is with many other courses. Because all eighteen holes were laid out in such a natural setting, there were no saplings around. No transplanted bushes. The thousands of trees that stand on the Tapawingo grounds today have been there long before Tapawingo was conceptualized.

During a press-conference luncheon, Player spoke of the architectural strategy when building Tapawingo.

"When you have a piece of property like this, it's important not to try to get too cute," he said. "With forest and water, you really can't go wrong if you just use your head. Sometimes it's just a matter of getting out of the way."

Staffers at Tapawingo are custodians of Player's masterpiece, and they take the responsibility seriously. They know that one slip in the upkeep would contrast mightily with the rest of the course, so every inch of the grounds is monitored for conditioning. The hardwood forests and lakes rarely require attention; the greenskeepers want to make sure the man-made additions live up to the beauty of their surroundings.

Tapawingo is not just a beautiful golf course; it can be a very demanding track as well. It is fairly long at just over 7,100 yards, and danger lurks on every hole. The holes wind through the woods, and many of them run adjacent to the Meramec River. Nature provided hardwoods and the river as hazards, but Player added a little trouble of his own.

Bunkers and water hazards make for additional perils at Tapawingo. The Woodlands nine, part of the original twosome before the Meramec Course was added, features many holes in which Player installed more than enough hazards to keep players honest.

The par-4 and par-5 holes on the Woodlands are of average length, but the par 3s are where you are forced to bring everything you have to the tee. Not only are they tough, they are plentiful. There are three par 3s on the Woodlands Course, two of them checking in at 200-plus yards and the other measuring 190.

Seven of the nine holes on the Prairie Course are of fairly average length, though each poses threats to the unwary player. The par-3 8th stretches your ability to hit the green from 210 yards, but it isn't the true monster of the course. That distinction goes to No. 4 — a prodigious par 5 that reaches 606 yards from the tips. The 4th hole on the Prairie Course requires one of the most demanding shots at Tapawingo. Water comes into play if you miss your drive to the right. If you hit your drive true, you're still not out of trouble. The hole not only is a tortuous 600-plus

yards, the approach to the green is straight uphill. There is no room for error on the Prairie 4th, which parallels the tale of Tapawingo's creation.

"We didn't want to make a mistake with this one," Player said. "With a property like this, you want to make sure you get it right."

AFTER YOUR ROUND

Going to the city:
Sunset Hills is just sixteen miles southwest of St. Louis, so the city lights are well within reach. The Gateway Arch is one of the top tourist attractions in the country. The arch is the tallest national monument in the United States at 630 feet, and each year more than 1 million visitors ride trams to the top of the arch. If the Blues are in town, a hockey game might be in order. You can also check out the St. Louis Zoo, the City Museum, the Missouri Botanical Garden, and the Anheuser Busch Brewery tour.

CHIP SHOTS

Course contact info:
(636) 349-3100,
www.tapawingogolf.com

Par: 72
Yardage: 7,151 yards

Rating: 55.1
Slope: 144
Notable: Tapawingo has been tabbed as the toughest course in the region by several publications, so players of mid- to high-handicaps should not play from the back tees. This is a bit of advice public-access players sometimes ignore, which only slows down play for everyone on the course. The tips are reserved only for those who are confident they can handle a stern challenge.

On the green
◔ $60

SCORECARD - WOODLANDS NINE

Hole	1	2	3	4	5	6	7	8	9	out	
Yardage	390	387	190	525	456	208	585	210	569	3,520	
Par	4	4	3	5	4	3	5	3	5	36	

SCORECARD - PRAIRIE NINE

Hole	1	2	3	4	5	6	7	8	9	out	
Yardage	400	153	410	606	469	439	394	210	550	3,631	7,151
Par	4	3	4	5	4	4	4	3	5	36	72

MONTANA

CANYON RIVER GOLF CLUB
MISSOULA, MONTANA

Golf course marketers often use wildlife population as a selling point; a way of proving their course is natural and environmentally sound. The marketing team at Canyon River Golf Club doesn't have to say a word about its bravest and most curious furry friend.

A fox that makes constant appearances on the course — morning, noon, and twilight, and mostly on the back nine — needs no introduction. She's become a bit of a local legend in and around Missoula. She traipses on fairways and goes one step further: she frequently swipes golf balls. The Canyon River has not yet added a "fox free drop" provision to their course rules, but they just might.

Canyon River's foxy golf-ball thief has had a tangible impact. A restaurant at the club is called "The Fox Den" and course staffers are considering marketing merchandise with a fox logo. The four-legged visitor does indeed prove that Canyon River is nature-friendly, and it's a place smart golfers put on their rotation. In fact, you could say players who enjoy frequenting Canyon River are sly as a fox.

Canyon River snakes through thick pine forest and the native grasses of western Montana. Lakes and marshes throughout the property are both natural and potentially perilous. These federally protected environmental features on the property were used to the benefit of the golf course, both to beautify and to keep players aware of the elements.

The Lee Schmidt-Brian Curley design is located in East Missoula on the banks of the rushing Clark Fork River. The striking changes in elevation will alter your strategy as well. Vistas of the surrounding mountains accompany players throughout the round, and the course is forgiving to those who need a break or two. The fairways supply ample landing room, so if you keep it reasonably straight, you can avoid the tall, natural grasses adjacent to the pines.

Many of the elevation changes at Canyon River are natural, so Schmidt and Curley were able to avoid moving an exorbitant amount of earth during construction. The layout melds with the surrounding landscape to form a seamless meeting of golf course and nature.

There are no cookie-cutter holes. Because of the natural aspects, the fairways follow the land formations that preceded them. One of the more intriguing holes is the par-3 14th, short in distance but long on memories. The 168-yarder features a fifty-foot drop from tee to green, and the putting surface is almost completely surrounded by trees. The hole is a prime example of Great Northwest golf, including a waterfall and a pond to the right side of the green.

There are many reasons to visit Canyon River at least once, and repeat visits are recommended if your schedule allows. Locals have gone crazy over the place since it opened in 2006.

Crazy like a fox.

AFTER YOUR ROUND

Take a hike: Montana is a beautiful state, and I highly recommend that you stay outdoors as much as you can if weather permits. The 5,500-acre Blue Mountain Recreation Area, just two miles west of Missoula, offers a place to do just that. Lolo National Forest Nature personnel worked closely with Missoula-area recreation groups to establish an intricate trail system that includes a nature center highlighting various wildlife species and plants native to the area. It's a great way to enjoy the pure air of the Great Northwest. Go ahead, take a deep breath.

Campus culture: There are cultural selections in Missoula, which is home to the University of Montana. The Montana Museum of Art and Culture is located on the campus, and there are also drama and dance productions at the university's Montana Theater.

CHIP SHOTS

Course contact info:
(406) 721-0222,
www.canyonrivergolfclub.com

Par: 72
Yardage: 6,948 yards

Rating: 72.2
Slope: 123

Notable: Canyon River was named one of the "Top 10 New Golf Courses You Can Play for Under $75" by *Golf Digest*. Considering that greens fees don't come close to $75, that's quite an honor. The course is part of a master-planned community with home prices starting in the $425,000 range.

On the green
◐ ◐ $60

Beautiful evergreens, crisp greens, mountain views, and even some rustic homes are part of the Canyon River experience.

OTHER PUBLIC COURSES IN MONTANA WORTH A VISIT
- Big Mountain GC, Kalispell
- Old Works, Anaconda

SCORECARD

Hole	1	2	3	4	5	6	7	8	9	out	
Yardage	398	470	181	396	467	523	241	338	571	3,585	
Par	4	4	3	4	4	5	3	4	5	36	
Hole	10	11	12	13	14	15	16	17	18	in	total
Yardage	392	531	190	461	168	525	187	343	566	3,363	6,948
Par	4	5	3	4	3	5	3	4	5	36	72

MONTANA

WHITEFISH LAKE GOLF CLUB
(SOUTH COURSE)
WHITEFISH, MONTANA

There is small window of opportunity to enjoy this Montana mountain golf course in all its splendor. Altitude and climate keep the season from starting until June in most years, and snowflakes have been known to drift home in May. But if you plan your visit at the right time of year, sliding through that barely open window, the round that waits at Whitefish Lake Golf Club will reward your sense of keen timing. It takes some effort to get there, but it's worth the flight, the drive, and the walk.

The best way to get to Whitefish Lake from out of town is to fly into Kalispell – population 35,000 – a place the locals in northwest Montana call "the city." From there, just stay on US 93 North to Whitefish Lake – but keep your eyes peeled. There is no road sign that lets you know that you have arrived at Whitefish Lake, so watch for a parkland-style golf course and turn into the log-cabin-style clubhouse. They'll let you know you're in the right place.

CHIP SHOTS

Course contact info:
(406) 862-4000,
www.golfwhitefish.com

Par: 72
Yardage: 6,597 yards

Rating: 70.5
Slope: 122
Notable: Whitefish Lake Golf Course is the only 36-hole facility on the shores of Whitefish Lake, but that's not the only lake on the property. Lost Coon Lake adds to the watery views.

On the green
◉ $48

The South Course opened in 1994, and the John Steidel design joined the already established North Course. From the minute you walk into the clubhouse, and then make the trek to the first tee, you realize that this is woodsy, mountain golf at its finest. Nothing fancy, no unnecessary intrusions. The folks at Whitefish Lake are to be commended for allowing nature to speak for itself. A description of the holes is enough to understand where you are. You cannot give an accurate account without offering some sort of natural feature as you relate the hole-by-hole experience.

The first few holes play along a deep valley, with a perfect look at the front range of the Rocky Mountains. You start climbing through the woods on No. 6, and the par-3 7th forces a carry of Lost Loon Lake to hit the lush, green target.

The woodsy climb continues on No. 9, and the clubhouse is nowhere to be seen. You don't head towards the house until you've finished the 15th hole.

Whitefish Lake sits about forty miles from the Continental Divide and about twenty miles from Glacier National Park. The golf courses are microcosms of all that the Montana outdoors has to offer. They rise to nearly 6,000 feet, a level where the views are pure, the air is thin, and a golf ball will soar like one of the bald eagles roosting in the miles and miles of deep woods.

It might be difficult to take advantage of that thin air, however, because there are so many distractions on the tee. No, there are no cars driving by, or homes choking the fairways. This is Montana, remember? The distractions are the elk, deer, turkeys, and even the occasional black bear. If you're a nature lover, stay focused or you'll feel like you've contracted a case of wildlife-driven Attention Deficit Disorder.

Ignoring the wildlife in your backswing is a necessity on the golf course, but in order to maximize your visit to the area it is highly advised that you delve into the beauties of Mother Nature. When the northwest Montana locals aren't swinging away on the fairways of Whitefish Lake, they're kayaking the rivers, fishing the lakes, and hiking the 750 miles of trails that wind through Glacier National Park.

Many of the natives, however, don't use their kayaks and fishing rods as much from June to October as they do the rest of the year. There are more than a few golfers in these parts. And they're agile enough to slide through the golf season's narrow window.

The multiple, yet beautiful hazards on the 429-yard, par-4 11th at Whitefish Lake's South Course are not to be trifled with.

AFTER YOUR ROUND

Local lodge: Whitefish Mountain Resort at Big Mountain not only provides a nice place to stay while you're in Whitefish, but the proximity to the mountains provides numerous recreational activities. You can "walk in the treetops" on a Big Mountain swinging bridge, or take the "Glacier Chaser" gondola to the 7,000-foot, peak summit. Hiking, bike riding, horseback riding, you name it. There's mountain fun for everyone.

SCORECARD

Hole	1	2	3	4	5	6	7	8	9	out	
Yardage	427	401	174	407	389	470	241	402	317	3,228	
Par	4	4	3	4	4	5	3	4	4	35	
Hole	10	11	12	13	14	15	16	17	18	in	total
Yardage	514	429	548	354	348	204	146	361	465	3,369	6,597
Par	5	4	5	4	4	3	3	4	5	37	72

NEBRASKA

WILD HORSE GOLF CLUB
GOTHENBURG, NEBRASKA

Wild Horse Golf Club, in all its minimalistic simplicity, may be the quintessential example of combining outstanding golf with a price tag that leaves you with enough cash for a healthy lunch after your round. Quality does not suffer for price, nor is bargain sacrificed for the excellent conditions.

This pristine golf course situated on peaceful prairieland is a perfect mix. *Golfweek* has rated it as one of the "Top 20 Modern Courses in America" and you can play the beautiful facility for under $50. *Golf Digest* and *Golf Magazine* have also discovered this inexpensive Nebraska gem. More important than the plaudits from the national publications, however, are the reactions of those golfers who don't have to unload their wallets when loading up their clubs.

When constructing Wild Horse, Dan Proctor and Dave Axland teamed up to make sure the natural lay of the land was largely undisturbed and they kept the cost of building the course in check. The pair built the course for less than $3 million — a modest amount by today's standards — on a 330-acre plot of land. Proctor and Axland's understanding of the property could not have been hurt by the shaping work they did for Ben Crenshaw and Bill Coore at Sand Hills Golf Club, a private facility in nearby Mullen, Nebraska.

That's the magic here. The same kind of land, the same people shaping the earth. But instead of paying for a country club membership at Sand Hills, we all can plunk down a couple of twenties, play a wonderful round of golf, and leave the place with some walking-around money.

Proctor and Axland are to be commended for their restraint, but they did have a little help. Prairie winds sculpted the huge and plentiful bunkers at Wild Horse, providing rugged land and toughening the challenge. Native grasses are allowed to grow thick in strategic areas, providing precarious situations in the absence of trees or water.

No, this is not Scotland. It's Gothenburg, Nebraska, and that's the 405-yard, par-4 1st hole at Wild Horse Golf Club.

The course plays to just less than 7,000 yards from the tips, but it's a tricky 7,000 yards. Wind plays a distinct role at Wild Horse, and can make up to a three-club difference when choosing which stick to play.

Anticipation on the first tee of most courses is a normal phenomenon, and that feeling is heightened upon first glance of the course at Wild Horse. The rippling, mound-filled fairway is pockmarked by scraggly bunkers and cocooned by blowing fescue. The rest of the world has seemingly disappeared. No housing developments, no highways, not much of anything except great golf, a few tumbleweeds, and the occasional jackrabbit. It is Great Plains golf at its finest. And, best of all, it comes with a great, plain price.

AFTER YOUR ROUND

Pony up: Gothenburg was the site of a Pony Express station from April, 1860, to November, 1861. Its mission was to deliver mail between St. Joseph, Missouri, and San Francisco. You can visit the Pony Express schoolhouse or the bunkhouse on a tour of the old station.

Grassy attraction: The Sod House Museum stands adjacent to a full-scale replica of an authentic sod house, the type that was used by early settlers. This museum area also features a barn, windmills, and life-sized barbed-wire sculptures. The barn-shaped museum houses memorabilia and photographs taken during the pioneer era.

CHIP SHOTS

Course contact info:
(308) 537-7700,
www.playwildhorse.com

Par: 72
Yardage: 6,964 yards

Rating: 73.6
Slope: 134
Notable: Wild Horse opened in 1998, and its success seemed, in part, to spur a rush of excellent public golf courses to the upper midwest. Hawktree in Bismarck, North Dakota; Red Rock in Rapid City, South Dakota; and Bully Pulpit in Medora, North Dakota, were built within six years of Wild Horse's debut.

On the green
⬤ $38

OTHER PUBLIC COURSES IN NEBRASKA WORTH A VISIT
- Arbor Links, Nebraska City
- Bayside GC, Brule
- Quarry Oaks GC, Ashland
- Wilderness Ridge GC, Lincoln

SCORECARD

Hole	1	2	3	4	5	6	7	8	9	out	
Yardage	405	431	537	171	376	548	364	451	185	3,468	
Par	4	4	5	3	4	5	4	4	3	36	
Hole	10	11	12	13	14	15	16	17	18	in	total
Yardage	408	126	442	208	559	342	445	548	418	3,496	6,964
Par	4	3	4	3	5	4	4	5	4	36	72

As a golfer and his caddie approach the Bali Hai clubhouse amid the tropical Polynesian setting, it's hard to imagine this is on the Las Vegas Strip, just a chip shot from the desert.

NEVADA

BALI HAI GOLF CLUB
LAS VEGAS, NEVADA

You've heard the age-old axiom, "What happens in Vegas, stays in Vegas." But there is a new truth about Sin City, and it focuses on a luxurious public golf course amid the glaring and blaring decadence of the Strip.

When it comes to Bali Hai Golf Club, what happens in Vegas absolutely should *not* stay in Vegas. After playing Bali Hai, it would selfish to keep the experience to yourself.

Las Vegas golf is no secret. Increasingly, tourists include golf clubs among their must-have cargo when visiting. There is off-the-chart, high-end golf, more affordable golf, desert golf, golf that attracts PGA Tour players, and resort golf.

And then there's golf on the on the Strip. After the famed Desert Inn imploded and the accompanying golf course was destroyed in 2001 to make room for Wynn Las Vegas, Bali Hai became the sole golf venue within a roll of the dice of the hotels and casinos. It's almost surreal to drive past sunrise gamblers, bypass the casinos' ostentatious entrances and take the next driveway down the Strip into a . . . golf club. Even more surreal is the Polynesian tropical theme both in the clubhouse and on the course.

And the Bali Hai experience isn't just some muni tucked downtown. Yes, you use the Mandalay Bay Resort as an aiming point for a few holes (and as an aiming point, the golden megastructure serves fairly well), but the golf course is in outlandishly outstanding shape.

It's not what you'd expect when the rest of the immediate area is concrete and steel. The contrast, as you might imagine, is not happenstance. Bill Walters, who made a fortune as co-founder of a sports-betting syndicate, spent a good chunk building Bali Hai. Walters Golf comprises four Las Vegas courses, and Bali Hai is its Strip special. Walters dropped $32 million to build Bali Hai and give it a somewhat unlikely South Pacific feel. Some 3,500 palm trees and more than 100,000 flowers were planted, and black lava rock was used to enhance the exotic ambience. Seven lakes with beach-style bunkering, two creeks, and $300,000 worth of crushed white marble help to further evoke the South Seas atmosphere.

Bali Hai is a breath of fresh air for Las Vegas. Most of

the other courses around are desert golf, and that makes sense. But this course proves that there's another way. The expense of creating this other way has been handed down in the form of pricey greens fees. But you can't beat the convenience and lush experience right on the Las Vegas Strip. And, if you happen to hit it big on the tables, what better way to spend your winnings than on a tropical paradise next door to the place where you won the loot?

Another facet that makes Bali Hai unique is its journey to being a par-72 layout. There are four par-5s, five par-3s and nine par-4s. The par-4s leave the most distinctive golf-specific memories at Bali Hai. They are a virtual Murderer's Row, including the 468-yard 3rd, the 482-yard 8th and the 486-yard 17th. You can take out the driver. And then take it out again, and again, and again.

There's plenty to see in Vegas. Plenty to do. But, more and more, all the playing is not done at night. With the proliferation of quality golf, and a beautiful golf course right down the street, there's also plenty of fun to be had during the day.

And you can repeat the stories. Even after you leave town.

AFTER YOUR ROUND

A strategic exercise: It's impossible to include a fraction of post-golf activities Las Vegas has to offer, so this "After Your Round" entry presents my personal strategic plan to help you balance golf with nightlife. As difficult as it may be, get to bed early so you can be up and on the course before the rest of the crowd. I went to bed at about midnight the night before playing Bali Hai and I awoke at 5:00 a.m., showered, and was on the first tee by 6:00. Early Las Vegas mornings are chillier than you might expect in December (which is when I visited) so bring a pullover that you can

strip off when things warm up a bit. The beautiful thing about such an early tee time is that if you finish your round by 10:00 a.m., you can take a two-hour nap and wake up at noon to re-start your day of play. You're still up before many of the folks who stayed up all night, and you've already gotten in eighteen holes.

Buffets away: The world knows about the plentiful and bountiful Las Vegas buffets. But if you're looking for another option, you might want to head back to the place where you started your day. A meal at Bali Hai is guaranteed to be a different brand of dining than you've ever experienced inside a clubhouse. The restaurant is open for extended lunch, so don't wait until dinnertime. There is great contemporary American cuisine seasoned with Asian influences to go along with the course's Polynesian theme.

CHIP SHOTS

Course contact info:
(888) 427-6678;
www.balihaigolfclub.com

Par: 71
Yardage: 7,004 yards

Rating: 73.0
Slope: 130
Notable: You think it's easy producing a South Seas ambience in the middle of the desert? Try this on for size: Bali Hai pays an annual water bill of more than $500,000.

On the green
○○○ $169

OTHER PUBLIC COURSES IN NEVADA WORTH A VISIT
- Boulder Creek GC, Boulder City
- Cascata GC, Boulder City
- DragonRidge CC, Henderson
- Las Vegas Paiute Golf Resort (Wolf Course), Las Vegas
- Oasis GC, Mesquite
- Rio Secco GC, Henderson
- Shadow Creek GC, North Las Vegas
- Wynn GC, Las Vegas

SCORECARD

Hole	1	2	3	4	5	6	7	8	9	out	
Yardage	341	538	468	324	392	168	550	482	208	3,471	
Par	4	5	4	4	4	3	5	4	3	36	

Hole	10	11	12	13	14	15	16	17	18	in	total
Yardage	526	190	440	468	250	546	141	486	486	3,533	7,004
Par	5	3	4	4	3	5	3	4	4	35	71

NEVADA

LAS VEGAS PAIUTE GOLF RESORT
(SNOW MOUNTAIN COURSE)
LAS VEGAS, NEVADA

It's an unusual sight. A welcome, but unusual sight.

It doesn't take long, maybe thirty minutes, to go from the craziness of Las Vegas to a sense of serenity — right in the middle of nowhere.

Driving along Route 95, heading north from the Vegas Strip, the setting is a picture postcard of nothingness. And then, out of nowhere, off in the distance, you see a building rising from the sand. A mile off the exit you begin to see the lush, green fairways of a simply stunning golf course. This emerald marshmallow appears to be a mirage floating above the desert.

Welcome to the Las Vegas Paiute Golf Resort. Welcome to golf paradise.

Forget, for a moment, all that the resort has to offer. Forget the three Pete Dye golf courses, including the Snow Mountain Course, the first course on the property and the track that gets my vote.

The scenery alone is enough to keep many players shaking their heads for eighteen holes. Sometimes, you find yourself standing on the tee and staring into the mountains. This is when you must pinch yourself, look away, and grab a club.

It's that awesome. Perhaps it's the feeling of absolute solitude that contrasts so mightily with the mania you left behind at the craps tables and roulette wheels. Or maybe it's the striking green with

the mountainous backdrop. Whatever the reason, Paiute Resort's Snow Mountain Course provided me with one of the best golfing experiences I've ever had.

Located about thirty minutes from the Vegas Strip, the Paiute Resort is one of the area's most impressive sights — and this is in a land full of sights to see. The rolling, green fairways cut through the desert like a rattlesnake looking for its next meal.

The desert isn't the only sandy spot at Snow Mountain. The many bunkers within the course seem to go perfectly with the sand surrounding it. And adding to the sense that you're seeing a mirage, there are several water hazards that blend into the rich, green turf.

Dye has become known for drawing up special challenges throughout his more than thirty-year career as a golf course architect. He has accomplished that and more at Paiute, and his trademarks are obvious — from the railroad ties around bunkers and water, to the elevated greens throughout Snow Mountain.

Snow Mountain plays to more than 7,100 yards from the back tees, and it's a manageable course from that distance for experienced golfers. The course is fairly open, so it gives players a chance to swing away. There are dips and valleys and hazards with which to contend, but the thin desert air is too much to resist. Take out that driver and give it a rip.

There are no trees in the desert, although there is plenty of wild brush and more than a few cacti. Water comes into play on seven holes, including Nos. 16, 17, and 18. Another Dye staple — deep, steep bunkers around the greens — is evident at nearly every hole. The bunkers sit well below the level of the hole, and they can present some pretty nasty escape attempts depending on your lie.

Snow Mountain features a variety of hole lengths, and it really adds a lot of fun to the round. You never know what to expect at the next tee, only that it will be an interesting hole to tackle. Three par 4s play less than 400 yards and one par 5 measures more than 600 from the tips to the flagstick.

There are plenty of jackrabbits, iguanas, turtles, lizards, and other desert creatures around Snow Mountain. Rattlesnakes are also native to this area, so it isn't advisable to go chasing after your ball if it strays off course. Just let the ball go. That way you can make sure that what plays in the desert stays in the desert.

CHIP SHOTS

Course contact info:
(800) 711-2883,
www.lvpaiutegolf.com

Par: 72
Yardage: 7,146 yards

Rating: 73.9
Slope: 125
Notable: It seems Pete Dye just couldn't stay away from this desert land in the middle of Paiute Indian country. He built three courses, one at a time: first came Snow Mountain, then Sun Mountain, then Wolf. The Bird Golf Academy is another highlight, with private or group instruction. The collection of teaching pros have more than 400 combined years of instruction under their belts.

On the green
◐◐ $129

Pete Dye's trademark bunkers and lush green grass are on Snow Mountain's 4th hole, set in the middle of the Nevada desert.

AFTER YOUR ROUND

A magical time: There are dozens of shows in Las Vegas from which to choose, and one of the more mystical is *Chriss Angel's Believe*. Angel takes audiences on a mystifying journey through the haunting inner workings of his mind and the surreal world created by Cirque du Soleil performers in this combination of video, live stunts, and unbelievable illusion.

More Cirque: *KÀ* by *Cirque du Soleil* at the MGM Grand tells a thrilling adventure story about twins who are separated by an attack on their Far Eastern Palace. Stunts and athleticism combined with drama and music are presented on a stage surrounded by elements that make you feel like you are part of the set. I've seen Cirque du Soleil shows in Orlando, Florida, and also in Vegas, and this was my favorite of their productions.

SCORECARD

Hole	1	2	3	4	5	6	7	8	9	out	
Yardage	389	426	557	180	458	562	337	198	421	3,528	
Par	4	4	5	3	4	5	4	3	4	36	
Hole	10	11	12	13	14	15	16	17	18	in	total
Yardage	418	611	427	342	192	456	198	529	445	3,618	7,146
Par	4	5	4	4	3	4	3	5	4	36	72

BREAKFAST HILL GOLF CLUB
GREENLAND, NEW HAMPSHIRE

There has not yet been a lot of golf history made at Breakfast Hill Golf Club, mainly because the outstanding New England facility is only about a decade old. But that isn't to say the 170-acre property lacks a fertile past.

The Sewall family has owned the land on which Breakfast Hill sits for more than two centuries, working rich New Hampshire farmland until 1956. Luke Sewall soon began envisioning the possibility of a championship golf course on the property, and his dream was realized in June 2000. Like the land his family tilled for 200 years, Sewall's perseverance has resulted in a fruitful place to play golf. The family still plays an active role: Mary Ann Sewall is owner, and sales and marketing director.

Fruits and vegetables no longer grow on their property, but in their place is emerald-green turf and thick rough. We're in New Hampshire, which means pines, pines, and more pines. Granite boulders are also native to the land, and the holes are often creatively situated to make the rocky hazards come into play.

The growing-in of a layout usually takes about ten to fifteen years, according to generally accepted standards of golf course maturation. By that time, the course and natural land have melded, planted trees have grown, and vegetation placed throughout the track has had plenty of time to take hold. Breakfast Hill is now in that time frame, and the course is in its prime.

The patient wait for the full grow-in has paid off, but Breakfast Hill has been a must-play in New Hampshire from day one. Brian Silva saw to that when he designed the course, which is about an hour's drive north of Boston — one of many cities near the centrally located facility. Those visiting Portsmouth, New Hampshire; Newburyport, Massachusetts; Andover, New Hampshire; and Portland, Maine, also can make a quick trip to Breakfast Hill. In other words, if you're in the right part of any of three states you're within driving distance.

Oh, yes. Driving distance. One of the most enjoyable and scenic holes on the course is the 14th, which is within easy driving distance of any of the four tee boxes you choose to use. Ranging from 86 to 177 yards, the hole is deceptive from the tee, which can spell trouble. Tall trees make for a dangerous picture in the back of the green and thick vegetation in the front provides a protective border.

Read closely because here comes some important local knowledge to avoid the junk on No 14. The hole is much shorter than it looks. The majority of mis-hits land in the thick trees in the back, eliminating any shot at par. Aim for the middle or left side of the two-tiered green and remember to ignore your instincts: play one club up.

Another favorite is the topsy-turvy, par-4 10th. The left side of the fairway cants to the center, which forces you to aim left off the tee to avoid rolling into the trees just off the right rough. But a bunker and an outcropping are on the left side, so you really have to be careful to clear the hazards with your drive. If you do get by the ledge and the sand, however, you have a solid shot at birdie. The hole checks in at just 362 yards from the back tees, so it's worth a good rip off the tee for a short approach to the putting surface.

Early morning rounds are suggested. It's the most peaceful time of day, and besides, it just makes good sense. At a course named Breakfast Hill, can you think of a healthier way to start the day?

AFTER YOUR ROUND

Make a splash: Water Country, a soaking-wet adventure, is just five miles away in Portsmouth. The wet and wild Dragon's Den and Double Geronimo are two of the fourteen slides or pools to give power to your shower.

A drier day: For those who'd rather stay dry, the Great Bay Discovery Center in Greenland offers a trail and boardwalk amid upland hardwood forests, freshwater wetlands, a salt marsh, and mudflats. It may not be as wild as Water Country, but there is plenty of wildlife: eagles, osprey, waterfowl,

---

CHIP SHOTS

Course contact info:
(603) 436-5001,
www.breakfasthill.com

Par: 71
Yardage: 6,493 yards

Rating: 71.5
Slope: 131
Notable: When Breakfast Hill opened, it had been nearly 40 years since a course was built on the New Hampshire coast. The rarity, plus the pristine golf and a practice area that includes driving areas and chipping and putting spots, makes Breakfast Hill a must-stop if you're looking for one of the area's top golf experiences.

On the green
○ $47

Breakfast Hill employs a rock formation, combined with a bunker, to keep players from hitting to the right of the fairway as they near the 17th green.

and several more species are readily visible.

Your fill at the Grille: There's an excellent, variety-filled menu for all three meals at the Breakfast Hill Grille, but let's pay special attention to – no surprise here – breakfast. Homemade corned beef hash, thick-cut brioche French toast, blueberry and strawberry pancakes, eggs Benedict or Florentine, and custom-made omelettes are fantastically filling. Lunch and dinner are also worth a stop if you play an afternoon round: Cobb salad, Reuben melt, spicy BBQ burger, marinated steak tips, blackened beef quesadilla, and baked haddock are among the delectable offerings.

OTHER PUBLIC COURSES IN NEW HAMPSHIRE WORTH A VISIT
- The Balsams Grand Resort (Panorama Course), Dixville Notch
- Mount Washington Resort GC, Bretton Woods

SCORECARD

Hole	1	2	3	4	5	6	7	8	9	out	
Yardage	380	490	399	179	525	141	408	356	363	3,241	
Par	4	5	4	3	5	3	4	4	4	36	
Hole	10	11	12	13	14	15	16	17	18	in	total
Yardage	362	473	572	311	177	359	395	158	445	3,252	6,493
Par	4	4	5	4	3	4	4	3	4	35	71

NEW HAMPSHIRE

OWL'S NEST RESORT & GOLF CLUB
CAMPTON, NEW HAMPSHIRE

Variety is a hallmark of northern New England golf, a part of the country that appreciates the game and the different looks it can take. There is a place — about two miles inland from the New Hampshire coast — where one course and one community succeed in capturing nearly every feature of the region's layouts.

At Owl's Nest Resort & Golf Club, there are some tough holes, with tight fairways and tiny, flat greens. Another hole might give you a generous fairway with a large putting surface. Some fairways are flat; others are built on rolling land. There are elevated tees, elevated greens, long holes, and short holes. And don't forget the White Mountains. Those views don't hurt.

Mark Mungeam had to use his imagination when he transformed an enormous sand pit into a golf course. His charge was to create a course that would serve as the centerpiece of a master-planned resort community. He left nothing in the bag when formulating the Campton layout.

The fact that the course is part of the landscape for residents who are regular visitors is one of the biggest reasons variety was such a consideration when constructing Owl's Nest. It's one thing to create an interesting golf course for players who might come two or three times a year. But for folks who play a couple of times a week and live two doors down from the club-house, it takes quite a golf course to keep them interested.

There is nothing mundane about Owl's Nest, where you can expect a little bit of everything. Water hazards come into play on five holes, and a few of the hazards pre-date the golf course. There are some man-made ponds, but wetlands and the Pemigewasset River comprise very real wet dangers.

The Pemi (as it's known by the locals) comes into play on the 5th hole, a 190-yard par-3 that produces peril for those who do anything but plop one on the green. The river is on the left, and more water on the right. It is a pretty sight, and also ominous, but it's best to ignore the views and focus on the golf ball. You'll need all the concentration you can muster.

No. 4 is one of those "toughies" that produce contrast at Owl's Nest. After playing the par-4 3rd, you immediately come upon a 542-yard par-5. The river comes into play again, this time on the right side, and it has a big effect on your tee shot. The best way to get a solid angle toward the green for your second shot is to play your drive to the right side of the fairway. But if you play too far right, your golf ball might end up swimming in the Pemigewasset River.

While the golf course and residential area co-exist nicely, they don't intrude upon one another. The real estate isn't in danger of being bombarded by errant golf balls because it allows the course enough room to flow smoothly.

"I think that's one of the reasons we get the recognition we continue to receive," Mungeam said, shortly after receiving a rating from *Golfweek* as one of New Hampshire's top tracks.

Success has not stopped Owl's Nest personnel from looking forward. Another nine holes will add another selling point to the community, not to mention even more variety to the golf experience.

CHIP SHOTS

Course contact info:
(888) 695-6378,
www.owlsnestgolf.com

Par: 72
Yardage: 6,818 yards

Rating: 73.3
Slope: 136
Notable: The folks who live at Owl's Nest don't have to go far to play one of New Hampshire's best golf courses. Builders were careful not to let the real estate crowd the golf. This philosophy has led to several national magazines giving recognition to Owl's Nest in several categories — including a "Top Residential Golf Course Development," and one of the "Top 100 You Can Play." No less than seven publications have given Owl's Nest awards in fifteen various categories over the years.

On the green
⛳ $64

AFTER YOUR ROUND

A whale of a trip: Departing from State Pier off the tiny New Hampshire coastline in Hampton Beach, you can go deep-sea fishing or take a fun, whale-watching trip.

Local history: At the Campton Historical Society, you'll learn about the Blair Bridge, originally built in 1829 and then rebuilt in 1870 when arsonists destroyed the original. Also on display are other 1800s structures, including the Town House and the 1903 Carriage House.

The back nine is the spot for scenery lovers at Owl's Nest, and No. 12 is a perfect place to take in the view.

Hole	1	2	3	4	5	6	7	8	9	out	
Yardage	400	433	441	542	190	343	213	380	541	3,483	
Par	4	4	4	5	3	4	3	4	5	36	
Hole	10	11	12	13	14	15	16	17	18	in	total
Yardage	152	356	428	521	220	282	473	526	377	3,335	6,818
Par	3	4	4	5	3	4	4	5	4	36	72

The 4th at Portsmouth takes a late and pesky left turn on the way home.

NEW HAMPSHIRE

PORTSMOUTH COUNTRY CLUB
GREENLAND, NEW HAMPSHIRE

Persistence paid off for those who wanted a quality place to play at Portsmouth Country Club. In 1901, a group of Portsmouth businessmen hired Alex Findlay to build a golf course and five weeks later, nine holes were finished. Then, in 1933, nine more holes were added. But this is far from the end of the story.

The U.S. government took control of the property in the early 1950s to build a New Hampshire bomber base, seizing the land by eminent domain. By 1956, the government no longer had use for the property, and Robert Trent Jones, Sr. was hired to design another layout. The result was one of the finest golf courses in an area dotted with decent tracks.

The people of Portsmouth, and those who visit, are grateful for the dedication to golf shown by everyone at this country club. What would you rather have in your backyard, a bomber base or a golf course? That's an easy choice, as is a decision to play on one of New Hampshire's top tracks.

Several of the Granite State's fine golf courses lie in the White Mountains, but a trip toward the shore of Great Bay unveils the Portsmouth Country Club, one of the best coastal layouts in the entire New England area. The Robert Trent Jones, Sr., design was opened in 1957 and has built a reputation as one of the state's best courses — public or private.

Jane Blalock, who won twenty-seven tournaments and more than $1.2 million on the LPGA tour, learned the game at Portsmouth and is a shining example of the benefits that come from growing up on a challenging golf course. She started playing at thirteen, and says she was "weaned as a golfer" at Portsmouth. She was the New Hampshire and New England junior champion in 1963, and carried that success into a career spanning twenty-plus years.

Blalock credits her training at PCC as one of the contributing factors.

"When I've hosted charity tournaments on this course, the pros always say, 'No wonder you can play the wind. You grew up on this monster.'"

Wind indeed is a near constant at Portsmouth, and players discover early in the round the advantages of keeping the ball low. One of the prime examples of how wind affects play comes at No. 14, the toughest and most scenic hole on the course.

The 14th is a dogleg left and the green sits at the extreme end of an isthmus that juts far into the Great Bay. The putting surface is lengthy, but it is but a thin ribbon of green that offers little welcome to those trying to avoid the surrounding waters.

The approach shot is not the first time you see perilous waters at No. 14. Water comes into play off the tee, on your second shot, and on the approach. And, if you don't happen to hit the green on your third shot, you're not done with the water yet. Landing in a greenside bunker means you better be accurate blasting out or you might just wind up in the bay.

The "coming out of a chute" effect is not unique to No. 14. Many holes at Portsmouth force low, line drives off the tee to stay out of the wind between the surrounding trees to the landing areas. The fairways open up nicely a hundred yards or so from the tee, and you can score if you're hitting it straight.

But watch out for the water hazards that come into play on five holes. None of them are nearly as intrusive as the bay on No. 14, but there are several that can cause you fits if you don't offer them respect.

Respect should come easy at Portsmouth Country Club. When you consider how hard these people had to work to get this course off the ground (twice), it's not difficult to doff your cap.

AFTER YOUR ROUND

Bery good time: The Strawbery Banke Museum features quaint and educational presentations on colonial history, gingerbread houses, sewing exhibits, Tom Sawyer tales, and many other subjects. Many mansions dot the Greenland and Portsmouth area, including the Moffatt-Ladd House and the Wentworth-Coolidge Mansion — the home of New Hampshire's first colonial governor. Several mansions are open to the public for a fee.

CHIP SHOTS

Course contact info:
(603) 436-9791,
www.portsmouthcc.net

Par: 72
Yardage: 7,072 yards

Rating: 74.1
Slope: 127
Notable: Portsmouth Country Club has played host to many prestigious tournaments, including the 2009 New England Amateur Golf Championship.

On the green
$65

Hole	1	2	3	4	5	6	7	8	9	out	
Yardage	401	445	390	516	175	443	530	226	403	3,529	
Par	4	4	4	5	3	4	5	3	4	36	
Hole	10	11	12	13	14	15	16	17	18	in	total
Yardage	435	539	472	171	525	341	167	445	448	3,543	7,072
Par	4	5	4	3	5	4	3	4	4	36	72

NEW JERSEY

ATLANTIC CITY COUNTRY CLUB
ATLANTIC CITY, NEW JERSEY

Abner Smith had no idea when he lined up his shot on Atlantic City Country Club's 12th hole, more than 100 years ago, that he was about to create a term that would become a part of golf vernacular forever. Quite by happenstance, a purely smote shot combined with a comment by someone in his weekend-outing foursome made history.

The group from suburban Philadelphia approached the par-3 12th just as they had the first eleven. Smith stood over his ball on the windy day and struck one right on the nose. The shot plopped on the green, rolled toward the hole, and stopped mere inches from the cup. After he sank the easy putt for a 1 under par, the historic phrase was uttered: "That was a bird of a shot," making reference to Smith's tee shot.

Players at ACCC started using the term "birdie" when they scored 1 under par on a hole, and visitors to the club took it back to their own clubs back home. The term spread . . . and spread . . . and spread. Although there is some disagreement on what year the event occurred — some say 1899, others 1903 — the birth of the birdie does not seem to be a clubhouse myth.

"It's been well documented," says Kenny Robinson, the caddie master and the main man behind the pro-shop counter at the club.

A story by golf historian William Kelly offers credence to the approximate time of the term's origination by tracking down records of its earliest use. He documents what is believed to be the first written reference in 1911 when an article in *McCleans Magazine* reported " .

. . Lansborough followed with a birdie, straight down the course about 215 yards."

British golf writer Bernard Darwin wrote in 1913 about the American term that had not yet caught on in Great Britain: "It takes a day or two for the English onlooker to understand that . . . a 'birdie' is a hole done in a stroke under par."

The coining of such a term at a club that opened in 1897 gives a clear picture of Atlantic City Country Club's standing in the storied history of American golf. The origination of "birdie" may have been an accident, but ACCC's place in golf lore is quite by design.

The course has stood the test of time amazingly well. It is still considered New Jersey's top daily-fee layout, and while tradition is rich, the maintenance practices are up to date. The dedication to upkeep produces immaculate conditions that rival any private club in the country.

No. 14 is one of the "featured" holes (which seems a more classy term than "signature") at ACCC. "Salt Marsh," as No. 14 has been known for more than a century, is a short par-4 at 339 yards, but don't let the abbreviated distance fool you. The skilled player can occasionally drive the hole because the prevailing wind is strong and at the player's back. But that kind of aggressive play can lead to scorecard-altering consequences. Any shot short of the green brings the salt marsh into play, which, of course, swallows any chance at par. Even a successful conservative shot off the tee leaves a forced carry off the marsh to the green.

Standing on the "Salt Marsh" tee, it's incredible to think that players at the turn of the twentieth century were facing the same challenge. Although it was unthinkable to carry the marsh with a drive in those days, the views and the second shot over the marsh were precisely the same.

Keeping up with modern standards while not intruding on golf lore is sometimes a difficult mix. But the folks at Atlantic City Country Club have found the perfect equation.

AFTER YOUR ROUND

Another look: Today, the nearby action features something completely different than it did in 1897. Casinos within walking distance include the Trump Taj Mahal, Harrah's, Caesars, Showboat, and Bally's. But the Atlantic City area offers more. Steel Pier amusement park is a great place for kids to have as much fun as the parents do at the gaming tables. Giant slides, a double-deck carousel, a Ferris

CHIP SHOTS

Course contact info:
(609) 236-4401,
www.atlanticcitycountryclub.com

Par: 70
Yardage: 6,577 yards

Rating: 72.0
Slope: 128
Notable: A sampling of the tournaments held at the Atlantic City Country Club and those who won them give an indication of the club's justifiably celebrated history: the 1901 U.S. Amateur (Walter Travis), the 1948 U.S. Women's Open (Babe Zaharias), and the 1990 U.S. Senior Open (Don January).

On the green
◐ ◐ ● $100

Crisp fairway, thick rough, pristine sand, manicured greens, and a stately clubhouse offer a complete picture of the historic Atlantic City Country Club.

wheel, helicopter rides, dragon jets, trampolines, and bumper cars are some of the attractions that offer helter-skelter amusement.

OTHER PUBLIC COURSES IN NEW JERSEY WORTH A VISIT

- Ballyowen GC, Hardyston
- Neshanic Valley GC, Neshanic Station
- Pine Hill GC, Pine Hill
- Royce Brook GC (East Course), Somerville
- Sand Barrens GC, Swainton
- Scotland Run GC, Monroe Township
- Seaview Resort & Spa (Bay Course), Absecon
- Twisted Dune GC, Egg Harbor Township
- Vineyard GC at Renault, Egg Harbor City

SCORECARD

Hole	1	2	3	4	5	6	7	8	9	out	
Yardage	450	368	353	144	445	592	452	196	452	3,452	
Par	4	4	4	3	4	5	4	3	4	35	
Hole	10	11	12	13	14	15	16	17	18	in	total
Yardage	488	432	134	553	339	190	400	157	432	3,125	6,577
Par	5	4	3	5	4	3	4	3	4	35	70

A pond on the left and trees on the right frame a narrow strip of entrance to the West Course's 15th green. Brave players have a chance to carry the water to cut distance from the hole.

NEW JERSEY

BLUE HERON PINES GOLF CLUB
(WEST COURSE)
COLOGNE, NEW JERSEY

Atlantic City is a great place to play. You can shop near the piers, and there's casino action twenty-four hours a day. The town is a virtual playground, and we're not talking swing-sets, monkey bars, and merry-go-rounds. Not all of the recreation, however, is centered in the amped-up downtown sector. There's another brand of fun in the area. You can play a great round of golf.

There are a number of excellent golf courses within a stiff ocean breeze of the casinos and shopping areas. Located fifteen minutes from the boardwalk and less than an hour from Philadelphia is the thirty-six-hole Blue Heron Pines Golf Club, housing two courses that *Golf Digest* rated "four-star."

With a rating of well over 70 and a slope in the mid- 130s, Blue Heron's West Course has plenty of star

power. There is challenge and distance for even the most skilled player, but five sets of tees also make it possible for even us average public-access guys to have an enjoyable round.

The West is a straightforward, sturdy, daily-fee course that cuts through the Jersey pines. It isn't an easy course, by any means, but there aren't any tricked-up holes that you would call unfair.

Before Stephen Kay designed the course, he toured some of the famed tracks in the area. Kay realized he was in excellent company with nearby layouts such as Pine Valley in New Jersey and Bethpage Black in New York.

By the time Blue Heron opened in 1993, it was clear Kay had held his own, even among other prime courses. He has called Blue Heron one of his best designs.

"To me, one of the defining characteristics of a great golf course is the better golfer you are, the tougher the course plays," Kay said during a news conference to announce the course's opening. "In other words, it challenges the low handicappers without bringing the middle and high handicappers to their knees. I think that is true of Blue Heron Pines."

After stepping off the 18th green, most players offer rave reviews of Blue Heron's West Course as they traipse to the clubhouse. The fairways are like carpet and the greens are even smoother. The rough, however, is another matter. It is deep, thick, and penal — not a place you want to be.

Among the West's highlights is No. 14, a 518-yard par-5 that resembles "Hell's Half Acre" on the 7th hole at Pine Valley. Then comes the 421-yard, par-4 15th, which many Blue Heron staffers label the toughest test on the course. From the back tees, No. 15 demands a 200-yard carry over waste area. Then players must deal with a precarious pond to reach the green.

Blue Heron added the East Course in May, 2000, and the Steve Smyers design has given players another option at the 350-acre property. The East is a stark contrast to the West's traditional parkland-style layout, where water hazards come into play on seven holes.

The East is an American links-style course, with wide fairways, large greens, and many deep and menacing bunkers. It is a bump-and-run, fast-and-firm exercise in golf.

You might expect to pay top dollar for a club as striking as Blue Heron Pines, but stay-and-play packages actually make it quite reasonable. It's also advisable to examine options other than prime time to save on greens fees. Even if you pay top dollar, the price is within reason. Blue Heron is one of those places you might make special arrangements to visit. For instance, if you play once a week at your local muni during the summer, you might want to skip a week, save your shekels, and visit Blue Heron.

AFTER YOUR ROUND

Down by the boardwalk: After hitting the links, there's plenty of time to hit the tables. On my visits to Atlantic City, I've found that while it's no Vegas, the downtown area has revitalized itself to become a pretty hopping place to be. Blue Heron Pines is only fifteen minutes from the casinos, where neon glitz serves as quite a contrast to a peaceful day on the course. Don't forget your sunglasses.

Phinding Philly: Atlantic City is less than an hour from Philadelphia, a city that serves as a symbol of our nation's independence and as a pillar of its history. It is also a very family-friendly metropolis, with attractions such as the Philadelphia Zoo, Independence National Historical Park, and the Please Touch Museum. Other fascinating family activities include seeing the Liberty Bell up close and standing next to a Tyrannosaurus rex at the Academy of Natural Sciences.

CHIP SHOTS

Course contact info:
(609) 965-1800,
www.blueheronpines.com

Par: 72
Yardage: 6,805 yards

Rating: 72.8
Slope: 135
Notable: Besides two high-quality and contrasting golf courses, Blue Heron Pines features a 36,000-square-foot practice range with three greens and bunkers. There is also a 19,000-square-foot clubhouse, housing a restaurant and pro shop with a full line of equipment and apparel.

On the green
◉◯ $79

SCORECARD

Hole	1	2	3	4	5	6	7	8	9	out	
Yardage	315	180	533	183	413	412	323	575	420	3,354	
Par	4	3	5	3	4	4	4	5	4	36	
Hole	10	11	12	13	14	15	16	17	18	in	total
Yardage	395	130	415	374	518	421	218	451	529	3,451	6,805
Par	4	3	4	4	5	4	3	4	5	36	72

NEW MEXICO

PAA-KO RIDGE GOLF CLUB
SANDIA PARK, NEW MEXICO

The name Dye sits atop, or near the top, of nearly all lists of modern-day golf architects – Pete Dye has reached legendary status for the world-renowned courses he has constructed, and just as much for the unique style he has developed. But there's another Dye in town.

This sheriff is Ken Dye, one of the hottest architects around, and perhaps his best work sits twenty minutes east of downtown Albuquerque, New Mexico. Ken Dye created a natural-feeling work of art in Paa-Ko Ridge Golf Club and the staff at the twenty-seven-hole facility further enhances the atmosphere with a humble pride that is obvious upon the first step into the clubhouse. They have a great club and they know it. Of course, it isn't hard to figure out. Suburbia is left behind; no real estate here. Rounds are brisk at the foot of the Sandia Mountains, several holes are of the jaw-dropping variety within canopies of juniper and piñon evergreens, and a profound peace increases with every progressing step.

Even more unbelievable than the beauty, however, are the stunningly low greens fees. At the right time of season, at twilight, you can get on Paa-Ko Ridge for about forty bucks. The average price is about $75, which is still quite remarkable when you consider courses of this quality often cost twice as much to play. It's a paradise for all players, but it's particularly attractive for those of us accustomed to paying this price for local munis. This place is worth a special trip to Sandia Park, whether it's a trek of forty miles or four hundred.

Several ranges are visible at different points on the course, and they aren't the only ups and downs that are part of the Paa-Ko Ridge experience. Some of the elevation changes on the golf course itself are striking and downright precarious. Two par-3s fall off 100 yards from the tee to the green, and the view of your ball sailing toward the green with the mountains as a backdrop is one of those "I'll never forget this" moments.

Indeed, Paa-Ko Ridge is filled with postcard views, but don't think it's a walk in the park. It measures a whopping 7,562 yards with some monster holes along the way. One of the par-3s measures more than 225 yards and two others come in at more than 250. Sure, there is help from the massive drop to the greens and the high elevation, but No. 14 commands a 272-yard shot to the green.

Whew. Paa-Ko Ridge is a toughie throughout, and the finishing three are perhaps the biggest treats on the course.

The 16th is one of those golf-poster moments, and it's also great fun to play. Water on the left keeps you honest on the 228-yard par-3, and mastering the multi-mound green is no easy task.

Yet another elevated tee kicks off No. 17, and it offers perhaps the best view on the course. Five surrounding mountain ranges can be seen from this hole, there is a

Huge, ominous bunkers are a common sight at Paa-Ko Ridge, as is the majesty of the Sandia Mountains.

ninety-foot drop to the landing area, and you can take in the labyrinth-like runs of three nearby ski resorts. It's fairly difficult to concentrate on hitting the ball, even if you do get the opportunity to belt it off a cliff.

The finishing hole is bittersweet. The 474-yard par-4 is a great hole, demanding a carry over a gulch to another multi-tiered green. It's a challenging chore, but it's fun. What isn't so enjoyable is the realization that the round is over.

You almost can't help looking over at No. 1 to see if it's clear. You just might be able to get off for the third and final nine on the property.

AFTER YOUR ROUND

Folksy fun: Fans of art have many options after enjoying Ken Dye's Paa-Ko Ridge masterpiece. Artists call New Mexico a wonderful place to display their works because so many of the residents are fans of multicultural exhibits. Two examples are Tinkertown Museum, a quaint and colorful folk art museum that has called New Mexico home for more than a quarter century; and Guilloume Fine Arts, which features drawings, bronze editions, and oil paintings by Colombian immigrant Guiloume (one name . . . you know these artist types). The Gallery of the Sandias is also a popular stop.

CHIP SHOTS

Course contact info: (866) 898-5987, www.paakoridge.com

Par: 72
Yardage: 7,562 yards (first 18)

Rating: 72.0
Slope: 138
Notable: Architect Ken Dye used a minimalistic approach at Paa-Ko Ridge: "I am most pleased with what I didn't do here," he said upon completion of the twenty-seven holes. "I saved as much of the rock outcropping and native vegetation as I could. I disturbed as little land as possible."

On the green
$75

OTHER PUBLIC COURSES IN NEW MEXICO WORTH A VISIT

- Black Mesa GC, La Mesilla
- The Championship GC, University of New Mexico, Albuquerque
- Pueblo de Cochiti GC, Conchiti
- Sandia GC, Albuquerque
- Santa Ana GC, Santa Ana
- Taos CC, Taos
- Twin Warriors, Santa Ana Pueblo

SCORECARD

Hole	1	2	3	4	5	6	7	8	9	out	
Yardage	429	394	604	183	562	327	496	265	477	3,737	
Par	4	4	5	3	5	4	4	3	4	36	
Hole	10	11	12	13	14	15	16	17	18	in	total
Yardage	416	449	541	386	272	640	228	419	474	3,825	7,562
Par	4	4	5	4	3	5	3	4	4	36	72

NEW MEXICO

PINION HILLS GOLF COURSE
FARMINGTON, NEW MEXICO

Ken Dye must have a thing for New Mexico. In 2000, he wrapped up his design at Paa-Ko Ridge Golf Club, a stunning public course and one of the best bargains in the Southwest. But he had already put himself on the map in the Land of Enchantment in 1989, constructing a golf course that would later be named the No. 1 municipal track in America.

No doubt about it, Dye digs New Mexico. And his masterful digging in the dirt resulted in the creation of Pinion Hills Golf Course, the pride of Farmington and the first of what would become a brilliant Dye twosome.

Pinion Hills is a 200-mile northwestern journey up U.S. Route 550 from Paa-Ko Ridge, about a three-and-a-half hour drive. Let's see, you get up at 6:00 a.m., hit your first drive at 6:45 at Paa-Ko Ridge, and by 11:00 you're done; drive to Pinion Hills, step up to the first tee about 3:30 p.m. and finish up in time for a late supper. Now that sounds like a day to Dye, er, die for. Sorry.

Sandstone canyons, lengthy arroyos, and plenty of rock outcroppings beautify Pinion Hills, and the course sits perfectly within the environment — coloring the area with deep, green turf and alluring, blue aqua.

The course is beautiful, but it also can be a beast. The 7,000-plus-yard challenge requires length off the tee, but you can't just rip away. Doglegs, tricky bunkers, those pretty but pesky outcroppings, and the cavernous canyons will force you to call on strategy as well as brawn.

Much as he did with Paa-Ko Ridge's pleasing and punishing finishing holes, Dye saves his best for last at Pinion Hills. Only this time he added a quirk: the highlights of a round filled with super moments don't come on the very last holes of the day. They come on the final hole of each nine.

No. 9 measures nearly 600 yards and is the longest hole on the course. Don't think about reaching this in two unless you're feeling sharp as a razor and are ready to strike the ball like a laser.

Conservative play on the outward nine's finisher is the smart play, and it would be advisable even if the length were a bit shorter. The quest for par, let alone birdie, is compounded by two arroyos that split the fairway into three sections. Length, as you see, is no guarantee of par.

In spite of the arroyos, it is imperative to stay in the fairway on No. 9, especially on your second and third shots.

Bunkers are everywhere, particularly on the right side. Miss left, and you might be OK, but an errant shot right almost certainly means trouble.

No. 18 is a par-4, and like No. 9, you have to be long and straight. A large bunker on the right side narrows the fairway where your drive might land, and then the fairway takes a gentle bend right to the green. The hole checks in at 471 yards, fairly hefty for a par-4, and it plays even longer with a prevailing head wind.

The wind in your face can significantly slow down your ball, but there is one good thing about that breeze. Depending on the strength and frequency of the gusts, it might also slow your walk toward the 18th green. This allows a few more seconds to soak in the waning moments of a sparkling round.

CHIP SHOTS

Course contact info:
(505) 326-6066,
www.fmtn.org, click on
"attractions," scroll down
to "Pinion Hills Golf Course"

Par: 72
Yardage: 7,222 yards

Rating: 73.9
Slope: 139
Notable: When *Golf Digest* named Pinion Hills the "No. 1 Municipal Golf Course in America" in 2002, the Farmington facility bested community-owned tracks such as San Diego, California's Torrey Pines and Farmingdale, New York's Bethpage Black — both of which have hosted the U.S. Open.

On the green
$41

AFTER YOUR ROUND

A treasure trove: Farmington is engulfed by baubles of scenic sites and historic happenings. Chaco Canyon, Shiprock Pinnacle, Monument Valley, old trading posts, and Aztec Ruins National Monument are nearby and each makes for an eye-opening and educational visit. The "Aztec" ruins — just a few miles from Farmington in the northwest corner of New Mexico — were mistakenly thought by early white explorers to be relics of the Mexican Aztec civilization. In reality, the ruins go back to the twelfth century and were created by tribes indigenous to the region. It is presumed that the ruins are from the Mesa Verde Tribe, which had close ties with Chaco culture. Examples of Chaco ruins can be found fifty-five miles south of the Aztec ruins.

No. 6 at Pinion Hills is a boulder-filled beauty tucked neatly out of view from the rest of the world.

SCORECARD											
Hole	1	2	3	4	5	6	7	8	9	out	
Yardage	411	438	453	169	358	228	417	563	597	3,634	
Par	4	4	4	3	4	3	4	5	5	36	
Hole	10	11	12	13	14	15	16	17	18	in	total
Yardage	438	422	235	528	348	157	441	548	471	3,588	7,222
Par	4	4	3	5	4	3	4	5	4	36	72

NEW YORK

BETHPAGE STATE PARK
(BLACK COURSE)
FARMINGDALE, NY

All golfers can gain access to play Bethpage Black, a public course that has become the stuff of legend. But anyone with a high handicap better bring plenty of golf balls. In fact, a sign at the entrance reads: "Warning — The Black Course is an Extremely Difficult Course Which We Recommend Only for Highly Skilled Golfers."

That seems to be a pretty clear indicator of what can be expected. Players face narrow fairways, high roughs, well-placed bunkers, and small greens to make the Black a mind-boggling test from No. 1 all the way through to No. 18.

And when the U.S. Golf Association grows ankle-high rough and turns the greens into sheets of ice for the U.S. Open, anyone but a PGA Tour pro better look for cover on one of the other four courses on the Bethpage State Park property.

Bethpage Black is not only regarded as public royalty in the world of golf today, it has a history that goes back nearly eighty years. In the early 1930s, famed architect A.W. Tillinghast was hired to design three golf courses to add to the two that already existed. The demand for golf was growing, and Tillinghast built the Red, Blue, and Black courses to keep up with a new hunger for the game. The thirst to play golf at Bethpage seems as unquenchable as ever today, with an average of more than 30,000 rounds played annually.

Tillinghast was the architect of many world-famous courses, and Bethpage Black was one of his last. Many golf historians consider the Black Course to be Tillinghast's masterpiece.

The popularity of Bethpage Black makes it difficult for players to get on the course, but it is completely public and available to all if a spot opens up. The other four courses are pretty decent substitutes, but that's all they are. Imagine if Babe Ruth had four younger brothers who were .300 hitters. They'd be pretty decent players, but Babe Ruth is Babe Ruth.

The Black is what brings 'em back.

The price is another amazing aspect of all the Bethpage courses. Residents of New York pay in the $50 range to play the Black, and non-residents pay $100. The other courses are a bit cheaper, but the inexpensive price

The 4th hole at Bethpage Black offers little room for error. Bunkers dot a thin fairway and also provide ample protection for an elevated green.

tag to play a U.S. Open course isn't equaled anywhere in the nation.

The price of admission may be inexpensive, but there are severe prices to pay when a golfer gets out on the walking-only golf course. The yardage, rating, and slope in our "Chip Shots" section are all from the championship tees, but even from the middle tees, Bethpage Black rates as one of the toughest courses in the northeast.

In addition to difficulty, PGA.com rates Bethpage Black one of the world's most beautiful courses. Joe Rehor, director of golf at Bethpage for twenty-nine years, says he recalls the days when the course was less than the picturesque place to play that it is today. The raw material has always been there, but a renewed sense of appreciation by state officials resulted in increased maintenance funding to restore Bethpage Black's beauty.

Tillinghast's design always has been considered excellent, but several renovations and improvements needed to be made to bring conditions up to the prestigious level of the Black Course today. Drainage upgrades, regrassing, tree trimming, and various other projects restored the luster.

Despite the incredible number of rounds the course

The options are wide, including zoos and aquariums, hiking, nature preserves, a game farm, theater, amusement parks, museums and many, many other activities. After playing the best public-course bargain in America, there are plenty of equally enjoyable highlights ahead. The Long Island Game Farm Wildlife Park & Children's Zoo is one of the top family attractions in the area. The zoo, which celebrated its fortieth year in 2009, is located in Manorville, a forty-five-minute drive from Farmingdale. In addition to lions, tigers, zebras, and an eighteen-foot giraffe, there are prize-winning sunflowers and other farm-and-garden exhibits.

CHIP SHOTS

Course contact info:
(516) 249-0707,
http://nysparks.state.ny.us/golf/info.asp?golfID=12

Par: 71
Yardage: 7,279 yards

Rating: 76.6
Slope: 148
Notable: Any golfer can gain access to the monster that is Bethpage Black, except, of course, when the U.S. Open comes to town. The national championship was won here by Tiger Woods in 2002 and made a return appearance in 2009.

On the green
◯◯ $100 (New York residents pay $50)

hosts each year, Rehor has figured out a masterful way of keeping the course well conditioned to preserve its reputation. The course is closed on Mondays, but that's not going to stop a persistent player, who will eagerly come back another day for the chance to play a round at Bethpage Black.

AFTER YOUR ROUND

It takes a village: Farmingdale is a village with a population under 10,000, but this small town happens to be on Long Island, a big-time center of recreation and attractions.

 OTHER PUBLIC COURSES IN NEW YORK WORTH A VISIT
• Atunyote GC at Turning Stone Resort, Verona
• Bethpage State Park (Red Course), Farmingdale
• Leatherstocking GC, Cooperstown
• The Links at Hiawatha Landing, Apalachin
• Montauk Downs State Park GC, Montauk Point
• Saratoga National GC, Saratoga
• Shenendoah GC at Turning Stone Resort, Verona
• Tallgrass CC, Shoreham

SCORECARD

Hole	1	2	3	4	5	6	7	8	9	out	
Yardage	430	366	181	522	455	411	576	220	397	3,558	
Par	4	4	3	5	4	4	5	3	4	36	
Hole	10	11	12	13	14	15	16	17	18	in	total
Yardage	477	444	486	566	165	463	487	213	420	3,721	7,279
Par	4	4	4	5	3	4	4	3	4	35	71

The 180-yard, par-3 12th is a perfect illustration of the difference between the mania at Cameron Indoor Stadium and the serenity at Duke University Golf Club.

NORTH CAROLINA

DUKE UNIVERSITY GOLF CLUB
DURHAM, NORTH CAROLINA

College basketball fans everywhere are familiar with Duke University. National championships, Coach K, and decades of excellence are staples of Blue Devils basketball. There is one other aspect of the program that is just as prominent: the bouncing, bare-chested, wig-wearing, face-painting fans in Cameron Indoor Stadium.

The Duke University Golf Club shares some of these same characteristics. It is an outstanding golf course that has been around for decades. Like the national championship banners hanging from the rafters in the stadium, the golf course has a few prizes of its own: it has been host to the NCAA National Championship and the course has been rated as high as "No. 2 Among North Carolina Public Courses" by *Golf Digest*.

But luckily for golfers seeking a serene round, the golf course strays from the basketball arena in one very important regard. The "Cameron Crazies" yell and scream in the stadium, but at the golf course they assume a quieter tone that befits the dignity of Duke.

The golf course sits just across from the ivy-walled campus and is a jump shot away from the raucous atmosphere of the basketball arena. It is a peaceful, sleeping giant among courses in North Carolina, a state loaded with behemoths in the world of illustrious public golf courses. The loudest sounds on this part of campus will come from your foursome partners or from the birds chirping as they nest in the Carolina pines.

Class is a word laced into virtually everything associated with Duke University, and the golf course, more than a half-century old, is a tradition-rich example.

Built in 1957, the layout was designed by the great Robert Trent Jones, Sr. The tight, mounded fairways are lined with huge pines from manicured tees to slick greens. A feeling of solitude prevails once you get past the 2nd hole; the pines envelop the senses and block out the rest of the world.

Par-3s are intriguing aspects of the Duke layout, a prevalent trait of many of Jones's course designs. The lengths are 159, 172, 180, and 216 yards, and club selection isn't the only issue — errant shots are harshly penalized. Even if your tee shot finds the mark, par is no guarantee. Curvaceous putting surfaces can create 3-putts if your first shot doesn't cozy up to the pin.

Former Duke President Preston Few and two coaches — Wallace Wade and Eddie Cameron — first envisioned a campus golf course in the early 1930s. The trio inspected portions of the Duke Forest, surveying possible sites. Famed golf course architect Perry Maxwell drew up plans in 1941, but instead of a golf course, the university changed directions and built the Duke Faculty Club on that plot of ground.

Construction on an adjacent piece of property was scheduled to begin in the mid-1940s, but the onset of World War II delayed the project. Plans resurfaced at the war's conclusion, and Jones was called in to mold the new property — chosen for its blend of elevation changes amid mildly rolling terrain.

"A great architect should create the illusion that the golf holes were on the ground just lying there, waiting to be grassed over," Jones said.

This quote reveals his philosophy of golf-course design in general, but he could have been speaking specifically about his masterpiece at Duke. The Cameron Crazies might not set foot on the place, but they don't know what they're missing.

CHIP SHOTS

Course contact info:
(919) 681-2288,
www.golf.duke.edu

Par: 72
Yardage: 7,045 yards

Rating: 73.9
Slope: 137
Notable: This golf course's commitment to quality is spelled out in the first line of its Mission Statement: "The Duke University Golf Club believes in four core values: integrity, honesty, respect and cooperation." That's been the philosophy at the golf course since it opened in 1957. The same philosophy has held true since 1838 when Methodists and Quakers in the present-day town of Trinity founded Duke University. The school moved to Durham in 1892 and has been there ever since.

On the green
○ $45

AFTER YOUR ROUND

Come to Cameron: If you happen to play the Duke course during an overlap of the golf and college basketball season, you won't be disappointed with the quality of hoops nor with the zany atmosphere at Cameron Indoor Stadium. I've been to plenty of games during my years covering sports, but I can't think of an experience quite like Duke basketball.

Going to the chapel: The Duke University Chapel was built in the early 1930s and the tower of the chapel soars 210 feet above the campus. It is open for viewing year-round, and is another facet of the university that — like the golf course — offers a peaceful look at the university.

Planting a seed: In 1920, after fundraisers came up short in their efforts to create a lake in the valley near Anderson Street in Durham, the first seed was planted in Sarah P. Duke Gardens. Since then, it has become a beautiful garden spot. After a peaceful day on the golf course, serenity can continue with a visit to Duke Gardens.

OTHER PUBLIC COURSES IN NORTH CAROLINA WORTH A VISIT

- Grove Park Inn Resort & Spa, Asheville
- Linville GC, Linville
- Mid Pines Inn & GC, Southern Pines
- Pinehurst No. 4, Pinehurst
- Pinehurst No. 8, Pinehurst
- River's Edge GC, Shallotte

SCORECARD

Hole	1	2	3	4	5	6	7	8	9	out	
Yardage	450	428	387	159	401	395	572	172	491	3,455	
Par	4	4	4	3	4	4	5	3	5	36	
Hole	10	11	12	13	14	15	16	17	18	in	total
Yardage	427	551	180	372	548	216	398	441	457	3,590	7,045
Par	4	5	3	4	5	3	4	4	4	36	72

PINE NEEDLES LODGE & GOLF CLUB
SOUTHERN PINES, NORTH CAROLINA

Don't bother trying to select the best hole at Pine Needles Lodge & Golf Club. Even the folks who run the club can only narrow it down to five. This collection of beauties — Nos. 3, 5, 10, 11, and 18 — are what they call the "key holes."

There's something else to consider: the other thirteen aren't bad, either.

Those lucky enough to play Pine Needles undoubtedly will agree that the course is magnificent, but no one at the club will take offense if your opinion differs on the "key holes," or even your "favorite hole." Pine Needles' superior reputation is recognized worldwide, and there must be millions of combinations making up visitors' Pine's peaks.

Famed architect Donald Ross designed Pine Needles, which opened in 1928, and it originally latched onto the coattails of the legendary Pinehurst next door, which drew visitors from the north and beyond. Pine Needles' success was not immediate and it went bankrupt during World War II. Soon, however, when Warren and Peggy Kirk Bell led a group of investors in the purchase of Pine Needles in the mid-1950s, it began to draw attention.

Today, the Bell family still runs the operation, which has pulled free of the need to rely on Pinehurst's fame and has formed a magnificent reputation of its own. The course's status took a leap when it played host to the 1996 U.S. Women's Open, and jumped even further after a stunning renovation in 2004.

Pine Needles closed for nearly six months to achieve a difficult goal. The renovation was designed to stay true to Ross's original layout while at the same time meeting the standard of the new breed of golfer and incorporating the latest in club and ball technology.

John Fought was given the duty: he added 300 yards to the course, reshaped bunkers, cut back trees that had grown to form unwanted canopies over once-strategic areas, and enlarged greens to add challenge to putts. The golf world took notice in a big way. The U.S. Women's Open revisited in 2007, and Fought's work was met with rave reviews.

And what of those key holes? Each combines beauty with intrigue, but each in its own way.

No. 3 (pictured) is perhaps the most scenic on the course, including wetlands, a pond that forces accuracy off the tee, and a large, sloping green surrounded by pines. It is a par-3 that measures less than 150 yards, but anything less than precision makes the hole seem much longer.

There's the par-3 5th, where you reach the highest point on the front nine; the par-5, dogleg-left 10th, where bunkers and a pond can swallow shots; the 11th, which requires a tee shot through a chute of pines; and the 18th, a beauty of a finisher with a chance at a short approach shot. But that green can be difficult — to hold and to putt.

Whether it's the key holes or the rest of the course, you can be assured that the conditioning will be pristine year-round, even when some other courses in the area might be thirsting. When the greens were reworked in 1994, conditioning and challenge were given equal priority.

Pine Needles is one of the foremost public-access golf courses in the country, and it includes one of the most pleasurable resort experiences around. One other reason to visit: you get to pick your own favorite five.

AFTER YOUR ROUND

Golf, golf, and more golf: Perhaps not "what to see," but "whom to see" is a suggestion at Pine Needles. There is an outstanding staff at the Pine Needles learning center, founded by the legendary Peggy Kirk Bell. Putting greens, chipping areas, practice bunkers, and driving areas offer plenty of room to iron out your game. For those really serious about improvement, there's the Pine Needles Golf Academy — a three-day workshop that includes in-depth sessions on both the full swing and the short game.

CHIP SHOTS

Course contact info:
(910) 692-7111,
www.pineneedles-midpines.com

Par: 71
Yardage: 7,015 yards

Rating: 73.5
Slope: 135
Notable: Don't rule out playing Pine Needles, even though it is pretty pricey. Helpful hints to reduce costs: try to travel with several friends to get group rates, make sure to ask about the specials (including stay-and-play packages), and play during non-peak season.

On the green
●●● $140

This isn't a painting. It is Pine Needles No. 3: colorful, challenging, and peaceful.

A wild life: If you can tear yourself away from the golf course and the practice area, take a visit to Weymouth Woods Sandhills Nature Preserve. Located in Southern Pines, the preserve features 898 acres of wildflowers, streams, ponds, four miles of hiking trails, a beaver pond, and a museum with interactive exhibits.

SCORECARD

Hole	1	2	3	4	5	6	7	8	9	out	
Yardage	504	481	145	403	218	459	455	360	385	3,410	
Par	5	4	3	4	3	4	4	4	4	35	
Hole	10	11	12	13	14	15	16	17	18	in	total
Yardage	525	414	412	208	454	530	180	461	421	3,605	7,015
Par	5	4	4	3	4	5	3	4	4	36	71

NORTH CAROLINA

PINEHURST
(NO. 2 COURSE)
VILLAGE OF PINEHURST, NORTH CAROLINA

Pinehurst. That's all you have to say. One word. Not Pinehurst Golf Club, Pinehurst Country Club, or any other moniker that might be used to impress. The name Pinehurst is the only word necessary to evoke a premier golf experience.

And, believe it or not, we all can play it.

Located in the North Carolina sandhills, world-renowned Pinehurst is a 2,000-acre resort property. Tee times must be made well in advance, and they are a bit pricey, but a round at any of Pinehurst's eight courses — that's right, eight courses — is worth every minute of wait and every penny of cost.

The world-renowned golf cathedral has served as a championship golf site since legendary architect Donald Ross finished building the No. 1 course in 1895. Here's

a quick list of some of the major championships held at Pinehurst, but there isn't enough space to name them all because it has hosted more major tournaments than any other site in America: the 1936 PGA Championship, the Ryder Cup Matches in 1951, and the PGA Tour Championships in 1991 and 1992. Toss in a few U.S. Opens (the most recent in 2005), almost every major golf championship in America, and its deep-rooted relationship with the U.S. Golf Association, and you know this place is worthy of all the hype.

If, somehow, you still aren't convinced, just take in a round at any of the breathtaking courses on the property. One visit. You'll talk about it for the rest of your life.

Ross, Tom Fazio, and Robert Trent Jones, Sr., are among the famed designers who left their imprint at Pinehurst. There are old courses, new courses, short courses, and long courses. It is advised that you stay at Pinehurst for as much time as your funds allow, testing your game at a

Immaculate conditions and tests at every turn, such as the elevation changes and bunkers shown around the 5th green, make Pinehurst No. 2 a challenge even for the best golfers in the world.

variety of challenges in the get-away-from-the-world cocoon of golf.

No one walks way feeling unsatisfied when playing any of the eight layouts, and the prize of the bunch is No. 2. The second course built on the property is known for its turtleback greens and unique chipping areas, and its reputation as a great test of golf reached even higher levels during the course's first Open in 1999, won by the late Payne Stewart with a fifteen-foot putt on the final hole. Stewart was the only player to shoot under par at minus 1.

In 2007, the year of its 100th birthday, Pinehurst No. 2 received a special gift. The USGA named it the site of the 2014 U.S. Open, the third time in fifteen years that America's national championship has been played on the course. The U.S. Open's visits to Pinehurst in 1999 and 2005 represented the fastest turnaround for an Open since World War II. No course has ever hosted an Open three times in a fifteen-year span.

"Golfers of all skill levels have enjoyed Pinehurst No. 2 for a century, and we're honored that the USGA believes so strongly in the challenge it offers to the best golfers in the world," Pinehurst CEO Robert Dedman, Jr., said at a news conference when the announcement was made. "We look forward to another thrilling moment in our history as we continue our championship tradition."

It will be the tenth individual USGA championship to be held at Pinehurst, solidifying a longstanding relationship that began with the 1962 U.S. Amateur Championship.

CHIP SHOTS

Course contact info:
(800) 487-4635,
www.pinehurst.com

Par: 70
Yardage: 7,335 yards

Rating: 76.0
Slope: 137
Notable: There's plenty of tradition at Pinehurst, at both the PGA Tour and top-shelf amateur-tournament levels. In 1901, the famed club first hosted the North and South Amateur Championship, whose winners include Walter Travis, Francis Ouimet, former USGA president Bill Campbell, Jack Nicklaus, and Davis Love.

On the green
◦◦◦◦ $200+ (package rate includes one night accommodation at resort)

"This is a statement about Pinehurst," said David Fay, executive director of the USGA, at the same news conference, which was attended by golf dignitaries and media from across the nation. "The fact of the matter is there are some U.S. Open sites that the phrase should be 'Let's extend that contract' and that's what we've done with Pinehurst. 1999 and 2005 were so good, it was inevitable that we were going to come back, it was just a question of when."

AFTER YOUR ROUND

No need to leave: They call chefs "culinarians" at Pinehurst, and there are more than 100 on hand to see to your dietary desires. From four-diamond formal dining with award-winning wine lists, to casual family dining and lunch spots, you don't have to exit the Pinehurst doors to find every kind of food you crave.

Take a look around: The resort is both beautiful and active. A walk around the property is enough to satisfy scenery seekers, and there's swimming, wine fests, tennis and lawn sports, spa treatments, and activities for kids and the whole family. If you venture away from the resort, you can visit Revolutionary and Civil War sites — such as House in the Horseshoe and the Malcolm Blue Farm. The village and the area immediately surrounding Pinehurst offer the Sandhills Horticultural Gardens, village shopping, horseback riding, live music, and art galleries.

SCORECARD · NO. 2 COURSE, U.S. OPEN LENGTH*

Hole	1	2	3	4	5	6	7	8	9	out	
Yardage	405	472	384	568	476	224	407	467	190	3,593	
Par	4	4	4	5	4	3	4	4	3	35	
Hole	10	11	12	13	14	15	16	17	18	in	total
Yardage	611	478	451	380	471	206	510	190	445	3,742	7,335
Par	5	4	4	4	4	3	4	3	4	35	70

* No. 2 Course plays to 6,767 yards and par-72 when not hosting the U.S. Open.

The 16th hole at Tobacco Road gives a clear indication of the course's unconventional approach to golf course layout.

NORTH CAROLINA

TOBACCO ROAD GOLF CLUB
SANFORD, NORTH CAROLINA

Welcome to Tobacco Road Golf Club. You might want to put your safety helmets on.

This a winding, tumbling, sloping, swirling design through thick North Carolina forestland, and it may be a golf round unlike any you've experienced before. Without question, it is a memorable place to play. Golfers may not post their best score, but they certainly will remember the round.

It has been described as "Pine Valley on steroids" and "golf's rock and roll thrill ride." These are terms not usually associated with golf, but when it comes to Tobacco Road, conventional descriptions just wouldn't fit the bill.

There are legendary golf courses throughout the Carolinas — Pinehurst No. 2, Pine Needles, Hilton Head, and True Blue are a few examples. But Tobacco Road is the least expensive, and it still belongs in the same category as its well-respected neighbors.

For a pure, excellent public course, Tobacco Road is the place to play. Course designer Mike Strantz (1955-2005) understood his surroundings, both in the realm of Carolina competition and on a more narrow scope, the land he had to work with in Sanford, North Carolina.

It takes but one shot to realize Strantz hit it right on the head, and made Tobacco Road the place to play in the Carolinas. The requirement off the 1st tee, like virtually every spot on the golf course, laughs in the face of ordinary expectations.

Instead of getting a nice, soft start, players face a 558-yard par-5 that snakes through dunes and pinches. Perhaps the most intimidating tee shot on the course, the drive goes through a dune-surrounded choke point and lands on the other side. There is visibility if a perfect shot is played, but it has to be perfect.

There are five, average length par-3s on the golf course — all on the front nine — but they aren't gimmes. No. 3 checks in at 152 yards, No. 6 is 148, and No. 8 is 178. Like the rest of the Tobacco Road course, it isn't length that matters, it's smarts. Shot placement is of the utmost importance when playing a curvy course, and approach shots are critical to greens that reach near-dangerous slopes.

Proof that yardage isn't the challenge at Tobacco Road is the slope and the rating. It is almost unheard of for a course of less than 7,000 yards to have a mid-70 rating and a slope in the 150s. Such is the case at Tobacco Road.

A feeling of character is important to players when reliving their rounds over a cold beverage. The farmhouse-style clubhouse at Tobacco Road is authentic and warm. It was furnished using wood from old tobacco barns, and all the fixtures inside the clubhouse are North Carolina antiques.

Mike Strantz designed many golf courses in his short career, but Tobacco Road stands out as his most memorable legacy.

AFTER YOUR ROUND

Out on the farm: Gross Farms is a long-standing perfect picture of North Carolina farm country. And like Tobacco Road, this farm is open to the public. Fresh produce includes sweet corn, blackberries, strawberries, tomatoes, potatoes, sugar snap peas, butter beans, and plenty more. My family and I were lucky enough to visit Sanford in the fall, when Gross Farms features a corn maze and a pumpkin patch. For brave souls, there's a haunted maze and trail around Halloween time.

Drama scene: The Temple Theatre has been in operation for twenty-five years, offering professional productions as a staple of the Lee County cultural community. Well-known productions, such as *Moonlight and Magnolias*, *101 Dalmatians*, and *Little Women* are presented during a season that generally runs from September until May.

CHIP SHOTS

Course contact info:
(877) 284-3762,
www.tobaccoroadgolf.com

Par: 71
Yardage: 6,554 yards

Rating: 73.2
Slope: 150
Notable: Architect Mike Strantz was noted for his scenic, unique, and sometimes wild, roller-coaster designs. Tobacco Road certainly fits into that category. Strantz went on to create or renovate five more courses before his untimely death at age 50.

On the green
⬤ $69

SCORECARD											
Hole	1	2	3	4	5	6	7	8	9	out	
Yardage	558	377	152	525	333	148	411	178	427	3,109	
Par	5	4	3	5	4	3	4	3	4	35	
Hole	10	11	12	13	14	15	16	17	18	in	total
Yardage	441	531	419	573	194	387	326	142	432	3,445	6,554
Par	4	5	4	5	3	4	4	3	4	36	71

NORTH DAKOTA

HAWKTREE GOLF CLUB
BISMARCK, NORTH DAKOTA

Do you hear The Hawk calling?

Perhaps not, but if you listen closely enough while visiting Bismarck, North Dakota, it may just beckon you. Hawktree Golf Club, for those who know of its dynamic golf, has quite a powerful allure. Jim Engh, a native of nearby Dickinson, North Dakota, took extra care when designing Hawktree, a course stationed on a bluff that overlooks the wind-swept prairies that symbolize his home state.

It's a strategist's course, so much so that Engh says, "I have to fight being brain-tired after thirteen holes." Brain-tired? Now that's a thinking-player's golf course. And this from the guy who brought it to life.

A "thinking man's course" isn't restricted to those who are lucky enough to walk the fairways of Hawktree. Engh brought creativity to the table before the course even opened its doors. The use of black-coal slag in the bunkers is not only an extremely unique look, but it also presents players with a feel that may be completely new to their golf experience. The recycled, fine grain plays somewhat like regular sand, but it's different enough to alter the ease of achieving spin out of the bunker. More thinking required.

Avoiding the bunkers is paramount to putting little numbers on the scorecard. But it's no guarantee of success; native grasses in the rough — and plentiful and severe mounding surrounding the putting surfaces — force accuracy from tee to the green.

It didn't take long for Hawktree to make an impression, both for its excellence and affordability. When it opened in 2000, *Golf Digest* ranked it No. 2 in the nation on its "Best New Affordable Public Course" list. It is also generally regarded as one of the top courses in North Dakota, topping many lists of the state's best layouts.

Engh's pride in this course is evident, and his work is a creative outlet that in part was brought about due to an accident in his youth. A golf-cart spill resulted in injuries that left him with one kidney, reducing his athletic endeavors. But Engh's ability to immerse himself in golf is a strong compensation.

A young player at Hawktree braves a fly-over approach to the green while his caddie keeps a watchful eye.

He developed his golf-architecture business in his basement, and has since grown into one of the top designers in the game.

He has been known to push his courses to the edge, not to the point of gimmickry, but just close enough.

The mounding and bunkers at Hawktree are a couple of examples of that "push the envelope" philosophy. They force interesting golf shots that a player may not have faced before. Engh didn't have to create all the unique features at Hawktree. He used the natural elevation changes to his advantage.

Let's look at No. 3. The 164-yard par-3 goes eighty feet up, all the way to the must-hit green. Anything short rolls far back toward you, and the last thing you want to see is a golf ball that acts like a boomerang. Here's where you realize the importance of a golf cart. Walking is permitted at Hawktree, but unless you've brought mountain-climbing gear along, you might want to opt for wheels.

Think I'm kidding? No. 18 is a grueling finish that features a shot over a 150-foot elevation change to the green. And this is on your last shot of the day (hopefully). Toss in the wind that is often in a player's face on this challenge, and that final shot calls for a sprint through the finish line.

AFTER YOUR ROUND

A little culture: After an education in unique golf on Hawktree, hit Bismarck for education of another kind. Check out the Bismarck Art & Galleries Association to find out where to take in some the finest works in the area. There's also the North Dakota Heritage Center, the Gateway to Science, the Dakota Stage, and the North Dakota State Government Historical Society. Each is filled with art, artifacts, and exhibitions that provide excellent food for thought for the curious. Quite a cerebral finish to a day spent on a thinking-player's golf course.

Brewin' in Bismarck: They call them "brew pubs" and they offer a great way to check out the nightlife in Bismarck. Brew pubs differ from standard taverns in that they create their own unique beers and ales on site. Also, Bismarck's East 40 Chophouse & Tavern is an awesome chophouse, which also includes a tavern (are you seeing a pattern, here?). You'll find plenty of casual dining in Bismarck, where menus feature such eclectic dishes as fried shrimp, burgers and French fries, and orange-grilled salmon.

CHIP SHOTS

Course contact info:
(800) 620-6142,
www.hawktree.com

Par: 72
Yardage: 7,055 yards

Rating: 75.2
Slope: 137

Notable: Hawktree has teamed up with two other fine public tracks in North Dakota to form the Triple Challenge. For less than $150, you can play Hawktree, Bully Pulpit (three miles south of Medora), and The Links of North Dakota (in Ray, near Williston). If you can't play all three in one trip, the offer is good for one calendar year.

On the green
○ $65

OTHER PUBLIC COURSES IN NORTH DAKOTA WORTH A VISIT

• Bully Pulpit GC, Medora
• Links of North Dakota at Red Mike Resort, Williston
• Oxbow G&CC, Oxbow
• Riverwood GC, Bismarck

SCORECARD

Hole	1	2	3	4	5	6	7	8	9	out	
Yardage	410	467	164	412	554	376	569	194	447	3,593	
Par	4	4	3	4	5	4	5	3	4	36	
Hole	10	11	12	13	14	15	16	17	18	in	total
Yardage	547	356	483	230	540	203	326	219	558	3,462	7,055
Par	5	4	4	3	5	3	4	3	5	36	72

OHIO

THE GOLF CENTER AT KINGS ISLAND
(GRIZZLY COURSE)
MASON, OHIO

Maybe it's the Nicklaus name that draws them here. Or perhaps it's the roller coasters in the theme park next door. More likely, it's the outstanding golf on The Golf Center at Kings Island's Grizzly Course that keeps players coming back year after year.

And, we're not talking about just any players. The Grizzly has played host to PGA Tour, LPGA, and Senior Tour championships, and it is the course's versatility that has allowed this Cincinnati suburb to host the best players in the world.

The layout had to be extended to maximum yardage capacity when the PGA Tour visited from 1973 to 1977. The length was then brought down somewhat when the LPGA Championship — one of four LPGA "majors" — came to town from 1978 to 1989. And other adjustments were made when the Senior Tour held twenty-one consecutive annual tournaments at the Grizzly starting in 1980.

CHIP SHOTS

Course contact info:
(513) 398-7700,
www.thegolfcenter.com

Par: 71
Yardage: 6,504 yards

Rating: 71.2
Slope: 133
Notable: Kings Island was Nicklaus's final collaborative effort before he struck out on his own. The Golden Bear now has more than 300 courses in his design portfolio, including 10 in his home state. Here are a few Nicklaus numbers from his playing days: 73 official PGA Tour victories and 113 victories around the world. He won 18 major championships and was named "Golfer of the Century" by Golf Magazine and Golf Monthly.

On the green
$39

It took attention to detail to get the courses just right for the game's best, and it's that same kind of attention to detail that the everyday player at Kings Island's Grizzly can expect as well. This course is no roller-coaster ride, but it does have the potential to change its look depending on which of the three sets of tees you use to customize your game.

As you make your way around the tranquil twin nines on the Grizzly, it's hard to imagine that there's a teeming amusement park right next door. No dizzying commotion here. The ponds, the trees, and the overall serenity make you feel grateful to be in the middle of such a peaceful, wooded oasis.

World famous designer Desmond Muirhead, who had taken a design fledgling named Jack Nicklaus under his wing, was hired to co-create the Grizzly in 1972. Muirhead not only influenced Nicklaus early in his golf-course designing career, but his presence can be felt all over the golf course. A couple of Muirhead staples on the Grizzly include long, multi-carved fairways with large trees retained as natural hazards. These later became Nicklaus staples, and it started at Kings Island when he took Muirhead's lead and created his own lengthy and perilous holes.

Nicklaus, born and raised in Ohio and a graduate of Ohio State University, learned many lessons from his days with Muirhead, and it wasn't long before he formed Nicklaus Design. Since then, Nicklaus has become one of the most sought-after designers in the business.

And here's a little nugget of information that might not surprise you: Nicklaus owns the course record at the Grizzly. The Golden Bear shot a 62 in 1973 during the third round of the inaugural PGA Tour's Ohio Kings Island Open. The record has gone unmatched for more than thirty-five years.

The Golf Center at Kings Island has an eighteen-hole mid-length course called the Bruin that is geared toward family play. It's shorter than the standard eighteen-hole course, and it's easily walkable. The track gives players an opportunity to face a toned-down Nicklaus challenge, and the greens fees have also been scaled back to allow an entire family to play without emptying their pocketbook.

Playing the Bruin Courses will afford you the opportunity to experience a great little hole. The Grizzly is the best course, but No. 9 on the Bruin is one of the top holes on the complex. This designation may sound strange when you consider that it's just a 289-yard par-4. But the short distance, combined with design technique made for the thinking golfer, is what makes the Bruin's 9th hole so interesting.

The bunker is on the right side of the fairway at 163 yards, and ponds that begin at that point are on the left side. You must drive between the bunker and the first pond, but not too far because another huge pond begins at 195 yards and runs all the way to the front of the green. Mid-iron, wedge to the green, might not sound like much, but there is water everywhere and just enough sand to force precision.

The 9th offers an interesting challenge, but the Bruin is

Jack Nicklaus was born and raised in Ohio, and he made sure The Golf Center at Kings Island — a course in his home state — was a serene departure from the amusement park nearby.

no match for the Grizzly. That's where the true test of golf lies at Kings Island.

The Grizzly Course is actually made up of three, nine-hole courses that are played in eighteen-hole combinations. Because the professional tournaments were played on the north and west nines, that's the combination most people think of when they simply say "the Grizzly Course." There are other combinations to play, but if you get a chance it's advised to tackle the north and west nines.

AFTER YOUR ROUND

Park place: Let's see, the name of the course includes "Kings Island," so you have a pretty good clue that you won't have to travel far to find loop-de-looping entertainment and amusement park attractions. Roller coasters, simulators, games, and rides of all kinds are enough to

fill half a day after golf, or an entire day if you decide to leave your clubs in the trunk. I'm from southeast Michigan and I've often made the four-hour drive to Cincinnati, either for Kings Island golf or the amusement park. I've never experienced both on the same trip, however. Might be fun.

OTHER PUBLIC COURSES IN OHIO WORTH A VISIT
• Aston Oaks GC, North Bend
• Avalon G&CC (Avalon Lakes Course), Warren
• Boulder Creek GC, Streetsboro
• Cooks Creek GC, Ashville
• Elks Run GC, Batavia
• The GC at Stonelick Hills, Batavia
• Longaberger GC, Nashport
• Shaker Run GC, Lebanon
• StoneWater GC, Cleveland

SCORECARD

Hole	1	2	3	4	5	6	7	8	9	out	
Yardage	366	186	374	518	163	402	377	215	489	3,090	
Par	4	3	4	4	3	4	4	3	5	35	
Hole	10	11	12	13	14	15	16	17	18	in	total
Yardage	403	500	422	450	175	310	218	390	546	3,414	6,504
Par	4	5	4	4	3	4	3	4	5	36	71

A canopy above and a creek below add beauty to the 11th hole, and they also create a chute-like effect off the tee.

OKLAHOMA

KARSTEN CREEK GOLF CLUB
STILLWATER, OKLAHOMA

This is Oklahoma?

Well, not exactly. It's Oklahoma State. University, that is. Karsten Creek Golf Club, the home course of Oklahoma State University, is generally considered to be one of the best college golf courses in history.

Back to the question of the course's location. Thick woods and mellow-mounded terrain may not feel like Oklahoma, but Tom Fazio has a great way with illusion. This is not North Carolina. We are truly in Oklahoma.

It isn't that Fazio tore up the natural landscape and created his own environment. Stately oaks, native to Oklahoma, line the fairways. He avoided creating artificial hills

or valleys, and the property remains Oklahoma-rugged. But lush green fairways, crisp white sand, and rich conditions are not exactly what most imagine when conjuring a picture of central Oklahoma.

The terrific golf and the wicked challenge — particularly when playing the Cowboy tees — are also decidedly genuine.

In fact, understanding how Karsten Creek can test you does not even require a trip to the first tee. A clubhouse peek at the scorecard reveals a monumental course length stretching to more than 7,400 yards, including three par-3s measuring more than 200 yards and a fourth at 198.

Oh yeah, and those are the short holes.

The par-5s range from 542 yards to – are you ready for this? – 623. You could pipe two consecutive 300-yard shots on No. 9 and be a quarter of a football field away from the green. Former Oklahoma State running back Barry Sanders would have to play three great games to rush for 623 yards. And we're expected to make it in three shots.

Say it ain't so, Mike Holder.

Whether looking to lay blame for the prodigious challenge or offer thanks for the incredible golf course, Holder is your target. The former golf coach and current athletic director at Oklahoma State convinced Fazio to design the course in hopes of creating one of the country's most rigorous courses on the Oklahoma plains. The result is a splendid and sometimes torturous success.

Karsten Creek and Lake Louise — which is surrounded by the final three holes — are named in honor of the late Karsten Solheim, founder of Karsten Manufacturing (the manufacturer of PING golf clubs), and his wife Louise, both of whom were longtime boosters of the Oklahoma State golf program.

Holder spearheaded the effort to make Karsten Creek a reality, and the Solheims provided a large chunk of the financial backing. Speaking of finance, a $4.5 million clubhouse was completed in June 2001. Built in mountain-lodge style, it measures an expansive 20,000 square feet. You think good things come in small packages? Not at Karsten Creek.

The Cowboy trophy case is large as well, and this is born of necessity. Oklahoma State's NCAA golf championships number in the double figures and the program continues to be one of the nation's most elite. Karsten Creek does nothing to hurt OSU's efforts to recruit the top talent in the country.

Long golf course, spacious clubhouse, roomy trophy case, and a big-time recruiting tool. Cowboy, when you come to Karsten Creek, you'd better be ready to pony up.

AFTER YOUR ROUND

Around campus: You could venture out to Town & Gown Theatre in the Round, or visit the Sheerar Museum, but many activities don't require a trip off campus. There are plenty of Oklahoma State sporting events to attend, and don't forget to check around campus for musical performances and student theater. Past productions have included *Romeo and Juliet*, *Pirates of Penzance*, and *Crimes of the Heart*.

CHIP SHOTS

Course contact info:
(405) 743-1658,
www.karstencreek.com

Par: 72
Yardage: 7,407 yards

Rating: 74.8
Slope: 142
Notable: When Karsten Creek opened in 1994, it was named the "Best New Course in the Country" by *Golf Digest*. Not bad for a public facility. Another rarity at a public course? Caddies are available from May 15 to August 15.

On the green
◐◐ $125 (when accompanied by club member; higher rates when not accompanied by club member)

OTHER PUBLIC COURSES IN OKLAHOMA WORTH A VISIT
• Bailey Ranch GC, Owasso
• Forest Ridge GC, Broken Arrow
• Chickasaw Pointe GC, Kingston
• University of Oklahoma GC, Norman

SCORECARD

Hole	1	2	3	4	5	6	7	8	9	out	
Yardage	542	458	198	349	481	350	206	459	623	3,666	
Par	5	4	3	4	4	4	3	4	5	36	
Hole	10	11	12	13	14	15	16	17	18	in	total
Yardage	477	209	351	425	570	217	471	471	550	3,741	7,407
Par	4	3	4	4	5	3	4	4	5	36	72

OREGON

BANDON DUNES GOLF RESORT
(PACIFIC DUNES/BANDON DUNES COURSES)
BANDON, OREGON

"Peerless" is a word that should not be tossed around casually. Credibility is at stake if hyperbole becomes habit.

It is with full knowledge of this risk that Pacific Dunes, designed by Tom Doak —or perhaps its sister course, Bandon Dunes, designed by David McLay Kidd — could very well be labeled as the No. 1 public-access golf course in America. Perhaps non-purists could take issue with the walking-only policy, but that is but a nitpick. When you consider that both courses are on the same property, "peerless," could apply.

These two courses at Bandon Dunes Resort are nearly flawless, and a third — Bandon Trails — surely doesn't hurt the cause. It was announced in 2009 that a fourth course — Old Macdonald — was on the way. The proof of Bandon's excellence is in the effort that golfers are willing to make to reach this rugged and perfect property. The resort is 4 1/2 hours from Portland and 1 1/2 hours from Eugene. When Bandon opened with one course in 1999, at least three hours of round-trip driving were necessary from the nearest point of legitimate civilization to reach it. The area has been built up slightly, and Pacific Dunes has been added, but drive time is still a factor.

David McLay Kidd already had a solid reputation in the design world when he took on Bandon Dunes, and he relished the challenge of making something magical.

When the course opened in 1999, *Golfweek* immediately named it second on its list of "Best Modern Courses in America." This list included both private and public courses. Bandon Dunes has not slipped a bit since then. It annually ranks in the top three of *Golfweek*'s "America's Best Courses." Once again, this list isn't restricted to club members' courses. Anyone can play. You just have to want to.

Tom Doak knew he had quite an act to follow when he was hired to design Pacific Dunes a few years after Bandon Dunes opened, and he has succeeded mightily on all counts. The routes of the holes at Pacific Dunes are varied, but the beautiful scenery is a constant that you'll appreciate. Natural grasses, dunes, mounds, a smattering of trees, and that far-reaching, panoramic view of the Pacific to the west surround all the holes.

There may be one or two more highly rated courses in the country, but Pacific Dunes tops most lists, with Bandon Dunes following closely. If you want to play the best public track that the country has to offer, peerless Bandon Dunes Golf Resort is the place to go.

CHIP SHOTS
(Pacific Dunes)

Course contact info:
(888) 345-6008,
www.bandondunesgolf.com

Par: 71
Yardage: 6,635 yards

Rating: 71.5
Slope: 129
Notable: Tom Doak knew he was blessed when he was called upon to create Pacific Dunes. He commented, "Every architect dreams of building among the sand dunes, in the same terrain where golf was conceived in the British Isles. For me and my associates, Pacific Dunes is that dream come true ... Together with its big sister, Bandon Dunes, this must be the finest 36 holes of golf at any resort in the world."

On the green
◎◎◎ $165 (hotel guests or residents of Oregon)

No. 11 at Pacific Dunes is just 148 yards long, but every inch of it is rugged Oregon coastline.

AFTER YOUR ROUND

On the prowl: Prowler Charters' licensed fishing guides know the local hot spots. Half-day salmon and bottom-feeders fishing trips, and full-day halibut and tuna excursions are among the selections.

Sea horses: Bandon Beach Riding Stables offer horseback rides on the beach that are as peaceful as you might imagine. I took a ride as daylight dwindled, and wondered which was more beautiful — the golf course or the setting sun.

OTHER PUBLIC COURSES IN OREGON WORTH A VISIT

- Aspen Lakes GC, Sisters
- Crosswater GC, Sunriver
- Eagle Point GC, Medford
- Pumpkin Ridge GC (Ghost Creek Course), Cornelius
- Reserve Vineyards & GC (South Course), Aloha
- Running Y Ranch Golf Resort, Klamath Falls

SCORECARD - PACIFIC DUNES

Hole	1	2	3	4	5	6	7	8	9	out	
Yardage	370	368	499	463	199	316	464	400	406	3,485	
Par	4	4	5	4	3	4	4	4	4	36	
Hole	10	11	12	13	14	15	16	17	18	in	total
Yardage	208	148	529	444	145	539	338	208	591	3,150	6,635
Par	3	3	5	4	3	5	4	4	5	35	71

SCORECARD - BANDON DUNES

Hole	1	2	3	4	5	6	7	8	9	out	
Yardage	386	189	543	410	428	161	383	359	558	3,417	
Par	4	3	5	4	4	3	4	4	5	36	
Hole	10	11	12	13	14	15	16	17	18	in	total
Yardage	362	384	199	553	359	163	363	389	543	3,315	6,732
Par	4	4	3	5	4	3	4	4	5	36	72

OREGON

EASTMORELAND GOLF COURSE
PORTLAND, OREGON

Portland, Oregon, golf includes a surprising venue. Not surprising because it's in the Great Northwest; there are plenty of excellent courses in the region. But Eastmoreland Golf Course is a bit of a myth-buster.

It's a wonderful place to spend an afternoon with your clubs, and it's also a municipal course. This combination is difficult to accomplish because of tight budgets, although it can be done with dedication from community officials. Bethpage State Park's Black Course in Farmingdale, New York, is one example; Pinion Hills Golf Course in Farmington, New Mexico, is another. Like the powers that be in those cities, Portland officials know they have something special on their hands, and so do the area's golfers.

There's no reason to head for the hills just because you hear the word "municipal." Not in Portland. Eastmoreland is a scenic place to play, and the aesthetics are more than matched by the course's dedication to preserving the area's golf tradition that dates to 1918.

Eastmoreland is the oldest of four municipal courses in the Portland area. Rose City, Heron Lakes, and Progress Downs round out the foursome. All share a piece of Portland's golf history.

Back in 1918, there were several men of some influence in Portland who put together the idea of building a golf course. They began a committee that started with $3,000 in seed money, and their fund-raising efforts quickly ballooned to $250,000, an enormous amount of money for that time. Eastmoreland was soon opened to the public and The Portland City Championship held its first tournament there.

Eastmoreland's layout has held up well over the years, although the yardage that seemed prodigious nearly a century ago is considered more medium-length today. The staff, however, is long on service and offers more than just the basics. The facility includes a covered and lighted driving range, a full-line pro shop, and a tasty grill that is well known throughout Portland.

It may not be the longest course around, but the Eastmoreland layout includes several toughies. The par-4 2nd is lined on the right with out-of-bounds markers, and there is no bailout area on the left. Two solid, straight shots are required to reach the green in two. It's an achievable par, but there's little room for error.

Another highlight hole is the par-5 6th. A long hitter may be able to reach the 497-yarder in two if he has the nerve to cut the corner on this risk-reward beauty. Even cutting the dogleg, however, is no assurance of success. Bunkers guard the green to the right, forcing players to aim to the left side of the severely sloping green. It can be a birdie hole, but it takes some risk.

Eastmoreland is filled with hilly terrain that actually pays off some of the time. Out-of-bounds areas are plentiful, and they aren't very forgiving. So the mounds often help steer into the fairway what could have been an errant shot. But don't let that fool you into thinking you're out of the woods. The fairways are narrow and trees line every one of them.

The nines contrast nicely. The front has no water hazards with which to contend, and the back nine has several ponds, including two that force carries from tee to green on the par-3s.

There is much to enjoy within the white stakes at Eastmoreland, and the views of the outlying scenery are also memorable. Crystal Springs Lake, the Rhododendron Gardens, and Johnson Creek flank the course, and there is a variety of trees and shrubs that provide continuous color changes throughout the year.

Eastmoreland shrugs off the municipal myth. Pack up the clubs and go see for yourself.

CHIP SHOTS

Course contact info:
(503) 775-2900,
www.eastmorelandgolfcourse.com

Par: 72
Yardage: 6,529 yards

Rating: 71.0
Slope: 124
Notable: The 1990 National Public Links Tournament was held at Eastmoreland, and the facility is still the annual host of the Portland City Championship. One more important fact: Eastmoreland's grill is known throughout Portland as having one of the best burgers in town.

On the green
◯ $26

There is no place to hide at Eastmoreland's 12th. Reeds, trees, water, and sand make it imperative to land on the putting surface to make par.

AFTER YOUR ROUND

Contrasting adventure: Portland has a little bit of everything. Within a few minutes of the city, there are Pinot-producing wineries, kayak-friendly waterways, wildlife preserves, and the majesty of Mount Hood (elevation: 11,249 feet).

City sights: If you're more of a city boy (or girl), there's the Oregon Museum of Science and Industry, the Alameda Brewhouse, Burnside Skatepark, Clear Creek Distillery, Glenn & Viola Walters Cultural Arts Center, and so much more. You could stay in Portland a week, golf to your heart's content, and never run out of things to do when you're finished with your round.

SCORECARD

Hole	1	2	3	4	5	6	7	8	9	out	
Yardage	311	447	337	347	210	497	410	227	497	3,283	
Par	4	4	4	4	3	5	4	3	5	36	
Hole	10	11	12	13	14	15	16	17	18	in	total
Yardage	334	469	167	463	383	381	423	169	457	3,246	6,529
Par	4	5	3	5	4	4	4	3	4	36	72

PENNSYLVANIA

HERSHEY COUNTRY CLUB
(WEST COURSE)
HERSHEY, PENNSYLVANIA

OK, we'll get the obligatory puns out of the way: make sure and hit it on the sweet spot at Hershey Country Club; (chocolate) bar none, it's a great place to play; it's one tasty golf course. There are dozens of others, but let's do our best to leave them on the candy shelf.

Hershey Country Club is a complex that should be taken seriously. Yes, it's in the chocolate capital of the world, and was built by a chocolate baron. Sure, you actually smell chocolate as you traverse the layout, and the 5th hole's green is a few steps from Milton Hershey's historic mansion. But if there's any possible way to get chocolate out of your mind for a little while, the Hershey Country Club is well worth the focus.

Consider this: the 1940 PGA Championship was held at Hershey's West Course, and the famed track has also hosted the PGA Tour, the LPGA, and the Nationwide Tour championships. The town may be famous for chocolate, but the country club is renowned for its outstanding golf.

Smack dab in between Philadelphia and Baltimore, the Hershey Golf Collection features sixty-three holes of golf — the West and East Courses at Hershey Country Club, the Hershey Links, and the Spring Creek Golf Course.

Golf in Hershey isn't just an afterthought. Milton Hershey's presence can be felt throughout the town, particularly on the Hershey property, and his decision to make golf a part of the landscape is a decision praised by locals, vacationers, and national experts.

Hershey Country Club's

The West Course's signature 6th at Hershey offers a sweet challenge and an even sweeter view of Pennsylvania woodlands.

West Course reveals inventive par-4s, and a couple can be reached from the tee if you dare. The middle of the outward nine offers some great vantage points — Nos. 3 to 6 all feature elevated tees that give brilliant views of Hershey and beyond. Tourists flock to Hershey to take the tour of a pretty convincing simulated chocolate factory at the amusement park, but you can see the actual chocolate plant from the golf course. And your eighteen-hole round, no matter what course you play, will be as memorable as any tour you could take.

The West Course was designed by Maurice McCarthy and opened in 1930, and even though the course has achieved renown over more than seven decades, course management is not resting on its laurels. A course renovation, which resulted in an announcement that the West Course would close until spring 2010, brought excitement from Hershey golf staffers.

"Our focus is to preserve and honor the legacy of the West Course," said Ned Graff, Director of Golf at Hershey Country Club, when the course revamping was announced. "We want to be great caretakers of its legacy."

At the same news conference, Graff stressed that all the other courses on the Hershey property would remain

CHIP SHOTS

Course contact info:
(800) 437-7439,
www.hersheypa.com/accommodations/hershey_country_club

Par: 72
Yardage: 6,880 yards

Rating: 74.5
Slope: 136
Notable: The PGA Championship was still a match-event when Hershey played host in 1940. Byron Nelson defeated Sam Snead 1-up in the finals.

On the green
◉◉◉◉ $200 plus (includes one night accommodation in hotel)

traps all over the yard, and their difficulty level ranges from tricky to treacherous.

As stated earlier, this is a golf complex that is to be seriously considered when thinking of a place to visit. So serious, in fact, that after the opening paragraph, I've been able to concentrate solely on golf and put the sweetshop puns away. Chalk(olate) one up for me.

AFTER YOUR ROUND

One sweet place: What to do in Hershey, Pennsylvania, after playing Hershey Country Club? Mmmmmm . . . How about taking a tour of the simulated Hershey chocolate plant and spending the day at Hershey Park, a big-time amusement park with first-rate roller coasters and a dizzying array of other rides? My family and I stopped for two days in Hershey on the way to Atlantic City from Michigan for Dad to play both Hershey Country Club and the Atlantic City Country Club. I'm not sure which part of the trip was more fun — the Hershey sweets or the golf.

open during the renovation.

Graff gave details of the work, discussing the modernization of the drainage and irrigation systems, and raising the soil and turf quality to USGA standards.

The West Course has received many well-deserved accolades, but the East Course is no slouch. It, too, has hosted professional events — including the Nationwide Tour's Reese's Cup Classic. Three large, man-made lakes beautify the property and more than 100 bunkers do more than hold sand; they contain peril on every hole. There are

OTHER PUBLIC COURSES IN PENNSYLVANIA WORTH A VISIT
- The Club at Morgan Hill, Easton
- Great Bear G&CC, East Stroudsburg
- GC at Glen Mills, Glen Mills
- Hershey Links, Hummelstown
- Lederach GC, Harleysville
- The Links at Gettysburg, Gettysburg
- Nemacolin Woodlands Resort (Mystic Rock Course), Farmington
- Olde Stonewall GC, Ellwood City
- River Valley GC, Westfield

SCORECARD

Hole	1	2	3	4	5	6	7	8	9	out	
Yardage	437	568	354	307	176	345	550	232	389	3,358	
Par	4	5	4	4	3	4	5	3	4	36	
Hole	10	11	12	13	14	15	16	17	18	in	total
Yardage	442	354	180	568	354	501	517	182	424	3,522	6,880
Par	4	4	3	5	4	5	5	3	4	36	72

Petunias, thick rough, a lush fairway, and a view of the modern clubhouse combine to make No. 9 at Quicksilver Golf Club an excellent finish to the outward nine.

PENNSYLVANIA

QUICKSILVER GOLF CLUB
MIDWAY, PENNSYLVANIA

Certainly, every easy-chair golf fan in America has heard of Bob Murphy. He's that soft-spoken, down-home, friendly commentator on NBC golf telecasts. Before that, he used his trademark soft and smooth swing to win five times on the PGA Tour and eleven times on the Champions Tour.

He might remind you of your favorite uncle who took you out back for a few swings of the club. But after playing Quicksilver Golf Club, which was redesigned by Murphy and Sean Parees in 1990, you might be left with a question: What the heck got into Uncle Bob?

Murphy left his genteel manner in the bag when he gave Quicksilver some teeth. Make that fangs. The slope rating is 145, which translates into a major-league difficult golf course; there's a 615-yard hole, a long par-5 by any-one's standards; and two par-3s nearing 200 yards. Whew.

Even your favorite uncle had his surly moments, but most of the time he was fun to be around. The same runs

true for Quicksilver Golf Club: sometimes it's a bear, but it's great fun to play.

When Murphy first laid eyes on the Quicksilver layout, he knew the potential was there. He and Parees got it right with the redesign and the professional tours took notice. Murphy showed off the place to his Champions Tour competitors when he played four times at Quicksilver in the Pittsburgh Senior Classic. The club has also staged three Nationwide Tour tournaments and two Hooters Tour events.

There are many factors that play into the difficulty at Quicksilver. The course features ponds and creeks that come into play on eight holes, so if you're not on the money, make sure you've spent the money for a good supply of golf balls.

There are a few holes with wide fairways that afford chances to really let the shaft out off the tee. Often, how-ever, it is advisable to back off on the driver or even leave it in the bag. Three-wood is the play on many of the holes that feature target-golf landing areas or narrow fairways flanked by water and woods. Forgoing the driver might sound like odd advice at a course that measures more than

7,000 yards, but accuracy is paramount at Quicksilver. Sacrifice some distance to land on solid ground.

And what of the greens? There are some undulations that purists might not like, but the greens don't quite reach the point of being gimmicky. That's not to say they're not pushing the envelope. Pin placements are crucial and the staff seems to understand this. There are spots on the green that, if chosen to be a pin placement, would spell big trouble for the average player. Luckily, these slopes come into play only if you have a putt of fifteen feet or more. In other words, make sure your approach shot hugs the pin.

Another Quicksilver aspect to embrace is the combination of risk and reward. There are two consecutive "I dare yous" on the back nine. Nos. 12 and 13 are both doglegs that can be cut with perfect, long shots. But if you don't really crush it, the woods await. If you're really hitting well, give the dogleg cuts a go. But, if it's an average day, the middle of the fairway is the safe play.

The Quicksilver dichotomy of enjoyment mixed with difficulty can leave you with two reactions, depending on the round's outcome. On a good day, you'll rave about mastering a beautiful, grueling golf course. But a sub-par effort might leave you with a different reaction: "Hey, Uncle Bob, cut us some slack!"

AFTER YOUR ROUND

Steel curtain: How about an early Sunday morning round followed by a Steelers game? Quicksilver is only thirty minutes from Heinz Field and seven minutes from the airport. Tee time at 7:00 a.m., off the course by 11:00, kickoff at 1:00 p.m., at the airport by 6:00. Sounds like one of the greatest days in sports. Not quite as cool as the time I saw the Steelers-Browns game before driving two hours for a Bruce Springsteen concert, but pretty close.

Pure Pittsburgh: If you're looking to make your visit an "authentic" Pittsburgh experience, here are a few foods that got their start in steel country: Isaly's chipped ham, the Clark Bar, the Devonshire sandwich, Heinz Ketchup, Iron City Beer, the Primanti Bros. sandwich, and Klondike Bars. There's a meal in there somewhere, isn't there?

CHIP SHOTS

Course contact info:
(724) 796-1594,
www.quicksilvergolf.com

Par: 72
Yardage: 7,083 yards

Rating: 75.7
Slope: 145
Notable: Quicksilver opened in 1971, and was drastically overhauled 19 years later. Five lakes and nearly 80 bunkers, many added during the renovation, crowd the fairways and affect shot placement on almost every hole.

On the green
◯ $70

SCORECARD											
Hole	1	2	3	4	5	6	7	8	9	out	
Yardage	421	412	401	580	419	169	615	199	307	3,523	
Par	4	4	4	5	4	3	5	3	4	36	
Hole	10	11	12	13	14	15	16	17	18	in	total
Yardage	423	173	361	467	189	577	405	540	425	3,560	7,083
Par	4	3	4	4	3	5	4	5	4	36	72

Early morning mists envelop Newport National. When morning fog lifts, players are greeted to stunning views of the Sakonnet Passage.

RHODE ISLAND

NEWPORT NATIONAL GOLF CLUB
NEWPORT, RHODE ISLAND

It used to be that Newport, Rhode Island, was strictly a place of yachts, mansions, and tony, gated communities. The rich still maintain a stronghold over the place, to be sure, but there's a new game in town. Sort of.

The tradition of golf has been part of the landscape for as long as anyone can remember. Newport Country Club, for example, was a founding member of the U.S. Golf Association in 1894 and had hosted a U.S. Open and the first U.S. Amateur before the turn of the nineteenth century.

But, as you might expect, Newport Country Club is private, which keeps most of us from laying eyes on the place. But there is a welcome alternative. Public golf, and not the high-end variety, has made its way to this beautiful seaside city. This is the new game of which I spoke. It's still golf, but it's golf for all of us.

Newport National Golf Club, which opened in 2002, is one such venue. In an area that includes one of the most tradition-rich country clubs in America, Newport National charges no dues. Million-dollar yachts may dock nearby, but Rhode Island residents can smile, knowing they are playing a great round of golf for a reasonable price in the shadow of those yachts. Twilight, in fact, brings larger shadows and smaller greens fees. This is an irony you can live with. Out-of-state players pay a higher price at peak times, but deals are available for everyone during the off-season and at twilight.

Arthur Hills and Drew Rogers designed Newport National, which sits on 200 acres of fertile ground. The former site of shrub and tree nurseries is as rich in ocean views as it is in minerals in the soil. The Sakonnet Passage, the Atlantic Ocean, and Narragansett Bay are visible throughout the course.

Down-by-the-sea golf courses require turf that can stand up to the elements. Newport National achieves optimal conditions by using seaside bent grass on greens, tees, and fairways. The rolls are true and the look is fantastic.

But it can get deep at Newport National, and you don't want to get in over your head. We're not talking about the nearby waters; rather, it's the blowing fescue that can cause problems. It's knee-high in some places, although you'd really have to hit a crooked shot to land in those spots. But even a slight mistake can put you in the four-inch golden grass, which is just as difficult to deal with as the knee-high stuff most of the time. Land in the rough, and chalk up an extra stroke.

But an extra stroke here and there is a small price to pay when you take a look at your surroundings. The idea that Newport would welcome us public-access players to town is a new concept, indeed. When John Jacob Astor IV, Theodore Havemeyer, and three members of the Vanderbilt family opened Newport Country Club in 1893, it's doubtful they imagined that little more than 100 years later there'd be regular Joes and Janes swinging away down the road.

OTHER PUBLIC COURSES IN RHODE ISLAND WORTH A VISIT

- Exeter CC, Exeter
- Montaup CC, Portsmouth
- Winnapaug CC & Restaurant, Westerly

AFTER YOUR ROUND

Man, oh mansion!: Not sure whether this activity would spark envy or admiration, but one of the great things to do in Newport is to take a mansion tour. These magnificent homes were built in the nineteenth century, and it's definitely not a "when you've seen one, you've seen them all" experience. Mansions include Marble House, Rosecliff, Isaac Bell House, and Kingscote. Tour tickets are available at www.newportmansions.org.

See the sea: The 3.5-mile Cliff Walk above the ocean is spectacular, with views of huge waves fifty feet below. This is an envigorating hike and also a great way to see the real allure of Newport. There are also fishing expeditions, kayak rentals, and dinner cruises.

CHIP SHOTS

Course contact info:
(401) 848-9690,
www.newportnational.com

Par: 72
Yardage: 6,882

Rating: 74.4
Slope: 138
Notable: PGA Tour player Brett Quigley owns the Newport National course record with a 67.

On the green
$75

SCORECARD

Hole	1	2	3	4	5	6	7	8	9	out	
Yardage	522	400	168	179	327	449	437	567	391	3,440	
Par	5	4	3	3	4	4	4	5	4	36	

Hole	10	11	12	13	14	15	16	17	18	in	total
Yardage	390	550	366	152	565	410	182	412	415	3,442	6,882
Par	4	5	4	3	5	4	3	4	4	36	72

RHODE ISLAND

TRIGGS MEMORIAL GOLF COURSE
PROVIDENCE, RHODE ISLAND

There are several golf course architects who have received worldwide renown through the years, but few have inspired the acclaim given to Donald Ross. Referring to this designer as a "legend" is not overstating the case – he performed his magic on countless courses in the early part of the twentieth century.

His world-class golf course artwork is sprinkled throughout the country, and Rhode Island was the fortunate recipient of several of his masterpieces. Rhode Island Country Club, Warwick Country Club, Metacomet Country Club, and Wannamoiset Country Club are included in his Rhode Island layouts, but none are true public golf courses.

You want to play a Donald Ross course for a price that won't leave you shuddering? Make a visit to Providence, and take a walk on Triggs Memorial Golf Course. When you speak of Ross, you speak of history. Triggs opened the course in 1932 and it features Ross's trademark nuances and old-time layout techniques.

The technology to move earth was much more limited back then than it is today, so Ross and other architects of the time employed their imaginations within the confines of the land's natural contours. Triggs is no exception, and it is a property that includes moderate elevation changes that Ross used ingeniously.

The short par-5s are other historical features. In Ross's day, they were long enough to keep players honest, but today they are reachable in two if you have the power. The "short, long holes" are now risk-reward opportunities that might be even more fun than they were when Triggs opened its doors.

The 6th hole, the first of the par-5s, is a good example. At 445 yards, it is eminently reachable in 2, but it doglegs right and accuracy off the tee is just as important as length. After the dogleg, the hole plays downhill to the green, which makes it feel even shorter than its already modest distance. Small bunkers offer a touch of challenge in front of the green, but they come into play only if your approach shot is short and off the fairway.

The par-4s are somewhat affected by modern club and ball technology that can result in longer drives, offering shorter approach shots if you really pipe your drive. But challenging par-4s are where Ross made his name, and their difficulty holds up at Triggs. The 3rd is the longest at 457 yards,

and the out-of-bounds area runs on the left side for the entire length of the hole, so it is generally considered the most difficult challenge on the course. The slope on the green runs back to front, so approaches must land short of the hole for a safe uphill putt.

The par-3s play much the same as in 1932, and offer an exciting glimpse into the yesterdays of golf. Two measure exactly 200 yards and a third is 191. These were long par-3s in 1932, and their lengths hold up today.

No. 4 is the first 200-yard par-3. There is a bailout area up front if the combination of windy conditions and 200 yards puts a fright into you, but large bunkers on both sides protect it. Mounds crowd both sides of the green, so hitting the putting surface is imperative.

Triggs was built on 140 acres in a time when few homes were in the area, but it now rests in downtown Providence and is in a densely populated area of town. The course's variety of holes offers a great challenge, and its varied surroundings provide interesting shifts in ambience.

The atmosphere around the course is much different than it was more than seventy years ago, but the golf experience is much the same. Once you get to the layout's inner holes, the nearby hubbub becomes irrelevant.

AFTER YOUR ROUND

Small state, big attraction: Rhode Island may be the smallest state in the Union, but its capital of Providence offers an attraction that is big-time unique. The WaterFire Providence is an artful experience featuring an amazing sculpture on the three rivers downtown. The sculpture displays one hundred blazing fires, and it is an unforgettable sight at night. WaterFire Providence has attracted 10 million visitors and counting, all of whom come to witness a burnt-orange glow mingling with the city's skyline.

No. 13 at Triggs features a smallish green protected by stately trees, bunkers, and native Rhode Island grasses.

Hole	1	2	3	4	5	6	7	8	9	out	
Yardage	402	425	457	200	327	445	191	341	402	3,190	
Par	4	4	4	3	4	5	3	4	4	35	
Hole	10	11	12	13	14	15	16	17	18	in	total
Yardage	513	350	200	462	158	508	319	412	410	3,332	6,522
Par	5	4	3	5	3	5	4	4	4	37	72

SOUTH CAROLINA

HARBOUR TOWN GOLF LINKS
HILTON HEAD, SOUTH CAROLINA

Pete Dye has become one of the most well-known golf course architects in the world, but when he and Jack Nicklaus teamed to design Harbour Town in 1969, he was looking to make a name for himself. Nicklaus, of course, was golf royalty as a player, and his reputation as a designer took a giant leap when Harbour Town was finished.

Both Nicklaus and Dye have designed hundreds of courses since, but Harbour Town is where it all began. After it was completed, both shot to the top of the golf course design world.

Harbour Town, the annual home of the PGA Tour's Verizon Heritage, offers one of those rare opportunities to play the same course as Tiger Woods, Phil Mickelson, and friends. But this layout offers a little more. Players not only get to walk the same fairways as modern-day PGA Tour stars, but because the Heritage has been held at Harbour Town since 1969, Gary Player and Nicklaus played here too. And when Arnold Palmer won the first Heritage, Harbour Town was on its way.

Back before Hilton Head became a South Carolina mecca of golf, there was just one course on the island. Palmetto Dunes, designed by famed architect Robert Trent Jones, Jr., got it all started in the mid-1960s. When Dye saw Palmetto Dunes, with its large greens, wide fairways, and expansive bunkers, he wanted to do things a different way.

Eager to establish his own identity, Dye appeared to be playing devil's advocate to Jones's design. Harbour Town features tiny greens, narrow fairways, and pot bunkers.

The course has one of the world's best par-3 tests. All require carries over water or sand, and many are built up by what has become a Dye trademark — railroad ties as bulkheads for bunkers and hazards.

The course is part of Sea Pines Resort. You are not required to stay at Sea Pines to play Harbour Town, but if you have the opportunity you ought to take it. There are parks, walking trails, and other features that add to the area's laid-back ambience, preserving the character of the South Carolina lifestyle. Beach, marinas, horseback riding, and bike trails make this one of the most pleasant outdoor experiences imaginable.

Fishing, sailing, dolphin watching, nature preserves, and kayaking are just some of the other activities available there. But make no mistake: Harbour Town is the star of the show. And that star glows even brighter when the PGA Tour pros come to town each year in April.

Harbour Town became famous for the PGA Tour event it has hosted for forty years, but the course doesn't go to sleep after the Heritage. In fact, it wakes up with a vengeance. More than 40,000 rounds are played there annually, and the course is open to the public every day of the year — with the exception of the time it is being manicured for the PGA Tour event.

As Harbour Town became more well known and so many rounds were being played, conditions sometimes suffered. But when Dye returned to Harbour Town to lead a renovation and restoration in 2000, part of the effort was to create conditions that could endure more traffic. Drainage, regrassing, and moving several tees were among the many changes.

And what do players have in store? With the famed red-and-white Harbour Town lighthouse serving as a backdrop, and luxury yachts and vacation villas nearby, the area has come a long way since it opened in 1969.

But one thing hasn't changed: exemplary golf.

CHIP SHOTS

Course contact info:
(866) 561-8802,
www.seapines.com

Par: 71
Yardage: 6,973

Rating: 75
Slope: 146
Notable: Harbour Town is home of the PGA Tour's Verizon Heritage, and was named the "No. 1 Golf Course in All of South Carolina" by *Golf Magazine*. Hilton Head is loaded with golf courses — many of them high quality — but there can only be one king. Harbour Town wears the crown.

On the green
◯◯ $120

AFTER YOUR ROUND

Take a deep breath: The resort's Breathe Spa might be an unusual fit for a "sightseeing" category since you'll have your eyes closed for much of your visit. Several different massage treatments are available at this Daufuskie Island spot, including a golfer's massage that concentrates solely on muscles strained by golf. I tried one and loved it.

Silver Dew: Owned and operated by Bob Burn, this art shop features Burn's extraordinary pottery. He is a great storyteller, too, so leave some time to listen to his tales. His artwork is pure South Carolina, and much of it includes

The lighthouse at Harbour Town serves as a backdrop and one of golf's enduring landmarks

black beach sand from Atlantic shores. Burn, a self-taught potter, specializes in "silver dew" pottery — a one-of-a-kind earthy look. Each piece includes Daufuskie Island sand.

OTHER PUBLIC COURSES IN SOUTH CAROLINA WORTH A VISIT
- Caledonia Golf & Fish Club, Pawleys Island
- Dunes Golf and Beach Club, Myrtle Beach
- The May River Course at Palmetto Bluff, Bluffton
- Tidewater GC, North Myrtle Beach
- TPC Myrtle Beach, Murrells Inlet
- Wild Dunes Resort (Links Course), Isle of Palms

SCORECARD

Hole	1	2	3	4	5	6	7	8	9	out	
Yardage	410	502	437	200	530	419	195	470	332	3,495	
Par	4	5	4	3	5	4	3	4	4	36	
Hole	10	11	12	13	14	15	16	17	18	in	total
Yardage	444	436	430	373	192	571	395	185	452	3,478	6,973
Par	4	4	4	4	3	5	4	3	4	35	71

There are several carries off the tee that are great to view, yet you don't want to get too close a look. Anything but a tee shot clear of the junk forfeits any realistic shot at par.

SOUTH CAROLINA

KIAWAH ISLAND GOLF RESORT
(OCEAN COURSE)
KIAWAH ISLAND, SOUTH CAROLINA

Only a handful of courses have staged numerous international competitions, top amateur tournaments, and professional national championships. Even fewer have been featured in theaters from coast to coast. Among the few courses that can make such claims is Kiawah Island's Ocean Course, where the movie *The Legend of Bagger Vance* was filmed; it hit theaters in November, 2000.

The Ocean Course has been on the national stage for years, and its star power continues to burn. When it was announced that the 2012 PGA Championship was coming to Kiawah Island, it marked the first time one of golf's four major championships would make a stop in South Carolina.

Pros aren't the only golfers who come to play one of the best courses in the world. It has everything: acclaim,

reputation, beauty, and premium golf. But there is one thing missing — private-club restrictions that would prohibit public play. Come to Kiawah Island and you might just get on the Ocean Course. If tee times aren't available, there are four other tracks on the property that offer a sterling supporting cast for the star of the show.

When the Ocean Course opened in 1991 it was an instant trophy for an island resort alive with natural elegance. The best way to enjoy such ambience is to walk the course. Leave the carts behind so as not to miss any of the charm. Another tip? Bring a caddie if you can afford to spend the extra coin.

The caddie can watch your ball as you gaze at the ocean. Players rarely lose sight of the Atlantic as they make their way up and back on their eighteen-hole journey. In fact, the Ocean Course features more oceanside holes than any other course in the northern hemisphere. There are ten holes that directly abut the ocean and eight more that run parallel just 100 yards or so from the sea.

A wide variety of wildlife abounds, but perhaps the

wildest part of your round is the wind. The gusts not only alter golf shots, they also change the look of the course.

If they're strong enough, the breezes can shift the dunes on the course, squeezing or expanding a fairway in the process. Kiawah Island staffers say no other course in North America is as affected by the wind, and they further contend that only a smattering of United Kingdom layouts experience such course-altering gusts. From one round to the next, a player might experience up to an eight-club difference on holes depending upon the direction and strength of the wind.

Wind isn't the only fight players must wage when playing the Ocean. The prodigious length – it checks in at nearly 7,400 yards – and a masterfully challenging layout by Pete Dye create one of the toughest public-access tests in the world.

Yet Kiawah is not all blustery brute. One of the course's most difficult and scenic challenges is the 194-yard 14th. It's not an exceptionally long par-3, but it is an oceanside hole featuring an elevated tee and winds almost impossible to predict. Try choosing a club, then try using it to land on a green shaped like an upside-down bowl.

It isn't cheap to stay and play at Kiawah Island. But even if it takes some

money-saving and money-raising efforts throughout the year, it's worth the trip to the coast of South Carolina. Those who play golf here will enjoy a vacation loaded with priceless experiences.

AFTER YOUR ROUND

Quite naturally . . . : It's all about nature at Kiawah Island. On my one and only visit to Kiawah (and I sure hope to return soon), I took a tour that brought me face to face with alligators, exotic birds, reptiles, and dolphins. Pick your mode of transportation when exploring the island, salt marsh, or ocean. Bicycles, charter fishing boats, and kayaks are available. Clay tennis courts are on-property if a day on the course isn't enough.

Triple treat: Kiawah Island's Sanctuary Hotel features three dining options on the resort property — you can dine at the sports bar, enjoy poolside fare, or go very upscale. The spread at the breakfast buffet is huge and delicious; lunch by the pool makes for a nice afternoon; and a fancy dinner with ever-changing New American cuisine tops off a delectable day. Meals are not included in the stay-and-play packages.

CHIP SHOTS

Course contact info:
(800) 654-2924,
www.kiawahresort.com

Par: 72
Yardage: 7,356 yards

Rating: 77.2
Slope: 144
Notable: The Ocean Course has hosted the Ryder Cup matches, the World Cup of Golf, the UBS Cup, and the Senior PGA Championship. It is one of only 17 courses on *Golf Digest's* list of 5-star courses.

On the green
◯◯◯◯ $239 (includes one-night lodging in the resort)

SCORECARD											
Hole	1	2	3	4	5	6	7	8	9	out	
Yardage	395	543	390	453	207	455	527	197	464	3,631	
Par	4	5	4	4	3	4	5	3	4	36	
Hole	10	11	12	13	14	15	16	17	18	in	total
Yardage	439	562	466	404	194	421	579	221	439	3,725	7,356
Par	4	5	4	4	3	4	5	3	4	36	72

SOUTH CAROLINA

TRUE BLUE PLANTATION
PAWLEYS ISLAND, SOUTH CAROLINA

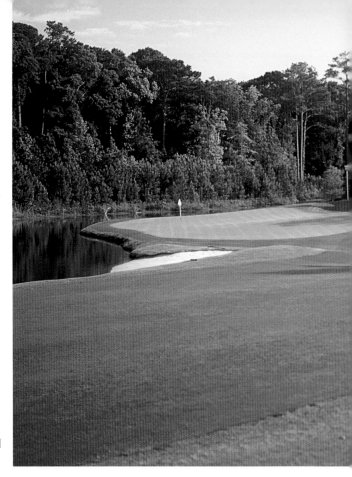

The world has heard of Myrtle Beach, the musical and manic Grand Strand locale where golf tourists flock to enjoy what is undeniably good golf, but in a goofy golf world. Myrtle Beach is a great place to be, but avoiding the throngs and finding a stress-free route to your tee time is as rare as a hole-in-one on a short par-4.

Never fear, you peace-seekers of the world, the Southern Strand has come to the rescue. True Blue Plantation is one of the string of excellent golf courses on the southern portion of the Grand Strand — an area that stands in starkly quiet contrast to the neon of the north. Pawleys Island, the home of True Blue, offers empathy for those in need of escape.

Caledonia Golf & Fish Club is perhaps the best known of the Southern Strand courses, but what True Blue lacks in fame it makes up for in a diverse combination of bravado and grace. Because of its leisurely beauty combined with risk-reward decisions that have caused many a player to wipe his (or her) brow, True Blue has been called the heaven and hell of golf. The moniker bears an ironic and uncanny resemblance to the whole of the Grand Strand — some parts are akin to golf paradise while others have become too crowded and commercialized.

Here, safely distant from all things amusement park-like, True Blue formerly forced players to strap in for a roller-coaster challenge. Recognizing this, the course was softened for the mid-range handicapper.

It used to be that if you weren't an exceptional player, you'd walk away from True Blue truly blue. But the course is a kinder place now, although still no walk in the park. If you've heard True Blue is too tough to play, it isn't altogether true anymore. Don't be afraid to visit if you take a golf trip to South Carolina. It is the most inexpensive of the Pawleys Island courses, but it is probably still more than you're used to paying at your hometown track.

Mike Strantz, who did the original layout, also came in to dial down the challenge just a touch. Always a striking course, True Blue now can be enjoyed by more of us. A huge waste area on the par-4 8th was filled in and no longer swallows drives. A mountainous amount of mounding has been removed from more than a dozen greens and TifEagle turf — which endures summer heat

and can be grown to slow down putts — was installed on the greens.

The changes have not altered the attractiveness of True Blue. The course is an eclectic mix, and the different looks of the holes keep players on their toes. Two of the first four holes are par-5s, allowing no wiggle room for those who might require a few minutes to get comfortable off the tee. There are three par-3s on the back nine, another unusual twist.

The par-5s might be the highlights of the course, and the best of those comes at No. 10. One yard shy of 600, it starts with a tee shot that soars (hopefully) and drops into a cavernous fairway. A large tentacle of a bunker juts into the fairway and comes into play on the second shot, forcing a carry to a soft landing from which to hit the approach.

Hitting into the 10th green is a bit tenuous, depending on pin placement. The entire right side is protected by sand, so you're OK if the pin is on the left side of the putting surface. But if it's on the right and you want to get close, the

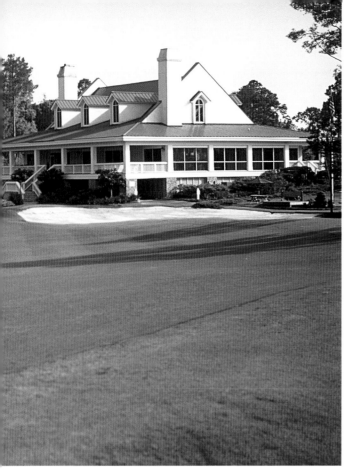

The 437-yard, par-4 18th — a tough but gorgeous True Blue finish — leaves little room for error either left, right, or up front.

AFTER YOUR ROUND

Strike up the Strand: The northward trek up the Grand Strand takes you to Myrtle Beach, where neon, mediums, and plenty of the miniature-golf/ninety-nine-cent-T-shirt establishments are the norm. Fun, if you looking for craziness, which some of us are from time to time. Head a few minutes southward from Pawleys Island for a different brand of the Strand at Georgetown, the third-oldest city in South Carolina. Trolley rides, horse-drawn carriages, and perhaps visits to Rice Museum and Kaminski House Museum offer a down-home, low-country atmosphere.

CHIP SHOTS

Course contact info:
(888) 483-6800,
www.truebluegolf.com

Par: 72
Yardage: 7,126 yards

Rating: 74.3
Slope: 145
Notable: From its opening in 1998 and continuing for more than a decade, True Blue has been named in a wide variety of "America's Best" lists. An extensive renovation didn't diminish the accolades, and because the course is easier now, True Blue experiences far more repeat play.

On the green
◎◎◎ $159

bunkers should never leave the corner of your eye.

True Blue is an eyeful. There is plenty to see in the way of ponds, creeks, and stately Carolina pines. But there isn't much to hear on the peaceful Pawleys Island layout — except for the pleasing sound of a purely struck golf ball.

SCORECARD

Hole	1	2	3	4	5	6	7	8	9	out	
Yardage	624	367	190	548	433	404	176	382	548	3,672	
Par	5	4	3	5	4	4	3	4	5	37	
Hole	10	11	12	13	14	15	16	17	18	in	total
Yardage	599	184	407	410	158	602	208	449	437	3,454	7,126
Par	5	3	4	4	3	5	3	4	4	35	72

SOUTH DAKOTA

THE GOLF CLUB AT RED ROCK
RAPID CITY, SOUTH DAKOTA

Talk about hitting the ground running. Ron Farris launched his golf course architecture career at the Golf Club at Red Rock, a course that by most accounts is the best public facility in South Dakota. And he did it for less that $3 million, a comparatively modest budget, and a big reason Red Rock can keep its rates surprisingly affordable.

When the Rapid City course opened in 2003, there was one question on most players' minds: "Where have you been, Ron Farris?"

Farris was able to keep construction costs down because so much of the natural terrain was perfect for a golf course. There wasn't a lot of earth to be moved to create elevation changes, although pockets of topsoil were relocated to areas of the Black Hills that were a little thin in the much-needed commodity. But that was about it and most of the heavy-duty land-moving work was done with just a bulldozer. When Red Rock visitors plunk down less than $50 to play such a great course, they invariably express

gratitude that Farris designed a course with the public golfer in mind.

Farris himself talked of a "minimalist approach" as he was building the course, and said, "We are going to let it be what it is." He understood the needs of the public player and wanted as many golfers as possible to see his first layout. Few go away unimpressed.

The track stretches to more than 7,100 yards and there are four tee boxes at each hole. Farris once again was keeping all golfers in mind with the placements of the tees. The tips are challenging enough for the skilled player, but a mid- to high-handicap player will be more comfortable from a closer tee. Sometimes multiple tees are merely an obligatory gesture, but here it is evident that Farris put thought into their locations.

Selecting a location in the Black Hills of South Dakota didn't hurt Farris's chances for a successful debut. The beauty of the course was in place when he arrived, and he was able to use native fescues and ponderosa pines to his advantage. Of course, beauty aside, there was the matter of creating a successful and challenging layout.

The 14th hole at Red Rock is probably as good a

The combination of difficult pin placements, such as this one at No. 4, and undulations can make putting at Red Rock an adventure.

place as any to begin a conversation about the most chal-lenging tests on the course. Get out the big club and hit it smartly off the tee if you expect a chance at par. The par-5 is 603 yards, and it takes three solid shots to get home in regulation. Length, however, is no guarantee of success.

The fairway takes five turns on the way to the putting surface. Some of them, obviously, can be cut, but they all demand thought. A perfect drive is the right side of the fairway, which gets you over the first dogleg and sets you up for a good angle on the second. The trickiest part of the hole comes just in front of the green, where a thin, horse-shoe-shaped strip waits if you happen to fall short. All of this is at the tail end of a 603-yard hole.

If there is a break to be found at Red Rock, it comes in the water-hazard category. There's just one pond on the course, but that includes a caveat. It welcomes you on the 1st hole of the inward nine, and it is a large protector of the 10th green. This hole also features a dogleg — a favorite Farris feature — and if you don't land on the right side of the fairway off the tee, you must carry the pond to the green.

The pond on No. 10 is no fun, and there are other troublesome spots at Red Rock. But no matter what difficulty you find, don't forget to be grateful to Farris for keeping the public golfer in his thoughts.

AFTER YOUR ROUND

Brave the caves: If you're looking for natural wonders, there's plenty to be seen in and around Rapid City. Top on the list is Black Hill Caverns, where logomites, stalagmites, stalactites, helictites, flowstone, and rare frost crystal can be seen. Not sure what some of these items are? Perhaps it's time to take a tour.

Roaring history: Concrete monsters interrupt the peace-ful landscape of Rapid City, but don't worry — they are confined to the perimeters of Dinosaur Park. The tourist attraction, which has been visited by millions since it was constructed in the 1930s, offers a sometimes cartoon-like and enormous look at the brontosaurus, the T-rex, and more.

CHIP SHOTS

Course contact info:
(605) 718-4710,
www.golfclubatredrock.com

Par: 72
Yardage: 7,114 yards

Rating: 75.3
Slope: 139
Notable: Red Rock has been compared to the Plantation Course at Kapalua in Hawaii for its ground-hugging style on a mountain slope. The course has been featured in the *New York Times* in a story on "Great Plains Pure Golf," and has been ranked five years running by *Golfweek* as the "No. 1 Public Course in South Dakota."

On the green
$49

OTHER PUBLIC COURSES IN SOUTH DAKOTA WORTH A VISIT
• Hart Ranch GC, Rapid City
• Hillcrest G&CC, Yankton
• Prairie Green GC, Sioux Falls
• Southern Hills Municipal GC, Hot Springs

SCORECARD											
Hole	1	2	3	4	5	6	7	8	9	out	
Yardage	340	586	406	376	217	477	395	225	520	3,542	
Par	4	5	4	4	3	4	4	3	5	36	
Hole	10	11	12	13	14	15	16	17	18	in	total
Yardage	434	426	155	405	603	214	495	385	455	3,572	7,114
Par	4	4	3	4	5	3	5	4	4	36	72

TENNESSEE

ROSS CREEK LANDING
CLIFTON, TENNESSEE

You might not stumble upon Clifton on your way to the grocery store, the mall, the movie theater, or much of anywhere else. But this rural community is part of a trail that will lead you there: the Tennessee Golf Trail.

And in Clifton you will find Ross Creek Landing — the most recent addition and perhaps the gem of the trail that includes twelve courses within an approximate 100-mile radius centered in Nashville. It's out of the way, so you might need a map, but the route — no matter how unfamiliar — is a journey worth the effort.

Ross Creek Landing is widely considered the best public-access course in Tennessee, and because it is on the Tennessee Golf Trail, there are deals to be had and tee times to be made. The trail features a map that will help you get to the courses, and each destination is a jewel in itself. All are in the Tennessee State Park system, and the Volunteer State government should be proud of the delightful dozen that it has banded as one.

To tie any negative connotation to these courses simply because they are state-park courses would be inaccurate and might lead you to decide against an experi-

ence you'd really enjoy. Of course, playing all the courses in one trip would take some dedication and some time, but there are those who have indulged in such a pure-golf excursion and haven't regretted the decision.

As if to prove they aren't backing down in their commitment to improving the trail, Tennessee's golf decision-makers hired Jack Nicklaus to design Ross Creek Landing, the fifth Nicklaus design on the route. This Clifton beauty at Ross Creek Landing was added in 2001 and has enhanced what was already a superb golf trail.

Nicklaus had a couple of unique features on the Ross Creek property, including two cemeteries that remain intact and an old barn through which the cart path travels. This barn, just before the first tee, is an indicator that more than a little thought went into making Ross Creek Landing a day on the course with nuances to remember.

It would be wise to forget about the cart ride to the 1st tee, however, because it takes focus to avoid trouble on your first drive of the day. There's a water hazard to the left on No. 1, forcing a linear drive to leave a decent approach to the reachable green. A safe drive leaves a decent shot, and a pretty good chance to start the day with a good number.

Ross Creek rolls gently alongside the Tennessee River,

A tranquil, early morning look at Ross Creek Landing's 11th: the flags are not yet in place and dew coats the fairway.

with plenty of holes that feature meandering meadows, woods, and wilderness. Marshes and natural ponds came with the territory and Nicklaus spun holes adjacent to the water features in a way that allows players the chance to simultaneously enjoy and disdain them — depending on how close they are forced to view them. Not a bad sight off the tee, but not too favorable if you're retrieving a ball from the precipice.

AFTER YOUR ROUND

B&B for me: There are a few bed and breakfast inns in the area, and staying at one is a warm and cozy way to feel immersed in the homey confines of Clifton. Getting up early with bacon frying is a pleasant contrast to more conventional lodgings. Southern hospitality and home cooking will give you a good start for a day at Ross Landing.

Miles from music: It's about a two-hour drive to Nashville, but if country music's on your mind, the 120-mile journey can take you there. The Grand Ole Opry, Ryman Auditorium, and the Country Music Hall of Fame are just a few of the yee-ha attractions.

CHIP SHOTS

Course contact info:
(931) 676-3174,
www.rosscreeklandinggolfclub.com

Par: 72
Yardage: 7,131 yards

Rating: 74.7
Slope: 137
Notable: *Golfweek* has named Ross Creek Landing the "No. 1 Public Course in Tennessee" a total number of five times, so if you have to pick and choose courses as you travel the Tennessee Golf Trail, Ross Creek should be top on your list.

On the green
○ $54

OTHER PUBLIC COURSES IN TENNESSEE WORTH A VISIT
- Gaylord Springs Golf Links, Nashville
- Vanderbilt Legends Club (North Course), Franklin
- Hermitage (The President's Reserve Course), Old Hickory
- Bear Trace at Harrison Bay, Harrison

SCORECARD

Hole	1	2	3	4	5	6	7	8	9	out	
Yardage	429	534	167	292	407	204	382	556	453	3,424	
Par	4	5	3	4	4	3	4	5	4	36	
Hole	10	11	12	13	14	15	16	17	18	in	total
Yardage	435	405	542	409	190	455	217	577	477	3,707	7,131
Par	4	4	5	4	3	4	3	5	4	36	72

CROWN COLONY COUNTRY CLUB
LUFKIN, TEXAS

The famed Colonial Country Club in Forth Worth, the legendary locale where Ben Hogan hung his hat, may always define golf in Texas. As far as storied golf tradition goes, it would be hard for any Lone Star State course to touch Colonial. But there is a place, 215 miles to the southeast in the town of Lufkin, that if judged purely on its golf course might just supplant Colonial atop Texas' list of best places to play. The name of that course? Crown Colony Country Club.

Before looking at the Crown Colony, let's give tribute where it's due: Colonial has hosted the Crown Plaza Invitational since 1946 — the longest running event on the PGA Tour — and its fairways have been graced by PGA Tour legends such as Hogan, Arnold Palmer, Byron Nelson, Gary Player, and Jack Nicklaus. As the Crown Plaza tournament continues, Tiger Woods, Phil Mickelson, and the rest of the modern crowd add to Colonial's legend.

But in spite of all the fame claimed by its neighbor to the north, and despite all the famed names who have played the Fort Worth club, there's one very important item offered by Crown Colony that Colonial can't touch: public-access golf.

That's where we come in. And, we're certainly glad the door to Crown Colony is open to the public player. The course is part of a master-planned community and there are memberships, but the immaculate conditions are there for all players to enjoy. Make a reservation, plunk your money down, and you're on one of the finest tracks in Texas. The course, which was designed by Robert von Hagge and Bruce Devlin and opened in 1979, is in sterling shape and offers a finely manicured test of target golf. Those targets are bordered by water on thirteen holes, and pines line all eighteen fairways, which feature gently rolling hills as well as more pronounced mounding.

This leads us to the Crown Colony greens, which throw the cookie-cutter approach out the window. Each putting surface is distinct in shape, style, and challenge. Some are circular, others are oblong, and a few defy the concept of previously known shapes. There are plateaus, turtle-tops, multi-tiered designs, and holes in a bowl. There's water on this side, sand over there, and many that cant into a thicket of nearby trees.

It is best to hit these greens without a roll-off — otherwise, trouble waits. And it's even more advisable to spend some time on the practice green before your round. It might not prepare you for all the shapes and slopes, but familiarizing yourself with the pace of the putting surface can't hurt. Every bit of ammunition helps when you bring out the flat stick at Crown Colony.

The club's diversity is exemplified perfectly by the fact that the two best holes on the course are the 183-yard 4th and the 582-yard 18th.

The par-3 4th forces a carry over water from tee to green, and that's it. Tee, water, green. The cart ride down the right side, the beauty of the hole, and the sternness of the tee-shot requirement enhance its simplicity.

At first glance, No. 18 seems nothing but a long, straightforward, par-5 hole. But looks can be deceiving. In fact, there are mounds and two pesky bunkers on the left side of the fairway, at the very place where you might be aiming your tee shot. Another bunker pinches the fairway where you'd hope the second shot would land. A tiny, L-shaped green awaits, made so thin by huge bunkers on both sides that the aiming point is incredibly difficult.

Start to finish, Crown Colony is among the premium courses in Texas. And there's plenty of competition in the largest state in the contiguous United States. The best part of all? It's ours for the taking.

AFTER YOUR ROUND

Texas toasting: If you need to get some pent-up energy out of your system, and you'd like to raise a glass or two full of refreshing libations, there's Wild Horse Saloon, a country-and-dance nightclub in Lufkin that can fit the bill. The club

---

CHIP SHOTS

Course contact info:
(936) 637-8811,
www.crown-colony.com, click on "club info," click on "golf."

Par: 72
Yardage: 6,692 yards

Rating: 73.2
Slope: 145
Notable: There has been confusion over whether Crown Colony is a private club or a public facility. Actually, it's both. It's semi-private, offering both memberships and the ability for the public to procure tee times. Don't be confused: in 2008, the *Dallas Morning News* named Crown Colony No. 1 in Texas on its "Best Courses You Can Play" list.

On the green
◉◉ $110 (when playing with a member)

Crown Colony's par-3 4th is 183 yards, and it's basically a green-or-nothing proposition.

is known around town as the hopping place to be if you're looking for fun.

Softer side: If you'd like something a little more laid-back after your round, try the Museum of East Texas, or the Texas Forestry Museum. You'll probably need to take a day off from golf for the Ellen Trout Zoo — home to more than 700 animals, including lions, giraffes, and hippos — but you're sure to have a wild(life) time.

OTHER PUBLIC COURSES IN TEXAS WORTH A VISIT
- Barton Creek Resort & Spa (Fazio/Canyons nines), Austin
- Barton Creek Resort & Spa (Fazio/Foothills nines), Austin
- Cowboys GC, Grapevine
- Horseshoe Bay Resort (Ram Rock Course), Horseshoe Bay
- River Crossing Club, Spring Branch
- Texas Star GC, Euless
- The Rawls Course at Texas Tech, Lubbock
- TPC Four Seasons Las Colinas, Irving

SCORECARD

Hole	1	2	3	4	5	6	7	8	9	out	
Yardage	540	385	583	183	381	388	138	359	390	3,347	
Par	5	4	5	3	4	4	3	4	4	36	
Hole	10	11	12	13	14	15	16	17	18	in	total
Yardage	437	379	195	503	185	380	481	203	582	3,345	6,692
Par	4	4	3	5	3	4	5	3	5	36	72

The 18th green at La Cantera is almost lost amid the splendor of the clubhouse, a creek, and its rocky surroundings.

TEXAS

LA CANTERA GOLF CLUB
(PALMER COURSE)
SAN ANTONIO, TEXAS

At La Cantera Golf Club's Palmer Course, there is no need to select one landmark hole, even a preferred nine, that's most memorable. Rather, it's the experience of the overall round that will keep players coming back.

All the holes are great, and you might even find one that you deem your own personal signature hole. But what's so unique here is the weaving together of individual holes to produce a colorful tapestry that will appeal to golfers of all stripes.

Arnold Palmer, who has signed a few autographs in his day, stamped his own signature on the place when he designed this gorgeous eighteen-hole layout at La Cantera. The Palmer Course, one of two tracks on the La Cantera property, didn't need any fancy gimmicks. The layout stands on its own.

"The King" knew after his first glance at the property that a magnificent golf course was possible. "The topography of La Cantera enabled us to use some of the natural highlights for the good of the golf course," Palmer said. "Rock outcroppings, dry creeks, and all that the Texas hill country has to offer. We knew there were some special possibilities."

The Palmer Course and its sister, The Resort Course, are part of a 1,600-acre master development that includes a Westin hotel adjacent to the golf facilities and a 24,000 square-foot clubhouse. The awards have poured in for the resort, the hotel, the courses (particularly the Palmer), the clubhouse, and even the pro shop. More than 100 honors from various publications around the country have been bestowed on La Cantera's eighteen-hole Palmer gem since it opened in 1995.

As you can see, there are many reasons to visit La Cantera. The No. 1 reason for golfers seeking a top-notch public facility is the exquisite Palmer Course. The Resort

Course is a fine layout, and it is designed to be a bit more forgiving for the resort golfer, but the Palmer is the choice for the seasoned player.

The Palmer Course is sculpted into rolling countryside just north of San Antonio. Elevated tee boxes offer fantastic views of the city, and oak trees line the fairways. The TifEagle greens are quick and curvaceous, and immaculate conditioning keeps them rolling true. The bent grass fairways are cropped tight to add length to drives struck soundly, and eighty white-sand bunkers dot the design.

The course doesn't tout a signature hole, but Arnold Palmer lists No. 18 as his favorite. Any time you finish your round with a 490-yard par-4 that includes a semi-blind tee shot, you leave the place with a lasting impression.

La Cantera, in all its splendor, remains a purely public course. It is advertised as part of a resort, and golf-accommodation packages are offered. But it isn't mandatory to stay at the resort to walk onto the course. Greens fees are reduced if you stay overnight, but the costs are fair even for walk-ons.

AFTER YOUR ROUND

Rollin' on the river: The world-famous San Antonio River Walk is the centerpiece of one of the most unique downtown districts in America. You can traverse the boardwalks or ride watercraft right through the middle of downtown to shop, eat, visit galleries, or catch a play. The River Walk is a great place to wander during the day, and even better when it is lit up at night. One San Antonio highlight is the Natural Bridge Caverns North Cavern Tour, an incredible world of natural beauty experienced by millions. This seventy-five-minute tour travels through a half-mile of the largest and most spectacular caverns in Texas.

CHIP SHOTS

Course contact info:
(936) 637-8811,
(800) 446-5387,
www.lacanteragolfclub.com

Par: 71
Yardage: 6,884 yards

Rating: 74.2
Slope: 142
Notable: Players who want to work on their game have a perfect opportunity at the Academy at La Cantera. The award-winning learning center includes spacious grass-hitting areas to work on short and long games, covered tee areas, and a state-of-the-art video system that is used to analyze a player's swing from several angles. The technology, combined with the expert PGA teaching pros available, will undoubtedly help your game.

On the green
◯◯ $125

Hole	1	2	3	4	5	6	7	8	9	out	
Yardage	390	449	540	188	448	399	204	204	436	3,258	
Par	4	4	5	3	4	4	3	4	4	35	
Hole	10	11	12	13	14	15	16	17	18	in	total
Yardage	415	300	363	200	573	573	556	156	490	3,626	6,884
Par	4	4	4	3	5	4	5	3	4	36	71

SCORECARD

The finisher at Thanksgiving Point — bunkers, mountains, and white picket fences.

UTAH

GOLF CLUB AT THANKSGIVING POINT
LEHI, UTAH

In a collection that contains more than 100 courses, you may quibble with some of my assessments – for example, what I call the best or the toughest course in a state may differ from your picks. However, there's one assessment that is not open for discussion: Utah's Golf Club at Thanksgiving Point is the l-o-n-g-e-s-t course in this book, totaling a mind-boggling 7,728 yards.

There are a few subcategories that also tell a lengthy tale. The par-5 11th, at 678 yards, is the longest hole in this book, and it's just one of the course's three holes measuring more than 600 yards. The back nine is more than 4,000 yards, including two par-4s of more than 460 yards and a par-3 that is exactly two-and-a-half football fields.

Sure, Thanksgiving Point is perched at more than 4,600 feet above sea level, but jeeze, you could be playing on the moon and 7,728 yards would be tough.

The course is laid out on 200 acres of picturesque mountain-desert landscape, and Johnny Miller designed a spectacular golf course on magnificent grounds. Think I'm kidding? Just look at the Thanksgiving Point photo above.

With all that this stunning track has to offer, it isn't a surprise that Golf Digest named it one of the "Top 10 New Courses in the Country" when it opened in 1997. To add to the accolades, Golf Digest also proclaimed it "No. 1 in Utah." Links Magazine called Thanksgiving Point one of fifteen "hidden gems." Do you blame me if I feel justified in heaping praise on this beauty, too?

In a book full of hidden gems, this course is not only the longest but also one of the most remarkable. Links may call it a hidden gem, but more and more golfers are becoming aware of its sterling-silver excellence. It would be wise to play the course before word gets out further.

The course's maintenance and purchasing budgets are huge, given Thanksgiving Point's enormous fairways, bark-covered berms that line fairways, and multiple flower gardens. The sheer magnitude of the place requires a course-and-a-half's worth of maintenance and supplies.

The length might be the first thing you notice on the scorecard, and it's pretty conspicuous when playing the course. But maybe even more prominent than the distance is the beauty. The Jordan River snakes here and there throughout the layout, stately pines envelop the fairways, and the rolling terrain includes extensive mounding and elevation changes. Vistas, brush, tumbleweeds, mountains — it's difficult to find a single piece of this huge property that warrants criticism.

It was almost required that Thanksgiving Point be a cosmetically spectacular golf course. It sits within an oasis in desert land purchased and developed by Alan and Karen Ashton, co-founders of the WordPerfect Corporation. There are acres of flower gardens that include roses, pansies, geraniums, and tulips; and vegetable gardens with tomatoes, carrots, squash, and pumpkins.

Indeed, the magnificent Thanksgiving Point is a course for which we should all give thanks.

OTHER PUBLIC COURSES IN UTAH WORTH A VISIT
- Coral Canyon GC, St. George
- Hideout GC, Monticello
- Sunbrook (Sagebrush/Creekside nines), St. George
- Wingpointe GC, Salt Lake City

AFTER YOUR ROUND

Thanksgiving days: Besides the obvious opportunity to view the spectacular Thanksgiving Point Gardens, there are other fun places nearby to visit, including the Museum of Natural History and the Museum of Ancient Life, with the largest display of mounted dinosaurs in the world. The Liberty Land Fun Center for kids has go-carts, laser tag, and carnival rides.

Taste budding: With flowers in bloom all around, patio dining in the café on site is a scenic delight. You can view the Thanksgiving Point Garden while eating sandwiches, soups, and gourmet salads. More formal dining is available at other restaurants on the property.

CHIP SHOTS

Course contact info:
(801) 768-7401,
www.thanksgivingpoint.com, click on "visit," click on "golf."

Par: 72
Yardage: 7,728 yards

Rating: 76.2
Slope: 140
Notable: Thanksgiving Point annually hosts The Champions Challenge — a father/son, father/daughter event that has included Jack Nicklaus, Johnny Miller, Billy Casper, Lee Trevino, and Craig Stadler.

On the green
◯◯ $85

SCORECARD

Hole	1	2	3	4	5	6	7	8	9	out	
Yardage	379	583	325	194	617	495	208	443	476	3,720	
Par	4	5	4	3	5	4	3	4	4	36	
Hole	10	11	12	13	14	15	16	17	18	in	total
Yardage	419	678	436	467	622	218	478	250	440	4,008	7,728
Par	4	5	4	4	5	3	4	3	4	36	72

VERMONT

THE GOLF CLUB AT EQUINOX
MANCHESTER VILLAGE, VERMONT

Neither the storied Equinox Golf Resort & Spa nor the golf course that is located on its 1,300 acres is quite as old as the Green and Taconic Mountain ranges that surround the luxurious grounds. But the resort was built before the United States became the United States, and the golf course was added the year Babe Ruth hit sixty home runs.

This celebrated resort has been part of the Manchester Village landscape since 1769, and it has welcomed through its doors such iconic personalities in American history as Mary Todd Lincoln, Ulysses S. Grant, and Teddy Roosevelt. It's unclear whether the Babe — an avid golfer — ever visited the Equinox or played its golf course, which opened in 1927, but it is apparent that this is one grand slam of a resort.

The golf may have come along 158 years after the resort was established, but the course is far from an after-thought. The great Walter Travis designed The Golf Club at Equinox, and Rees Jones knew better than to strip the layout of its original flavor when he tackled the course's renovation in 1992.

Jones added some length, but he didn't want to change the face of the place so he kept the distance under 6,500 yards. It isn't an overly difficult par-71 layout, but it's no pushover either. More scenic than challenging for the skilled player, it still presents plenty of difficulty for those in the resort-golfer category.

Weekend prices can top three figures, so it's best to come during the week and in non-peak season, when the rates are easier on your wallet (see "On the green"). But don't let the cost keep you from playing The Golf Club at Equinox. You'll be missing a golf memory well worth the price.

One of those memories is the 13th green, where the putting surface is reachable only after traversing a winding path that curls left toward the mountains through an amazing chute of enormous pines. The 423-yard par-4 is listed as

Large greens, such this one on No. 12, are a staple at The Golf Club at Equinox, as are the narrow fairways heading toward the mountains on No. 13 (left).

the fourth-toughest hole on the course, but it's close to the top in terms of awe-inspiring moments. And you'll find more than a few of those here.

When a golf course is part of such a stately property and is surrounded by magnificent mountains, it can be a dichotomous dynamic for a designer. Yes, there are advantages to having a layout that is so beautiful even before you turn over one shovel of dirt. But there is also more than a little pressure for you to create a design that will live up to the surroundings. Travis and Jones each met this challenge with aplomb.

The golf club's history was recognized when the Equinox was chosen in 2006 as the site for the first annual Orvis Cup Hickory Stick Shaft Pro-Am Tournament. The competition was the first North American professional championship to be played exclusively with hickory shafts since the days when they were the only sticks available. Hickory stick collectors were excited at the prospect of actually using their treasured clubs in competition. One rule made the event truly historical: players couldn't use any club that was manufactured after 1936.

It was fitting that hickory shafts — a true symbol of golf the way it used to be played — were being used on a course and resort with such historical significance. Hearing about "the good old days" is one thing, but actually watching equipment of the time being used right before your eyes is another.

Historical observation, respect for tradition, and playing the game with equipment used in 1927. The Babe would have been proud.

AFTER YOUR ROUND

Settle in: It seems a waste of time to travel off-property after you check into the Equinox. There are more activities at the resort than you can find in many cities. Spa treatments, hiking, biking, falconry, tennis, archery, and four-wheel fun are part of the action-packed possibilities. If you can't resist the urge to take a drive, there are boutiques, art galleries, antique shops, and shopping in Manchester Village. The Manchester Fine Art Gallery is a good place to spend an afternoon.

CHIP SHOTS

Course contact info: (800) 362-4747, www.playequinox.com

Par: 71
Yardage: 6,423 yards

Rating: 70.8
Slope: 129
Notable: *The New England Golf Journal* consistently ranks The Golf Club at the Equinox among the "Top Places to Play in All of New England." The golf course is not the only piece of the property that continues to stay "historical yet up to date." The resort underwent a multimillion dollar upgrade in 2009.

On the green
◎◎ $79

OTHER PUBLIC COURSES IN VERMONT WORTH A VISIT
- Okemo Valley GC, Ludlow
- Stratton Golf University (Mountain/Lake nines), Stratton Mountain
- Vermont National CC, Burlington

SCORECARD											
Hole	1	2	3	4	5	6	7	8	9	out	
Yardage	351	398	385	159	336	340	522	398	363	3,252	
Par	4	4	4	3	4	4	5	4	4	36	
Hole	10	11	12	13	14	15	16	17	18	in	total
Yardage	355	379	361	423	126	478	197	435	417	3,171	6,423
Par	4	4	4	4	3	5	3	4	4	35	71

After finishing No. 14 at Rutland, players can step off the elevated green and have a picturesque view of the 13th green in the distance.

VERMONT

RUTLAND COUNTRY CLUB
RUTLAND, VERMONT

Only five states in the country are smaller than Vermont, and yet there are more than seventy golf courses within just this one picturesque state. But because many are tucked in out-of-the-way locales, they sometimes don't get noticed. This isn't the case with Rutland Country Club, both because of its proximity to Route 7, one of the state's major highways, and because its excellence has made it conspicuous.

Vermont is not known as a golf destination, but there are quaint options loaded with charm and quality. It is a state worth visiting to play enjoyable golf, and Rutland Country Club is one of the must-stops along the way.

Located in the central part of the state about a mile from the heart of downtown Rutland, the second-largest city (population 17,292) in Vermont, Rutland Country Club is close enough to be handy but far away enough from city noise to provide you with the right amount of golf tranquility.

The semi-private track (don't worry, it's readily accessible to all) is a favorite of visitors as well as Rutland-area players. It is one of the highest-rated courses in Vermont and is certainly among the best in the central part of the state.

First incorporated as the Rutland Golf Club in 1897, the course is rich with history. Located in the clubhouse today are trophies, plaques, photos, artifacts, and equipment that go back to the turn of the twentieth century. Golf history buffs might want to leave extra time, either before or after a round at Rutland, to peruse the fascinating memorabilia. The collection offers not only a look into the history of Rutland Country Club, but also the tradition of golf in one of the oldest regions in the nation.

The course officially opened as the Rutland Country Club in 1902 after members purchased a farm from the Baxter family. Who could have predicted that their vision would be diligently maintained and sustained for more than 100 years? George Lowe built the original nine holes, and Wayne Stiles and John Van Kleek redesigned them and added nine more in 1928.

It is the tradition, along with the golf experience of today, that has helped it endure. The course is continuously hailed for its excellence, and repeat players are frequent. The fairways are in excellent shape and lead to greens that are considered to be the most challenging aspect of the course. They are slick and hilly, and you'd better use an uphill putt on the approach shots or you could be facing trouble.

The layout is short at just a touch more than 6,100 yards, but that can be a bit deceiving because it's a par-70. Two of the par-3s are plenty long — 205 and 223 yards — but the par-4s offer some great birdie opportunities. The par-5s are challenging, and the 539-yard 13th is the No. 1 handicap hole on the course — one of the infrequent occasions when a par-5 is deemed a layout's toughest hole.

Because the course was built on generally rolling property and was a former farm, its views of the countryside have a wonderfully calming effect. Steeples in the distance, rising from eighteenth-century churches, only enhance the ambience.

Rutland is a place to stop on any golf trip in Vermont. In fact, if you're in any part of New England and are looking for a peaceful round, it might be worth a swing through Rutland. You won't be sorry.

AFTER YOUR ROUND

Americana artwork: Plan on a trek to the Norman Rockwell Museum, less than five miles from the Rutland Country Club, and you've got a special day ahead. More than 2,500 works are included in the museum, highlighting his years in Vermont. Paintings, advertisements, calendars, and other works (including his world-famous drawings for the *Saturday Evening Post*) make for a charming and artsy day for learning about this legend of American art.

CHIP SHOTS

Course contact info:
(802) 773-3254,
www.rutlandcountryclub.com

Par: 70
Yardage: 6,134 yards

Rating: 70.5
Slope: 125
Notable: Rutland is semi-private, but don't let that fool you. If you happen to play (and pay) with someone who's a member, rates are extremely reasonable. (They're still just in the double figures if you aren't accompanied by someone with a club membership). A collared shirt is required and no denim allowed, but the atmosphere isn't that of a stuffy private club. My advice: make friends with a member and don't forget to bring a golf shirt.

On the green
$45 accompanied by a member ($80 if not accompanied by a member)

SCORECARD

Hole	1	2	3	4	5	6	7	8	9	out	
Yardage	393	409	170	481	223	415	361	372	308	3,132	
Par	4	4	3	5	3	4	4	4	4	35	
Hole	10	11	12	13	14	15	16	17	18	in	total
Yardage	314	323	205	539	393	129	365	336	398	3,002	6,134
Par	4	4	3	5	4	3	4	4	4	35	70

VIRGINIA

THE HOMESTEAD
(CASCADES COURSE)
HOT SPRINGS, VIRGINIA

It's all about history at The Homestead, the finest display of American golf tradition. The feel of yesterday is unparalleled, but that is not to say that today's golf experience isn't also exceptional.

Many times, golf is viewed as a sport for the rich, but The Homestead proves that isn't necessarily true. The resort is outstanding and the rates are reasonable for players who choose to stay there. Players accustomed to lesser public golf courses get a rare chance to view golf's history here.

The Old Course was the first course to open on The Homestead, beginning as a six-hole layout in 1892. It was expanded to eighteen in 1913. The Old Course was designed by the renowned Donald Ross, and the first tee is the oldest one in continuous use in the United States.

The Lower Cascades Course was constructed by Robert Trent Jones, Sr., and was opened in 1963. Lower Cascades waters rush in at higher elevations, but here they become a tranquil stream.

The jewel of the property is the Cascades Course. Like the other two Homestead layouts, the Allegheny Mountains serve as colorful and rocky surroundings. But somehow, some way, the Cascades Course seems just a little more beautiful. It might have something to do with the golf.

Annually rated among the top public golf courses in America by many respected publications, the Cascades Course was designed by the legendary William S. Flynn and opened in 1923. Instead of fighting the sometimes-inhospitable landscape, Flynn opted to embrace it. Such a concept not only beautifies the course, but adds to its strategy. More talented players have a chance to use the natural slopes to roll their shots to a desired location, and those players who need more forgiveness are not forced into difficult carries. It is a dream situation for a public-course player.

It's also not too shabby for legendary golfers, either. The late, great Sam Snead grew up in Hot Springs, and he learned to play the game on The Homestead's Cascades Course. It was the site of most of his early rounds, and there were more than a few bets made on the rolling layout. Word is, Slammin' Sammy didn't lose too many of them.

Snead didn't have far to travel when he played the Cascades, but visitors from out of the area should buckle their seat belts on the drive to The Homestead. There isn't much surrounding the road to your round other than trees and big-time Allegheny Mountain roads.

The nearest airport is about an hour away, and a ten-minute shuttle ride is required from The Homestead pro shop to the Cascades Course. You'll view such inconveniences as inconsequential when you're in the midst of a great round.

The three golf courses are longtime fixtures, but even before they were built, George Washington, James Madison, and Thomas Jefferson visited for the allegedly "healing waters" on the property.

The Homestead is a place to take in history – and to make a little golf history of your own.

AFTER YOUR ROUND

History lesson: The collection of golf books at The Homestead's library makes for one of the best golf history lessons in the world. No matter how deep you want to delve into past years of golf, you will find the information you seek at this one-of-a-kind golf resource.

The great outdoors: Fly fishing, falconry, hiking, shooting, and equestrian centers are among the activities available at The Homestead, and you never have to leave the property. Bowling, tennis, and croquet are also on site.

Fancy fare: Bring your jacket and tie because it's formal attire and fine dining in The Homestead's Dining Room. There is continental cuisine, live entertainment, and nightly dancing. It's not just nightlife, either. The Dining Room features a superb breakfast buffet.

CHIP SHOTS

Course contact info:
(800) 838-1766,
www.thehomestead.com

Par: 70
Yardage: 6,659 yards

Rating: 73
Slope: 137
Notable: The Homestead has hosted several U.S. Golf Association championships since the first round was played in 1923. The Cascades Course will be the site of the 2009 USGA Women's Senior Open.

On the green
◕◕◕◕ $225 (includes one night accommodation in the resort)

A picturesque shot of No. 16 on The Homestead's Cascades Course. No wonder Sam Snead liked to hang out here.

Kick back a bit: There are plenty of more casual options available, including a sports bar with a golf motif, and eateries with tableside preparation for French and American cuisine. Just a tip: if you're in a sports bar and they have steak on the menu, chances are it will be big. Really big.

OTHER PUBLIC COURSES IN VIRGINIA WORTH A VISIT

- Bay Creek Resort & Club (Palmer Course), Cape Charles
- Golden Horseshoe GC (Gold Course), Williamsburg
- The Homestead (Lower Cascades Course), Hot Springs
- The Homestead (Old Course), Hot Springs
- Independence GC, Midlothian
- Kingsmill Resort & Spa (River Course), Williamsburg
- Mattaponi Springs GC, Ruther Glen
- Riverfront GC, Suffolk

SCORECARD

Hole	1	2	3	4	5	6	7	8	9	out	
Yardage	394	419	283	208	576	369	432	158	457	3,296	
Par	4	4	4	3	5	4	4	3	4	35	
Hole	10	11	12	13	14	15	16	17	18	in	total
Yardage	375	198	476	438	408	229	525	515	199	3,363	6,659
Par	4	3	4	4	4	3	5	5	3	35	70

The juxtaposition of a carpet-smooth green on No. 4 against a snowy-mountain backdrop is a perfect example of a magnificent contrast at Semiahmoo.

WASHINGTON

SEMIAHMOO GOLF & COUNTRY CLUB
BLAINE, WASHINGTON

When Arnold Palmer designed Semiahmoo Golf & Country Club, he wanted to make sure all those who play golf — skilled players, mid- to high-handicappers, men and women — could enjoy their round at a top-notch layout. Multiple tees take care of the handicap differential, allowing players of all levels to tee it up and take a rip. The course consistently has been named among the country's best public courses since opening in 1986, proving that it's a great place to play.

There was another honor bestowed on the course that testifies to its success. In 2008, *U.S. Golf for Women* magazine named Semiahmoo one of "The 50 Best Courses for Women." It was the only Washington course to earn the accolade.

"It's an honor to be included," said David Shelton, director of golf at Semiahmoo. "We strive to make the playing experience great for everyone."

Arnold Palmer couldn't have said it any better.

When Palmer designed Semiahmoo, he wanted to create more than a top-notch golf experience. He wanted to create a feast for the senses. The course is nestled along the Pacific shore and offers views of snow-capped mountains and the San Juan Islands.

This tree-lined masterpiece allows you to relax and enjoy nature at its best. The golf challenge is stern but fair, water comes into play on five holes, and none of the bunkers are strictly cosmetic. All of them are good, but they were placed strategically and they are to be avoided lest your scorecard take a hit.

The fairways are generous and they are well maintained to produce a smooth, true roll. The greens are slick, and the rough gives you a chance to play out of it without too much difficulty.

Semiahmoo has been recognized by the Audubon Society for its co-existence with its natural surroundings, and there is plenty of nature to enjoy. The course is heavily wooded, the greens are spacious and contoured, and there's more than enough sand to remind you that this is a shoreline course — sixty-seven bunkers in all.

Golf Digest named the signature 11th hole one of "The Nation's Best Eighteen Holes You Can Play," and by all accounts it was a solid selection. No. 11 is a 371-yard, par-4 gem with a narrow bunker halfway down the right side and a lake just down the fairway from the bunker. Part of the lake juts in front of the green, so you are playing target golf to get home in two. The 11th is the trademark hole, but seventeen others have Pacific views — so take your pick.

After your round, there is a practice facility that includes a driving range, with putting and chipping areas. The clubhouse includes a restaurant, lounge, snack bar, banquet room, and an outdoor pavilion for special events.

If you are in the Seattle area and have time for a ninety-minute drive up Interstate 5, the trip to Semiahmoo will be worth the effort. And if you want to spend the night, the resort includes a 200-room hotel that has been named a "Silver Medal Resort" by Golf Magazine.

AFTER YOUR ROUND

On a clear day: Perhaps the most famous tourist attraction in Seattle is the Space Needle, which towers 605 feet. From the top of the Needle, visitors can see the Olympic and Cascade Mountains, Mount Rainier, Mount Baker, Elliot Bay, and the Seattle skyline.

Back on earth: If you're more of a grounded soul, how 'bout a ballgame? A Mariners game is a great way to spend a major-league afternoon or evening and the Seahawks reached Super Bowl XL after the 2005 NFL season.

CHIP SHOTS

Course contact info:
(800) 231-4425,
www.semiahmoo.com

Par: 72
Yardage: 7,005 yards

Rating: 73.9
Slope: 137
Notable: The Semiahmoo Resort is a 36-hole facility. Loomis Trail is the private sister course of the Semiahmoo Golf & Country Club. You may have to pay dues to play Loomis Trail, but Semiahmoo opens its doors to the public and provides a fine complement to its private companion.

On the green
◯ $55

OTHER PUBLIC COURSES IN WASHINGTON WORTH A VISIT
• Gold Mountain GC (Olympic Course), Bremerton
• Port Ludlow GC (Tide/Timber nines), Port Ludlow
• Suncadia Resort (Prospector Course), Roslyn
• Trophy Lake Golf & Casting, Port Orchard

SCORECARD

Hole	1	2	3	4	5	6	7	8	9	out	
Yardage	491	412	188	417	407	202	453	428	509	3,507	
Par	5	4	3	4	4	3	4	4	5	36	

Hole	10	11	12	13	14	15	16	17	18	in	total
Yardage	419	371	173	574	415	211	387	539	409	3,498	7,005
Par	4	4	3	5	4	3	4	5	4	36	72

WEST VIRGINIA

RAVEN GOLF CLUB AT SNOWSHOE MOUNTAIN
SNOWSHOE, WEST VIRGINIA

It's called Snowshoe, not Golfshoe, but there's a place in central West Virginia that proves sometimes names can be deceiving. Yes, this gorgeous gift of nature is known for its skiing, which predates golf by a good many years. But the growing reputation of its A-1 golf course in the foothills just might call for a name change. How about Snowshoe Mountain and Golf Club? Well, maybe not — yet.

But here's the next-best thing: the Raven Golf Club at Snowshoe Mountain. A pretty solid name at a very solid course.

Gary Player, who won 163 times in a career that spanned more than five decades, knows a thing or two about the way the game is played. If the Raven is any indication, he's also picking up quite a bit of knowledge about golf course architecture.

The Raven is a highlight for golfers who come to Snowshoe Mountain, an 11,000-acre complex that is the largest winter resort in the region and comprises rugged, mountain countryside as far as you can see. But, hey, let's talk summer — where the sight of the 4,848-foot summit is just as awesome as when the snow flies.

The course opened as Hawthorn Valley in 1993, and its name was changed to Raven Golf Club at Snowshoe Mountain when Intrawest Corporation purchased the resort in 2001. Whatever the name, it is now considered one of the top mountain golf courses in the United States. As far as West Virginia goes, *Golf Digest* has rated the Raven the "No. 1 Place to Play" in the category of public-access courses.

There's plenty of competition in West Virginia, and you don't have to go far to find it. Both Greenbrier, the three-course piece of golf history where Sam Snead used to hang out, and the Stonewall Resort in Clarksburg, an Arnold Palmer design, are about ninety minutes away from the Raven Golf Club.

There are several reasons why the Raven can take its place among such supreme layouts. The deep woods that

Rock outcroppings and natural mounding provide highlights throughout the Raven Golf Club at Snowshoe Mountain.

saturate Cheat Mountain, upon which the Raven is situated, are a major feature. Tons of wildlife, beautiful views of the mountains, and the stunning rock outcroppings that are a staple of mountain golf are other attractions here.

The course plays long and tough, particularly from the back tees. The hazards are placed in spots that almost always come into play, and approach shots force length and placement.

The Raven features a collection of amazing holes — some with monumental elevation drops, others that cross ravines, and more that cross a mountain stream that meanders to and fro. The hole that gets the most attention is the 548-yard 13th, which is among the top mountain holes in America.

The par-5 13th hole turns left twice, once after your drive and again on your approach, and there is a huge pond that runs virtually the entire length of the hole just to the left of the fairway. The right side is where you want to be for several reasons — chief among them being that it will help you avoid the water. Also, there's no way to reach the green unless you come at it from the right. The putting surface isn't visible until your approach, and not even then unless you come in from the right edge of the fairway. The 13th is one of the unique and glorious holes at Snowshoe Mountain. Maybe they'll think of renaming the place after all.

AFTER YOUR ROUND

Park it: The Snowshoe Mountain Bike Park is sculpted into the mountain, with twenty trails, and 1,500 feet of descent. The best part? It's all downhill. Chairlifts and shuttles take you to the top of the mountain.

Outdoors some more: At Snowshoe you'll find dune buggy tours, skeet shooting, cross-country mountain biking, water slides, pools, motorcycle rides, hiking, and nature walks. This is a vacation where indoors is meant strictly for bedtime.

Wheelin' and mealin': How about mixing a little adventure with a fantastic meal? I can't think of a better way than the Sunset Dinner Tour Adventure at Snowshoe. Get this: you hop into an off-road dune buggy and head to a remote backcountry hut for an unbelievable dinner while watching the sun go down. This is an idea I haven't heard of before, and as you ride into the sunset you'll surely enjoy this unique West Virginia experience.

CHIP SHOTS

Course contact info:
(877) 441-4386,
www.snowshoemtn.com

Par: 72
Yardage: 7,045 yards

Rating: 75.5
Slope: 142
Notable: Simply a magnificent bargain when you consider the accolades the Raven has received and the modest price you pay. This course has been named "The Top Public Course in West Virginia" by *Golf Digest*, and one of the nation's "Top Resort Courses" by *Golfweek*. If you pick the right time of week or the right time of season you can get in for less than $75. If you stay at the resort on a stay-and-play package, the price is even better.

On the green
⬤ $69

OTHER PUBLIC COURSES IN WEST VIRGINIA WORTH A VISIT
• Glade Springs Resort (Cobb Course), Beckley
• The Greenbrier (Old White Course), White Sulfur Springs
• The Resort at Glade Springs (Stonehaven Course), Beckley
• Stonewall Resort GC, Roanoke

SCORECARD

Hole	1	2	3	4	5	6	7	8	9	out	
Yardage	557	399	127	433	611	163	420	363	359	3,432	
Par	5	4	3	4	5	3	4	4	4	36	
Hole	10	11	12	13	14	15	16	17	18	in	total
Yardage	396	445	200	548	202	453	417	516	436	3,613	7,045
Par	4	4	3	5	3	4	4	5	4	36	72

WISCONSIN

BROWN DEER GOLF CLUB
MILWAUKEE, WISCONSIN

The milestones are starting to accumulate at Brown Deer Golf Club, strongly suggesting that Milwaukee's historic public course has not allowed advancing years to lead to qualitative decline.

Brown Deer celebrated its seventy-fifth anniversary in March, 2009, two years after playing host to the PGA Tour's fortieth annual U.S. Bank Championship. Not bad for a public course, just more than 6,700 yards, run by Milwaukee County.

You read correctly. A relatively short, municipal course that is open to everyone has also been staging a PGA Tour event for more than four decades. The eyebrow-raisers go on: Jack Nicklaus and Arnold Palmer have each played Brown Deer's PGA Tour stop and neither took the crown; and a Tour rookie named Tiger Woods played his first event as a professional at Brown Deer in 1996.

There is no questioning Brown Deer's versatility. Like a fawn that loses its spots, Brown Deer sheds its public-access muni style for one week a year to host the pros. After that, the pro shop doors once again swing open to Joe Public. And it's been that way since the very beginning.

When Brown Deer opened for business in 1934, Club President John Drake was quoted as saying, "Whether a man shoots 75 or 125 makes no difference. Every-

one not only is welcome, but has an equal opportunity for enjoyment and sharing in the prize awards. All club events are designed to care for the high handicappers as well as the better shooters."

Brown Deer is a traditional, parkland track whose beauty is lost on those looking for tricks. Do not expect 90-degree doglegs, gimmicky greens, or any feature bordering on slick artifice. The course is balanced, straightforward, and does not seek to shock. It is a homey layout, but not without its challenges.

Players will not find length at Brown Deer, but that's more than compensated for by the strategic demands of the course. Short par-5s offer layup areas or force difficult shots to the green; and the par-4s that don't seem to measure up in distance create risk-reward decisions that force a player to think.

When George Hansen designed Brown Deer in 1934, trophy courses or flashy resort showpieces didn't exist. Hansen created a solid course that reflects not only the era in which it was developed, but also the ability of pure, interesting golf course design to endure.

There has been a bit of flash on Brown Deer — not from any tricks the course might offer, but from some of the great players who have walked the fairways. One of those electric moments came from the aforementioned rookie in 1996, making his professional golf debut. Tiger Woods didn't win at Brown Deer that year, but he did have a little fun. Wearing his trademark Sunday red, Tiger aced No. 14 in the final round.

That hole-in-one by a player destined to be the greatest in golf history just adds to the legend at Brown Deer. Character exudes from every blade of grass, even as autumn fades. The rough grows thick and the greens roll a bit slower as the old beauty readies for her winter sleep. But as history proves, she will wake each spring for yet another season.

AFTER YOUR ROUND

Good times a'brewing: You can tour the Pabst Mansion, built in the late nineteenth century by Frederick Pabst, Milwaukee's "king of beer." Or head over to Miller Park to catch a Brewers game.

Milling around Milwaukee: A visit to the 200-acre Milwaukee County Zoo, home to 2,500 animals representing 300 species, is a great way to spend a day.

CHIP SHOTS

Course contact info:
(414) 352-8080,
www.browndeergolfclub.org

Par: 71
Yardage: 6,759 yards

Rating: 72.6
Slope: 132
Notable: Brown Deer is among the shortest golf courses to host a PGA Tour event, but who doesn't like to see the pros make birdies? Past winners include Greg Norman, Mark O'Meara, Corey Pavin, Kenny Perry, Scott Hoch, and Jeff Sluman. Here's some trivia to trot out over your next 19th-hole beverage: Ralph Guldahl was the first winner of the Milwaukee Open in 1940. Since then, there have been several sponsorship changes, and the Brown Deer tournament is known today as the U.S. Bank Championship.

On the green
◔◔ $79

No. 1 at Brown Deer Golf Club is the first hole Tiger Woods played as a professional in a PGA Tour event.

Another is at the Mitchell Park Horticultural Conservatory, where you can experience a desert oasis, tropical jungle, and floral gardens during the day, and take in an electrifying light display in the evening.

OTHER PUBLIC COURSES IN WISCONSIN WORTH A VISIT

- Big Fish GC, Hayward
- Blackwolf Run (River Course), Kohler
- The Bull at Pinehurst Farms, Sheboygan Falls
- Erin Hills GC, Hartford
- Geneva National (Gary Player Course), Lake Geneva
- Golf Courses of Lawsonia (Links Course), Green Lake
- University Ridge GC, Verona
- Whistling Straits (Irish Course), Kohler

SCORECARD

Hole	1	2	3	4	5	6	7	8	9	out	
Yardage	461	417	171	485	164	556	215	436	359	3,264	
Par	4	4	3	5	3	5	3	4	4	35	
Hole	10	11	12	13	14	15	16	17	18	in	total
Yardage	447	196	381	437	188	531	371	387	557	3,495	6,759
Par	4	3	4	4	3	5	4	4	5	36	71

A heavenly start at Whistling Straits: is that a halo shining above the first hole?

WISCONSIN

WHISTLING STRAITS
(STRAITS COURSE)
KOHLER, WISCONSIN

No doubt you have heard the Kohler name, or at least seen it from time to time as you washed your hands in sinks throughout the country. The Kohler family earned its fortune in the plumbing-fixture business before turning to the resort industry. And now, after the brilliant success of the Destination Kohler resort in the city that bears their name, the family is famous for building one of the premier golf destinations in America.

There are four earth-shaking courses on site: the Straits Course, the Irish Course, and the two courses at Blackwolf Run — the River and Meadow Valleys. All are breathtaking, but only one has held a PGA Tour major championship — the Straits Course. Blackwolf Run proved itself worthy of a major championship by hosting the LPGA Championship in

1998, but even this great course must take a back seat to the Straits.

No resort in the world houses four courses of such acclaim, and the tracks offer quite distinct styles. Meadow Valleys features rolling plains, while the Straits Course is a picture in rugged-links golf.

Those who remember watching the 2004 PGA Championship are familiar with the course's beauty and difficulty. The Wisconsin monster is more than 7,300 yards from the back tees, and there are more than 1,400 bunkers with which to contend. It may look like completely natural Wisconsin dunes land, but more than 800,000 cubic yards of dirt were moved in the creation of the Straits Course. The Kohlers — plumbing-fixture folks that they are — never were afraid of a little hard work.

The 619-yard 11th or the 592-yard 2nd struck many watching the PGA Championship in 2004. These are the attention-getters that go to great lengths to create big numbers on your scorecard. But the short par-4s are just as fun to play, perhaps more so for golfers who aren't quite ready for the PGA Championship.

One of the tricky little par-4s is No. 6, a 391-yard hole nicknamed "Gremlin's Ear." A drive struck down the left fairway allows a pretty solid angle to a tucked-away green. You can get away with being short and right, but this leaves a blind wedge to the green. This a fun shot, particularly if you hear the pleasing plop on the putting surface.

You know you've been through a tough round of golf when you get through with the Straits Course, or — as the case may be — it gets through with you. The Kohler family knew you might be whipped, so they constructed a huge stone clubhouse with timber and leather décor inside. These are the kinds of touches that drive the price to pocket-digging levels, as well as golf and dining that will knock your socks off.

While on the Whistling Straits grounds, it feels as if you are a million miles from civilization, but the courses aren't really that isolated. The resort is in central Wisconsin, a one-hour drive from Milwaukee and Green Bay and a little more than two hours from Chicago, so Kohler isn't nearly as remote as it feels.

The far-away feeling was more genuine before Pete Dye carved the Straits Course into the Lake Michigan shore. Since the course opened in 1998, however, the world of golf has turned its eyes on Kohler. And there are so many reasons why. Perhaps it's television coverage, word of mouth, or the golf gods giving approval to a heavenly golf experience.

The golf is out of this world, and the greens fees are pretty steep. This isn't a course the public player could tackle every day, but it's worth saving up the pennies for a while to take a trip to Whistling Straits.

Comfort is everywhere. The clubhouse is homey and the resort hotel is luxurious and warm. All in all, not a bad place to kick your feet up for a while. But don't forget to take off your golf shoes.

AFTER YOUR ROUND

Something spa-cial: Kohler Waters Spa offers more than fifty treatments. This is more than just an ordinary spa. It concentrates on water and its remineralizing qualities to promote health and relaxation. Each one of the unique remineralizing spa services nourishes and heals your body, in part by helping replace trace minerals, vital to well being and life itself.

Outdoor lure: River Wildlife, a 500-acre wilderness preserve, offers fishing, hiking, horseback riding, canoeing, and pheasant hunting within a chip shot of the resort.

Decisions, decisions: There are no fewer than ten places to eat in the Kohler Resort. Among them is an incredible breakfast buffet in the Whistling Straits clubhouse. There is a black-tie restaurant and there are delicious luncheon establishments as well. One more thing: you can't leave the place without trying either the stew, corn sausage chowder, or bratwurst — just a few Wisconsin specialties.

CHIP SHOTS

Course contact info:
(800) 344-2838,
www.destinationkohler.com

Par: 72
Yardage: 7,362 yards

Rating: 76.7
Slope: 151
Notable: Staffers call Whistling Straits "a throwback to the raw freshness of Ireland sculpted into the Wisconsin coastline." But even this description might not be enough. "Out of this world" would also be suitable.

On the green
◯◯◯◯ $200-plus

SCORECARD

Hole	1	2	3	4	5	6	7	8	9	out	
Yardage	405	592	183	455	584	391	214	462	415	3,701	
Par	4	5	3	4	5	4	3	4	4	36	

Hole	10	11	12	13	14	15	16	17	18	in	total
Yardage	389	619	166	403	372	465	535	223	489	3,661	7,362
Par	4	5	3	4	4	4	5	3	4	36	72

WYOMING

THE POWDER HORN
(MOUNTAIN/STAG COURSES)
SHERIDAN, WYOMING

There are three courses, three completely different looks, and far more than three good reasons why The Powder Horn is high on the list of Wyoming's golf-course communities. For some, it's just a walk out the backyard to the Mountain, Stag, or Eagle courses, but those of us who have to drive will find that The Powder Horn staff is just as welcoming. Whether it's a twenty-step walk or a 200-mile drive, it's the destination — not the origin — that counts most.

The golf courses here are beautiful and challenging, and though golf is the subject of these pages, if you are thinking about buying some real estate at The Powder Horn, there is a bonus beyond the beautiful twenty-seven holes of golf: Wyoming has no state income tax. Just a thought.

Now back to golf.

Situated on the cusp of the Big Horn Mountains, The Powder Horn somehow creates a perfect blend between rugged Western lifestyle and a picture of luxury. The surrounding mountains and rough-and-tumble terrain make it easy to imagine cowboys of the Wild West storming through on horseback, but there's nothing stormy about the velvety fairway, attention-to-detail manicuring of the course, and an immaculate clubhouse overlooking the pristine conditions. Little Goose Creek, weeping willows, aspens, and Russian sage add to the scenic landscape.

The original eighteen holes opened in 1997 and the third nine debuted in 2002. The visionaries who imagined The Powder Horn have created what was formerly 607 acres of Wyoming prairie into a golf course that makes it hard to believe from whence it came. Making the transformation even more unique is the Scottish feel on many of the holes, including a replica of the famed Swilcan Burn Bridge on the Mountain nine. Large and plentiful bunkers, rolling terrain from start to finish, and extra-large greens are other

Eye-catching features — both manmade and natural — are constant companions at The Powder Horn.

Scotland staples — all in the heart of Wyoming. A creek meanders through four holes, and several other ponds are capable of washing good scores away.

Variety of style is another Powder Horn specialty. Yes, there is a distinct Scottish touch, but on other parts of the course it's more traditional parkland Americana: thickets of large trees, target golf, approach shots over natural wetlands, and greens cut right into the woods, making you forget Scotland entirely. It is a wonderful dichotomy.

The city of Sheridan, where The Powder Horn is located, makes a claim of being "the golf capital of Wyoming." That might be a subjective call, but it's hard to argue about the excellence of the three courses within a chip shot of one another. Kendrick Municipal is a public-owned beauty, and Sheridan Country Club is a quality neighbor. Kendrick is the most affordable of the three, Sheridan comes next in terms of fees, and The Powder Horn finds its niche at the high-end of town — which, if you check "On the green," isn't particularly pricey.

AFTER YOUR ROUND

Finding your footing: Sheridan is known for its charming Main Street, with plenty of pieces of Old West history. Put on your walking shoes for a stroll through town to start a leisurely afternoon. Change into your boots for some nature watching and hiking, and then don the waders for a little fly-fishing on Little Goose Creek. Hunting, camping, and historic Native American battlefield tours are also available nearby.

CHIP SHOTS

Course contact info:
(307) 673-4800,
www.thepowderhorn.com

Par: 72
Yardage: 6,934 yards

Rating: 71.9
Slope: 122
Notable: The practice area is actually a two-fold experience worth penciling in if you have the time. Between the two facilities, there are huge, multi-tiered putting greens, large natural-grass tees, and short game areas — including bunkers.

On the green
◯ $61

OTHER PUBLIC COURSES IN WYOMING WORTH A VISIT
• Bell Nob GC, Gillette
• Jackson Hole Golf & Tennis Club, Jackson Hole
• Teton Pines CC, Jackson
• Three Crowns GC, Casper

SCORECARD

Hole	1	2	3	4	5	6	7	8	9	out	
Yardage	350	520	175	375	420	525	463	202	413	3,443	
Par	4	5	3	4	4	5	4	3	4	36	
Hole	10	11	12	13	14	15	16	17	18	in	total
Yardage	335	455	564	435	424	180	370	218	510	3,491	6,934
Par	4	4	5	4	4	3	4	3	5	36	72

The 4th hole at Banff Springs: pure majesty on the par-3 tester.

CANADA

BANFF SPRINGS GOLF CLUB AND JASPER PARK LODGE GOLF COURSE
BANFF, ALBERTA, CANADA

Somehow, there is envy as U.S. visitors look over the Spray River to an immaculate Banff Springs fairway dwarfed by a magnificent face of Alberta's Rocky Mountains.

The Canadians obviously know just how good they have it, and they have proven how much nature means to them just by the way they maintain it.

Those to the north understand the importance of what they have at Banff Springs Golf Club and Jasper Park Lodge Golf Course. These are two separate courses, but it seems impossible to mention one without the other.

The Banff Springs Golf Club is nestled in the mountains adjacent to the majestic Fairmont Banff Springs Hotel, which is more than a century old. The Banff Springs philosophy is based around blending in with the environment.

Jasper is a mountainous and wondrous trek from Banff, and there are two reasons to play it when you are finished

at Banff. One is the great golf, and the other is the drive between the two courses. One course shouldn't be played without experiencing the other.

The Banff Springs Golf Club (about 1 1/2 hours west of Calgary on the Trans Canada Highway), and Jasper (a three-hour drive from Banff) are the nature-laden focuses of this chapter. There are four other solid courses in the Banff area, but Banff Springs — and the beautiful route to Jasper — features waterfalls and snowcaps, bears, coyotes, and velvet-antlered deer. Nature's living glory is everywhere.

Flying into Calgary — "the big city," according to Banff locals — is the end of a plane trip, yet the beginning of a journey. Get that rental car (or U-Drive, as the Canadians like to say) and start looking for the Trans Canada Highway, heading west.

Once you arrive at Banff Springs Golf Club, you know you are onto something special. Stanley Thompson, a magical name in Canadian golf lore, created the original course. Thompson, who also designed Jasper Park Lodge Golf Course, was famous for his wit and innovation, and for an uncanny ability to let a course's surroundings become an integral part of the game.

The surroundings at Banff are sensational, to say the least. It would be folly to assume the golf could be as fantastic as the natural landscape, but it comes close. Thompson's layout brings in raging rivers, mountainous doglegs, and surreal elevation changes. "Beautiful," "fun," and "challenging" are all words that apply at Banff Springs.

After leaving Banff, wonderful golf is in your rear-view mirror, and more waits in Jasper. But do yourself a favor: forget about it for twenty-four hours. You will remember the drive to the last day of your life.

OTHER PUBLIC COURSES IN CANADA WORTH A VISIT

- Kananaskis Country GC (Mt. Kidd), Kananaskis, Alberta
- Le Geant, Mt. Tremblant, Quebec
- The Links at Crowbush Cove, Morell, Prince Edward Island
- Predator Ridge Golf Resort, Vernon, British Columbia
- Radium Resort (Springs Course), Radium Hot Springs, British Columbia
- Wolf Creek Golf Resort, Ponoka, Alberta

CHIP SHOTS - BANFF

Course contact info:
(403) 762-2211,
www.banffspringsgolfclub.com

Par: 72
Yardage: 6,793 yards

Rating: 72.9
Slope: 138
Notable: If players doubt whether they will see wildlife on the course, they need look no further than the scorecard. There are special provisions on it that give instructions on what to do if your ball lands in elk droppings or a hoof print.

On the green
○○○ $195 (Canadian)

SCORECARD - BANFF

Hole	1	2	3	4	5	6	7	8	9	out	total
Yardage	432	179	536	199	431	381	610	158	510	3,436	
Par	4	3	5	3	4	4	5	3	5	36	
Hole	10	11	12	13	14	15	16	17	18	in	total
Yardage	386	369	547	197	390	481	417	141	429	3,357	6,793
Par	3	5	3	4	4	5	5	3	4	36	72

SCORECARD - JASPER

Hole	1	2	3	4	5	6	7	8	9	out	total
Yardage	391	488	454	240	480	393	178	427	231	3,282	
Par	4	5	4	3	5	4	3	4	3	35	
Hole	10	11	12	13	14	15	16	17	18	in	total
Yardage	492	403	181	603	361	138	380	360	463	3,381	6,663
Par	3	5	3	4	4	5	4	3	4	36	71

CHIP SHOTS - JASPER

Course contact info:
(780) 852-3301,
www.fairmont.com/jasper/recreation/golf/

Par: 71
Yardage: 6,663 yards

Rating: 71.1
Slope: 124
Notable: Flatter and less of a challenge than its sister course, Jasper is still a great round of golf. The sport is not an afterthought by any means, but Jasper definitely possesses the "walk in the park" beauty that designer Stanley Thompson had in mind.

On the green
○○○ $150 (Canadian); Jasper is a touch less expensive than Banff, but still in the same price range.

GLEN ABBEY GOLF CLUB
OAKVILLE, ONTARIO, CANADA

Tiger Woods has hit countless remarkable shots in his career, but among the most incredible was the one that sealed victory at the 2000 Canadian Open, with a stunning 6-iron out of a fairway bunker to the 18th green of Glen Abbey Golf Club.

In the realm of Canadian golf, Glen Abbey has been among the leading and most famous facilities since it opened in 1976. Not only is it a fantastic public facility, but it has also hosted Canada's national championship — the Canadian Open — two dozen times. When you consider that the club is home to the Royal Canadian Golf Association and the Canadian Golf Hall of Fame as well, you'll understand why Glen Abbey has reached legendary status with golfers up north.

During Glen Abbey's thirty-year reign either at or near the top of Canadian golf's hierarchy of greatness, the rest of North America has taken notice.

Designed by Jack Nicklaus, Glen Abbey sits just west of Toronto, one of the slickest cities in Canada. There's plenty to do after your round, and you'll have plenty of golf to discuss. Whether it be your performance on the course, a visit to the Hall of Fame, or the artifacts of past Canadian Opens on display, there's a plethora of topics available as you enjoy a night on the town with a hot meal or a cold drink.

The course itself is enough to spark memories. The "Valley Holes" — Nos. 11 to 15 — feature drives off the sides of cliffs to fairways sixty feet below, carries over creeks, fairways with alarming cants, greens that slope drastically toward hazards, and, finally, a climb out of the valley at No. 16.

So many Canadians, along with visitors to the country, have played Glen Abbey because it is a public facility. This adds to its popularity and word has spread about the conditions and stiff challenge of the Nicklaus design.

The reputation of Glen Abbey as the premier course in Canada waned just a touch in the late 1990s when it no longer was the exclusive home of the Canadian Open, but two events restored its legend. The first came in the final round of the 2000 Canadian Open when Tiger Woods hit a 6-iron shot 218 yards from a bunker on the right side of

Tiger Woods nailed the 6th green at Glen Abbey (pictured) with a shot to be remembered in the final round of the 2000 Canadian Open.

the fairway to the green, leaving an eighteen-foot putt to the hole. The shot is regarded as one of the most spectacular, both of Woods's career and in recent PGA history. Tiger, of course, then sank the putt to win the tournament by one shot over Grant Waite.

Another fascinating Canadian golf moment that expanded Glen Abbey's aura also took place in the Canadian Open. In 2004, the nation was riveted when Mike Weir came within one stroke of becoming the first Canadian to win the event since Pat Fletcher claimed the prize in 1954. Vijay Singh beat Weir in a playoff, but the Glen Abbey drama captured the attention of Canada and much of the golf world.

AFTER YOUR ROUND

Cosmopolitan Canada: The hustle and bustle, the city lights, and the vast choice of post-golf activities might surprise first-time visitors to Toronto. The city offers the third-largest theater district in the world, several art galleries, museums, and countless nightclubs. For some high-in-the-sky fun, visit the CN Tower, the world's tallest freestanding structure.

OTHER PUBLIC COURSES IN CANADA WORTH A VISIT
- Angus Glen GC (South Course), Markham, Ontario
- Deerhurst Resort (Highlands Course), Huntsville, Ontario
- The Lake Joseph Club, Port Carling, Ontario
- Osprey Valley (Heathlands Course), Caledon, Ontario

CHIP SHOTS
Course contact info:
(905) 844-1800,
http://en.clublink.ca/golf, search "Glen Abbey Golf Club."

Par: 73
Yardage: 7,112 yards

Rating: 75.5
Slope: 140
Notable: Jack Nicklaus never won the Canadian Open, which Glen Abbey hosted for the twenty-fourth time in 2008. Even though he never hoisted the trophy at the course he designed, he finished second an astonishing seven times.

On the green
○○○ $140 (Canadian)

SCORECARD											
Hole	1	2	3	4	5	6	7	8	9	out	
Yardage	435	414	156	417	527	437	197	433	458	3,474	
Par	5	4	3	4	5	4	3	4	4	36	
Hole	10	11	12	13	14	15	16	17	18	in	total
Yardage	443	452	187	529	426	141	516	436	508	3,638	7,112
Par	4	4	3	5	4	3	5	4	5	37	73

The 7th hole at Highlands Links is labeled "Killiecrankie," and at 570 yards it can leave players a little cranky when they're finished.

CANADA

HIGHLANDS LINKS GOLF CLUB
CAPE BRETON,
NOVA SCOTIA, CANADA

There are two ways to appreciate a golf tour of this mountainous Canadian island that juts into the Atlantic, so far north that climate basically shuts it down six months a year and so far east that it leaves the Eastern time zone an hour in its wake.

Patient visitors to Cape Breton Island might think of the excursion as an opera: one that commences with beautiful and sometimes soul-touching arias, and then slowly builds to a crescendo that saves the most powerful moments for the curtain-closer.

Or, for those who prefer more instant-gratification, the trip can be considered a five-star, four-course meal in reverse — beginning with a delicious dessert and working backward

through two solid main courses before finishing with a tempting appetizer.

The extreme northern tip of the island, in the midst of a sprawling national park is where dessert awaits, and Highlands Links Golf Club — considered by many to be the finest public course in Canada — is where this member of the instant-gratification crowd chose to begin.

Highlands Links is the gem of the golf course consortium that markets itself as Cape Breton's "Fabulous Foursome," but the highlights of its three partners are only slightly less fabulous. After playing Highlands Links in Ingonish Beach, working southward down the world-famous Cabot Trail from Cape Breton Highlands National Park of Canada, the tour stops include Le Portage Golf Club in Cheticamp, Bell Bay Golf Club in Baddeck, and Dundee Resort & Golf Club in West Bay. The trail is about 300 kilometers (185 miles) in length and the courses are sprinkled along the way.

There is the classic design of Highlands Links, the modern look of Bell Bay, the scenery of Dundee, and the culture that mixes with the community at Le Portage. It makes for a very well-rounded golf experience if you get a chance to play them all.

It is no wonder Highlands Links represents the pinnacle. Stanley Thompson, the Canadian legend who built other northern beauties such as St. George's in Toronto, and Banff Springs and Jasper in Banff National Park (a few hours north of Calgary), designed the course.

Thompson created a course in Highlands Links that seems to change with the seasons. In the spring, even though the course was built in 1939, it takes on a semi-modern strategy of aerial golf because of the softness of the turf. In the summer sun, Highlands Links turns old school — hard and fast, and calling for many bump-and-runs. And in autumn, before Cape Breton shutters its windows for the winter, birch trees go yellow, maples go red, and golf goes colorful — vivid, in fact.

Perhaps the most scenic stretch, regardless of season, includes Nos. 15 and 16. The 15th is a 540-yard par-5, and, if a signature designation is required at a course with as lofty a reputation as Highlands Links, then No. 15 would receive it both for difficulty and photographic possibilities. A draw to the left is required off the tee to reach higher ground, where an angle to the green becomes possible. Then comes No. 16, a 460-yard uphill par-5 that also requires a left-side drive in order to go for an elevated green. These two holes add up to a 1,000-yard, par-10 — enough to simultaneously satiate and exhaust.

It doesn't matter which route you take to enjoy Cape Breton golf — north to south or vice versa. As long as you include Highlands Links in the trip, Cape Breton is a trip worth taking and an island worth enjoying. Top to bottom.

AFTER YOUR ROUND

Circle of paradise: Cape Breton has been ranked by several travel publications as one the most beautiful islands in North America. The Northumberland Strait to the northwest, the Strait of Canso to the south, and the Atlantic Ocean up the eastern coast surround the forest-filled island. The most talked-about tourist attraction is the island itself. Just get in the car, open the window, and enjoy the ride. I played four golf courses in four days when I visited Cape Breton, and I have to say that I enjoyed the drives on the roads as much I did the drives off the tees. There are many interesting places to stop along the way, including the Whitney Pier Museum, Alexander Graham Bell National Historic Park, St. Patrick's Museum, the Fortress of Louisbourg, and the continent's only single-malt whiskey distillery.

CHIP SHOTS

Course contact info:
(800) 441-1118,
www.highlandslinksgolf.com

Par: 72
Yardage: 6,592 yards

Rating: 73.3
Slope: 141
Notable: Highlands Links, considered by many to be the top public-access course in Canada, is part of the Cabot Trail. The trail, named for explorer John Cabot, is one of the most scenic drives in the world, winding around the rocky splendor of Cape Breton's northern shore before ascending to the incredible plateaus of Cape Breton Highlands National Park.

On the green:
◕◕ $72 (Canadian)

SCORECARD											
Hole	1	2	3	4	5	6	7	8	9	out	
Yardage	405	447	160	324	164	537	570	319	336	3,262	
Par	4	4	3	4	3	5	5	4	4	36	
Hole	10	11	12	13	14	15	16	17	18	in	total
Yardage	145	512	240	435	398	540	460	190	410	3,330	6,592
Par	3	5	3	4	4	5	5	3	4	36	72

CANADA

NICKLAUS NORTH GOLF COURSE
WHISTLER, BRITISH COLUMBIA, CANADA

As logic would dictate, the town of Whistler, nestled in the snowy mountains of British Columbia, has long been considered one of the premier skiing spots in North America. But word is spreading. There's another game in town.

When Arnold Palmer designed Whistler Golf Club in 1982, it was golf's first entry into the Whistler landscape. But it took nine years for another course to be added, and three more were introduced in the next three.

The quality and variety of the courses captured the attention of golfers in Whistler, the rest of Canada, and also in the United States. It's taken almost a decade since the last course opened for golf to secure a solid hold on the region, but the number of rounds played in the few warm months prove that the sport is far more than just a way to pass the time between ski seasons. Locals and visitors alike are wetting their whistle for golf.

Whistler Golf Club is the least challenging course in the area, and stronger golf waits at other courses within yelling distance of the Whistler village square. Big Sky Golf & Country Club, Furry Creek Golf & Country Club, and Chateau Whistler Golf Club are all public courses and all are excellent places to play.

Nicklaus North Golf Course is among the area's best, if for no other reason than its snaking seclusion on fairways through thick Canadian woods. Some might pick one of the other Whistler layouts for various reasons, but nature lovers will find much to enjoy at Nicklaus North.

CHIP SHOTS

Course contact info:
(604) 938-9898,
www.golfbc.com

Par: 71
Yardage: 6,908 yards

Rating: 73.3
Slope: 141
Notable: Jack Nicklaus's golf-course design career began with South Carolina's Bay Harbour in 1969, and he had designed many courses prior to setting his sights on British Columbia. But Nicklaus North was the first golf course in the world to bear The Golden Bear's name.

On the green
◎◎◎ $145 (Canadian)

Garbage cans are covered with heavy metal and warning signs are posted throughout the course, reading: "Be aware of bears." It's a challenging golf course, to be sure, and the sense of danger is heightened just a bit with the thought of a black bear growling during your backswing.

On Nicklaus North, it is wise to score early. There are birdies to be had as you start, but the course gets progressively tougher. The fairways are tight and lined with homes. Real estate is bothersome on many other courses but the multimillion-dollar, rustic-style homes on Nicklaus North are actually one of the scenic highlights. Far enough off the fairway so as to never come into play, the lodge-style homes blend beautifully with the mountainous background. Imagine 5,000-square-foot log cabins, glistening with a lacquered sheen that reflects the rays of sunshine. These are the homes at Nicklaus North.

The course has played host to Shell's Wonderful World of Golf matches, as well as skins games that have drawn Nicklaus, Greg Norman, Nick Faldo, Fred Couples, Ernie Els, and others to the Great North.

The finishing three holes at Nicklaus North provide lasting memories. The trio begins with a 425-yard par 5, a 226-yard par 4, and a 438-yard par 4. The distances, even from the tips, are not altogether daunting, but Green Lake, as well as gusts of wind and some well-placed hazards, make them, excuse the expression, a bear.

Golf has surely taken a foothold in Whistler, but there are a myriad of other activities to enjoy in the quaint village here. If you're exhausted after a round at Nicklaus North, then avoid the biking, horseback riding, and ATV treks. A nice walk through the brick streets to visit the local shops is a perfectly enjoyable alternative.

And don't worry about automobiles. Cars are prohibited in the village. Visitors drive to the outskirts of the shopping district, and hoof it over the cobblestone walks to the town square.

There is shopping at Whistler. There is skiing at Whistler. And, no longer a secret, there is golf at Whistler, too.

AFTER YOUR ROUND

One big cat: Cougar Mountain is a daring adventure, with ATV and Hummer tours, fishing, and horseback riding in the summer. I tackled Cougar Mountain on an ATV and our group was literally splashing through the clouds.

The par-4 4th at Nicklaus North is a shimmering example of British Columbia beauty.

Raging waters: Whistler River Adventures offers whitewater rafting on the Birkenhead, Elaho-Squamish, and Green rivers. I went with six others on a wild trip over the rushing Green. Jet boating tours are also offered, as well as fishing for trout, salmon, and steelhead.

Shopping on the cobblestones: For those with a taste for less active pleasure, the village square in Whistler is lined with quaint gift shops and offers plentiful mountain views.

SCORECARD											
Hole	1	2	3	4	5	6	7	8	9	out	
Yardage	390	197	518	465	416	179	366	514	376	3,421	
Par	4	3	5	4	4	3	4	5	4	36	
Hole	10	11	12	13	14	15	16	17	18	in	total
Yardage	185	555	225	564	432	437	425	226	438	3,487	6,908
Par	3	5	3	4	4	5	5	4	4	35	71

MEXICO

MOON SPA & GOLF CLUB
(JUNGLE/LAKES COURSES)
CANCUN, QUINTANA ROO, MEXICO

With so many birds to watch, reefs to dive, and history to absorb, the northeast tip of the Yucatan Peninsula has not historically been thought of as a golf destination. But the velvet fairways and emerald greens in Cancun belie that belief. There is some fantastic golf in this area of Mexico, and it's well worth taking a golf-exclusive trip south of the border.

The Jack Nicklaus-designed Moon Spa & Golf Club is among a handful of courses in or near Cancun in the Mexican state of Quintana Roo. Moon Spa, which opened in 2003, joins other exquisite golf tracks in the region, including Playacar Golf Club (designed by Robert von Hagge) and Playa Mujeres Golf Club (designed by Greg Norman).

Von Hagge and Norman's layouts are each of country-club quality, but when you consider that Jack Nicklaus, a man familiar with leadership in both competition and design, was the force behind the golf courses at Moon Spa, you know you're talking about an outstanding golf experience. Moon, without question, is the golf leader in the Northeast Yucatan.

Nicklaus designed three nine-hole courses at Moon — the Jungle, the Lakes, and the Dunes — and the Jungle is considered to be the leader. For the sake of clarity, the Chip Shots portion of this chapter focuses on the Jungle/Lakes combination — the longest of the three possible course pairings.

Moon Spa & Golf Club is a beautiful facility, and Nicklaus created the course knowing that many of those who play the layout will be tourists. With that in mind, its fairways are friendly and the front tees make for an enjoyable round for the mid-to high-handicap player. This isn't to say that the more skilled player will be bored at Moon. From the back tees, length is added as well as an additional focus on angles to the green.

Moon staffers know they have an excellent golf course, and they say they have learned a lot about setup after hosting the Mexican Open on more than one occasion. They have learned how to make the course more difficult when the event comes to Cancun, tightening the fairways and letting the rough grow.

The three nines can be made tough for the Mexican Open, but the challenge isn't the only toothy animal. Crocodiles, gray fox, aardvarks, deer, iguanas, and snakes-to-be-watched also add some teeth. Nature abounds on the course and throughout the Cancun area. Many of the tourist sights throughout the region are centered on natural beauty and wildlife, and Nicklaus took this into account when designing Moon. The wetlands and vegetation are not only present on the course, they come into play throughout the round.

While recognizing the natural beauty that surrounds the Moon property, Nicklaus knew he had to come up with something special. And the superintendent and greens keepers have kept up their end of the bargain. The upkeep is outstanding with manicured fairways, lush rough, and putting surfaces that allow for a consistently true roll.

One of the highlights of all the twenty-seven holes is the par-3 8th on the Lakes Course. It is labeled as the signature hole and plays to an island green. A rock wall surrounds the putting surface, building it up from the water. The green is an expansive 6,500 square feet, so while players are forced to hit the putting surface or land in the drink, the green is large enough to offer a fighting chance.

If you haven't been to Cancun for a while, you might have to add more baggage to the items you check in at the airport. Here's a little advice from those in the know: when you visit Cancun, don't forget your clubs.

This picture represents a pristine microcosm of the 27 holes at Moon Spa & Golf Club: immaculate fairways, sand, and greens, surrounded by spacious Mexican villas.

CHIP SHOTS

Course contact info:
(011) 52-998-193-2010, www.palaceresorts.com, click "golf," then "golf in Cancun."

Par: 72
Yardage: 7,201 yards

Rating: 75.3
Slope: 133
Notable: Moon Spa & Golf Club has been the site of the Mexican Open, and is one of the courses in Mexico vying for the first PGA Tour tournament in the country.

On the green
◯◯◯ $195 (U.S.)

AFTER YOUR ROUND

History and beauty: Tulum is an ancient Mayan city complete with amazing ruins that have stood up to the elements of the Caribbean. The city, about an hour's drive from Cancun, is situated on a cliff that overlooks the blue-green waters. The ambience is a combination of peace and beauty, and a portion of the sea that juts into a rock formation serves as a one-of-a-kind swimming area for visitors.

Barter for bargains: There are plenty of "regular" shopping areas in downtown Cancun, but a more authentic experience can be found in the markets on the outskirts of town that feature local handicrafts. A helpful hint: make sure you dicker. The first price is never the real price.

OTHER PUBLIC COURSES IN MEXICO WORTH A VISIT

- Acapulco Princess Golf Club, Acapulco, Guerrero
- Bajamar Punta Diamate, Tijuana, Baja California Norte
- Cabo del Sol (The Ocean Course), Cabo San Lucas, Baja California Sur
- Cabo Real Golf Course, Cabo San Lucas, Baja California Sur
- Cabo San Lucas Country Club, Los Cabos, Baja California Sur
- Cozumel Country Club, Cozumel, Quintana Roo
- El Tamarindo Beach & Golf Resort, Puerto Vallarta, Jalisco
- Palmilla Golf Club, San Jose del Cabo, Baja California Sur
- Playa Mujeres Golf Club, Cancun, Quintana Roo
- Playacar Golf Club, Cancun, Quintana Roo

SCORECARD - JUNGLE NINE

Hole	1	2	3	4	5	6	7	8	9	out	
Yardage	434	194	450	521	476	337	226	396	565	3,599	
Par	4	3	4	5	4	4	3	4	5	36	

SCORECARD - LAKES NINE

Hole	1	2	3	4	5	6	7	8	9	out	
Yardage	425	531	400	574	456	204	417	150	445	3,602	7,201
Par	4	5	4	5	4	3	4	3	4	36	72

JAMAICA

WHITE WITCH GOLF COURSE
MONTEGO BAY, JAMAICA

In a country full of bewitching legends, perhaps none is more intriguing than that of Annee Palmer, nicknamed the White Witch for casting spells and killing three husbands on her 4,000-acre sugar plantation in the nineteenth century. It seems fitting that Jamaica's most beguiling golf course shares her moniker.

White Witch Golf Course was blasted into the mountains of Montego Bay before it opened in 2000, and sits on the property formerly occupied by Palmer's plantation. Locals insist Annee still haunts the Rose Hall Great House, where she lived as mistress of the plantation. That may or may not be true, but it is undeniable that danger looms at every corner on the White Witch layout, created by Robert von Hagge and Rick Baril.

It is a daunting course from start to finish, featuring massive elevation changes carved right into the mountains. Von Hagge doesn't apologize for the course's difficulty, although he acknowledges it is a witch of a place to play.

"You think it's hard to play?" von Hagge said during dinner with me in Montego Bay. "You should have seen how hard it was to create. There was no topsoil. This is a beautiful piece of property, to be sure, but it's hard to explain what it took to turn it into a golf course."

Whatever it took, those who play White Witch are grateful that Von Hagge and Baril went to the trouble.

No walkers are allowed on White Witch, not that anyone in his right mind would tackle the course without the aid of an electric cart. Steep inclines make even riding the cart somewhat perilous.

Although the legend of the plantation mistress White Witch is a little spooky, it is best to leave all fears behind as you tackle the golf course. Even though it requires a player to be on target, there are just three blind shots on the course. You need to be careful on White Witch, but don't be intimidated or you won't have a chance at success.

The beauty of White Witch, along with its difficulty, is why von Hagge calls it his masterpiece. The elevation changes allow majestic perspective to take in the ocean views, and the Caribbean is never out of your vision as you make your way from hole to hole through the mountains.

No hole exemplifies the combination of elevation, challenge, and panorama like the par-5 10th. All three are offered in the extreme. The tee box is elevated some 100 feet over the fairway of the 621-yard hole, allowing a special vantage point to view the hole and the ocean as the backdrop. But it also affords players a clear vision of the monstrous challenge ahead.

The elevation of the tee gives players some bonus length on the drive, but 621 yards is still a ferocious length at any elevation. The 10th was originally laid out as the 1st hole when the layout was devised, but for a variety of reasons the nines were reversed. Perhaps Von Hagge didn't want to scare players off on the 1st hole.

The switch still leaves players with a dandy of an opening hole, another par-5. The 1st is 550 yards and also drops off sharply from the tee. The second shot is uphill, and then the third must be drilled perfectly into a plateau green.

Elevation can sometimes create an illusion that certain shots would be difficult and close to impossible. There is no doubt that the golf course is a tough challenge, but it isn't as grueling as it may seem. But it is tough enough.

A haunting history. A course torn into a mountainside. A challenge in a country you may only visit once. It is a golf course you will never forget.

The question is: are you ready?

AFTER YOUR ROUND

What to sea: The Caribbean Sea is visible from White Witch but you have a chance to get an up-close look from the beaches of Montego Bay. Resorts along the coastline have beaches reserved just for their guests, and I stayed at the Ritz-Carlton — with which the White Witch Golf Course is affiliated. The Ritz offers one of the most scenic and peaceful beaches in Montego Bay.

CHIP SHOTS

Course contact info:
(876) 518-0174,
www.whitewitchgolf.com

Par: 71
Yardage: 6,818 yards

Rating: 74.0
Slope: 139

Notable: It didn't take long for White Witch to capture the attention of golf aficionados after it opened in August, 2000. A short time later Hal Sutton took on Notah Begay at White Witch in one of *Shell's Wonderful World of Golf* events seen on national television. Later the same year, the World Junior Golf Championships were held at White Witch.

On the green
◯ $75

The par-3, 161-yard 17th at White Witch is a beguiling beauty, much like the legendary nineteenth-century White Witch herself — Annee Palmer.

Haunted house: A visit to Annee Palmer's former residence is a must. Our Jamaican tour guide did not smile as she took our group through the tiny mansion that's three stories high. It was obvious that the guide believed in the evil powers of the White Witch as she recounted tales of sightings and mysteries.

OTHER PUBLIC COURSES IN THE CARIBBEAN WORTH A VISIT

- Aruba GC, San Nicolas, Aruba
- Bahia Beach Plantation, Rio Grande, Puerto Rico
- Carambola GC, St. Croix, U.S. Virgin Islands
- Caye Chapel Golf Resort, Caye Chapel, Belize
- Four Seasons Resort Course, Nevis, West Indies
- Punta Borinquen GC, Aguadilla, Puerto Rico
- Royal Westmoreland, St. James, Barbados
- Sandy Lane GC, St. James, Barbados
- Tierra del Sol Resort, Spa and CC, Oranjestad, Aruba
- Westin Rio Mar Beach Resort and GC, Rio Grande, Puerto Rico

SCORECARD

Hole	1	2	3	4	5	6	7	8	9	out	
Yardage	550	189	412	453	402	507	414	183	420	3,530	
Par	5	3	4	4	4	5	4	3	4	36	
Hole	10	11	12	13	14	15	16	17	18	in	total
Yardage	621	160	342	427	164	353	567	161	493	3,288	6,818
Par	5	3	4	4	3	4	5	3	4	35	71

There is plenty of water with which to contend at Cable Beach's par-3 14th, and golfers can also get a peek at the sea in the distance.

BAHAMAS

CABLE BEACH GOLF CLUB
NASSAU, NEW PROVIDENCE ISLAND, BAHAMAS

Sun and sea aren't the only highlights in Nassau. A round of golf at the Cable Beach Golf Club adds to the experience and offers a new way to enjoy both these Bahamian pleasures. A sunny round awaits you almost every day in the Bahamas, and the sea is within eyeshot of the tourist-friendly Cable Beach course. If you haven't visited the Bahamas for a while, Cable Beach golf will undoubtedly surprise and delight you.

The course underwent a $4.5 million renovation in 2003, and added a lighted practice range two years later. A layout that had been in disrepair was suddenly transformed into a Caribbean beauty. Seaside paspalum was used to sod the course, a grass perfected by turf specialists to stand up to saltwater and ocean air.

The course doesn't abut the sea directly, but the water is close enough to affect the course. The ocean doesn't come into play on the course, but sixteen of the eighteen holes include small lakes and man-made water hazards. The ponds are often marshes filled with natural grasses, and with so many on the course, it's a difficult challenge to avoid every one of the hazards.

Cable Beach golf had been in existence since 1928, but after the course's renovation, which golf course architect Fred Settle called "more re-creation than renovation," the course in essence became the newest layout on the islands. It was regrassed, holes were reversed, and a sorely needed drainage system was installed during a two-phase project that vastly improved playability of the course.

The drainage system was an important facet because the network of lakes throughout the course posed a serious problem. But the addition of the new system has turned a negative into a positive. The same lakes that used to cause flooding now add beauty to the course.

During the renovation, only nine holes were open at a time, and now that all eighteen have been up and maturing for a few years, the people behind the project have had a chance to reflect upon the results. It isn't only Cable Beach golf personnel who are satisfied with the outcome; the players who visit the course also walk away content.

The course is laid out on 120 acres, the same parcel that was used in 1928. But the added golf knowledge of the staff and the maintenance techniques now employed at Cable Beach makes it feel like an entirely different course.

Cable Beach is a par-71 that plays to a modest 6,453 yards from the tips. The length allows golfers of all skill levels to enjoy themselves, an important fact to remember because many players don't come to the Bahamas strictly for golf. Even those public players who don't play frequently can visit Nassau and experience a pleasurable round.

Another pleasure? The price is extremely affordable when you consider you are playing a course in a resort area such as the Bahamas. Island courses often drastically hike up prices simply because of location, but players don't feel duped when they play Cable Beach.

The course is straightforward, just like the pricing structure. It is priced fairly throughout the day and becomes even more affordable at twilight time. And don't worry about transportation to the course. Many of the hotels on Cable Beach — which locals and tourists refer to as "resort row" — offer complimentary shuttles to the course.

The short length of the course forces players to add a little strategy to their game. You can't just rip out the driver and bomb away from the tee. Sharp iron play is a must in order to ensure proper angles to the putting surface.

CHIP SHOTS

Course contact info:
(242) 327-6000,
www.crystalpalacevacations.com/golf

Par: 71
Yardage: 6,453 yards

Rating: 72
Slope: 115
Notable: The golf season at Cable Beach is easy to remember: January to December. The high season is November to April. During this time, it is best to call ahead. During non-peak season, open tee times are the norm.

On the green
◐◐ $130

Once you've intelligently negotiated the course, there's another smart move to make: head back to the beach and enjoy the sun.

AFTER YOUR ROUND

Tips for tourists: The most simple and obvious sight to see when visiting Nassau is the sun-soaked beach. While there, I found swimming and sunning just as enjoyable as the golf. The beach may not seem to offer much recreation, but this is a place to relax — whether it be lying around or playing a round. When I ventured into Nassau to sightsee, I joined an organized tour and stayed with the group. Most locals are friendly, but there are areas in which care must be taken. Specialty shops (where dickering is almost expected) include handicrafts, jewelry and watches, leather goods, perfumes and cosmetics, and cigars. After the sun, a little fun in the casino might be in order. It was just the ticket for me.

OTHER PUBLIC COURSES IN THE BAHAMAS WORTH A VISIT

- Cotton Bay Club GC, Cotton Bay, Eleuthera
- Lucayan G&CC, Freeport, Grand Bahama Island
- Paradise Island GC, Nassau, New Providence Island
- Princess Emerald GC, Freeport, Grand Bahama Island
- Princess Ruby GC, Freeport, Grand Bahama Island
- South Ocean Golf & Beach Resort, Nassau, New Providence Island
- Treasure Cay GC, Treasure Cay, Abaco

SCORECARD

Hole	1	2	3	4	5	6	7	8	9	out	
Yardage	362	408	409	147	425	356	521	538	202	3,368	
Par	4	4	4	3	4	4	4	5	4	36	
Hole	10	11	12	13	14	15	16	17	18	in	total
Yardage	328	287	151	559	141	411	391	448	369	3,085	6,453
Par	4	4	3	5	3	4	4	4	4	35	71

Photo Credits

ACKNOWLEDGMENTS

Many thanks to Craig Yuhas, a wildly avid golfer and an old Detroit News buddy whose camaraderie and assistance with this project won't be forgotten; to Golf Channel's expert "televisionist" Brian Hewitt for writing the preface; and to Brad Klein, Golfweek's course architecture aficionado, for penning the foreword.

Direction, attention to detail, and encouragement from my editor, Mark Chimsky-Lustig, proved invaluable. Mary Baldwin and Charlotte Smith of Sellers Publishing, Steve Cooley, and Bob Holtzman were all vital members of Golf's Best-Kept Secrets team.

Scott Miller (www.scottamillerphotography.com), Kevin Frisch of Fusion Media Strategies, Brian Walters from Resort & Golf Marketing, and Rob Brown (www.robbrownphotography.com) also helped soothe an author's soul on particularly stressful nights.

This book certainly would not have been possible without the countless guided tours, patient explanations, and wonderful rounds of golf offered by public golf course owners, architects, pros, and personnel behind the counters. Their labor allows peaceful summertime recreation for those of us who crave the game but can't handle country-club membership fees.

Special thanks to my mother and father, John and Bunny Barr, who have always encouraged me to explore my writing. Thanks, mom and dad, for buying me my first set of clubs and for the countless rounds of golf we've played.